YOUTH QUESTIONS

Series Editors: PHILIP COHEN and ANGELA MCROBBIE

This series sets out to question the ways in which youth has traditionally been defined by social scientists and policy-makers, by the caring professions and the mass media, as well as in 'common-sense' ideology. It explores some of the new directions in research and practice which are beginning to challenge existing patterns of knowledge and provision. Each book examines a particular aspect of the youth question in depth. All of them seek to connect their concerns to the major political and intellectual debates that are now taking place about the present crisis and future shape of our society. The series will be of interest to those who deal professionally with young people, especially those concerned with the development of socialist, feminist and anti-racist perspectives. But it is also aimed at students and general readers who want a lively and accessible introduction to some of the most awkward but important issues of our time.

Published

Inge Bates, John Clarke, Philip Cohen, Dan Finn, Robert Moore and Paul Willis
SCHOOLING FOR THE DOLE?
The New Vocationalism

Cynthia Cockburn
TWO-TRACK TRAINING
Sex Inequalities and the YTS

Philip Cohen and Harwant S. Bains (eds)
MULTI-RACIST BRITAIN

Andrew Dewdney and Martin Lister
YOUTH, CULTURE AND PHOTOGRAPHY

Dan Finn
TRAINING WITHOUT JOBS: NEW DEALS AND BROKEN PROMISES
From Raising the School-Leaving Age to the Youth Training Scheme

Robert G. Hollands
THE LONG TRANSITION
Class, Culture and Youth Training

Angela McRobbie (ed.)
ZOOT SUITS AND SECOND-HAND DRESSES
An Anthology of Fashion and Music

Angela McRobbie and Mica Nava (eds)
GENDER AND GENERATION

Forthcoming

Desmond Bell
ACTS OF UNION
Youth Culture and Sectarianism in Northern Ireland

Philip Cohen and Graham Murdock (eds)
THE MAKING OF THE YOUTH QUESTION

Angela McRobbie
FEMINISM AND YOUTH CULTURE

Series Standing Order
If you would like to receive future titles in this series as they are published,
you can make use of our standing order facility. To place a standing
order please contact your bookseller or, in case of difficulty, write to us
at the address below with your name and address and the name of the
series. Please state with which title you wish to begin your standing order.
(If you live outside the United Kingdom we may not have the rights for
your area, in which case we will forward your order to the publisher
concerned.)

Customer Services Department, Macmillan Distribution Ltd,
Houndmills, Basingstoke, Hampshire RG21 2XS, England.

The Long Transition

Class, Culture and Youth Training

Robert G. Hollands

MACMILLAN

First published 1990

Published by
MACMILLAN EDUCATION LTD
Houndmills, Basingstoke, Hampshire RG21 2XS
and London
Companies and representatives
throughout the world

Phototypeset by Input Typesetting Ltd, London

Printed in Hong Kong

British Library Cataloguing in Publication Data
Hollands, Robert G.
The long transition: class, culture and youth
training. – (Youth questions).
1. Great Britain. Young persons. Vocational training
I. Title II. Series
370.11'0941
ISBN 0–333–46373–0 (hardcover)
ISBN 0–333–46374–9 (paperback)

To Helen's past and Joe's future

'Schools of the vocational type, i.e. those designed to satisfy immediate, practical interests, are beginning to predominate over the formative school, which is not immediately "interested". The most paradoxical aspect of it all is that this new type of school appears and is advocated as being democratic, while in fact it is destined not merely to perpetuate social differences but to crystallise them in Chinese complexities . . . The multiplication of types of vocational school thus tends to perpetuate traditional social differences; but since, within these differences, it tends to encourage internal diversification, it gives the impression of being democratic in tendency. The labourer can become a skilled worker, for instance, the peasant a surveyor or petty agronomist. But democracy, by definition, cannot mean merely that an unskilled worker can become skilled. It must mean that every "citizen" can "govern" and that society places him, even if only abstractly, in a general condition to achieve this.' – **Antonio Gramsci**, *Prison Notebooks* (1929–35)

'It is certainly the case that the vocationalist deluge which is now going on, both inside the schools and in the "further education and training" sectors, is designed specifically to freeze the existing social division of labour between the mental and the manual classes – between conception and execution, as Marx put it – and, within that, to make damn sure nothing much moves on the sexual division of labour and the ethnic division of labour either! But all that does is to reaffirm what we already knew: that education is critical for the maintenance or the transformation of the social division of labour. A political force which is determined to do something to begin to break down the expropriation of the people into their separate universes must formulate alternative ways of making the link.' – **Stuart Hall** (1983)

Contents

Foreword by Philip Cohen   ix

Acknowledgements   xiii

List of Trainees Interviewed or Referred to   xiv

1 Introduction: Class, Culture and Youth Training   1

PART I CULTURAL EXPERIENCES ON THE SCHEME

2 From School to Schemes ✓   23
3 Off-the-Job Training and Lifeskilling   44
4 Work Experience and the Trainee Identity   74

**PART II WIDER CULTURAL FORMS, SITES AND
            IDENTITIES**

5 Youth Differentiation, Training and the World of Work ✓101
6 At Home and Out on the Street: Domestic Labour and
   Public Space   123
7 Non-work Activity and the Substitute Wage:
   The Limits of Leisure   142
8 Divided Youth: White Racism and Male Sexist Practice   161
9 Youth Politics in Thatcherland   180
10 Conclusion: Youth Transitions and the Labour
    Movement   195

Notes 211

Bibliography 223

Index 231

Foreword: Transitions in Transition

To many readers the title of this book will inevitably evoke echoes of another work, written in more hopeful times. In *The Long Revolution* Raymond Williams set out to chart the social and cultural transformations set in motion by industrial capitalism as they worked their way through the institutions which shaped ordinary lives. In *The Long Transition* Robert Hollands has set himself a less ambitious, but no less daunting task: to examine the way in which working-class identities are being reshaped in and against the new regimes which have been set in place to produce the kind of youth labour required by post-industrial capitalism. It is, here, through what has been called the 'new vocationalism', that the ideology of the enterprise culture has been institutionalised in particular pedagogic and disciplinary forms, and a new generation of working-class children find themselves being schooled, or trained, for their subordinate roles in the political economy of Thatcherism. How they negotiate that experience, what resistances and accommodations they make to what is demanded of them, is the substance of the story which this book has to tell.

Raymond Williams, himself, in his later work, *Towards 2000*, pointed to what might be released by the kind of 'mobile privatisation' promoted by the Thatcherite dream; yet, ever alive to emergent contradictions, he also argued that this new individualism might also open up spaces in which non-traditional working-class identities could take root and flourish, and eventually produce new forms of struggle. In an address to the Cultural Studies Association in 1984 he even suggested that youth training schemes (YTS) were the most important arena for socialists concerned to renew the project of popular education; here the battle for young hearts and minds might well be won or lost.

Robert Hollands's study, almost uniquely, sets out to take up Williams's challenge; his book is concerned to renew the cultural analysis of class, to map out some of its more intricate and intimate positionings as they articulate the shifting boundaries of gender, generation and ethnicity. In particular he succeeds in showing how different types of training regime open up or close off specific identities for young people. The monolithic image of 'Thatcherite YTS' crushing the aspirations of 'young workers' crumbles before a more sophisticated and nuanced account, albeit one which is even more damning in its conclusions.

If the book avoids simplistic polemics, it is not, however, by retreating into a purely academic exercise of 'theorisation'. His method involves an ethnography which is both critical and compassionate; he neither patronises nor sentimentalises the young people he listens to; rather, he makes their voices heard within an interpretative framework which accords full weight to the wider resonances and hidden complexities of what they have to say. But the book does not stop there; it draws out the implications of this research for the development of new and more responsive youth policies within the labour movement; as such it makes a welcome and timely contribution to current debates around the Labour Party's policy review.

The book, however, offers cold comfort to those who think that school-leavers and youth trainees will make easy recruits for any political ideology, Right or Left. Instead what it points to is the real gulf which separates these young people's felt needs from their expression in any form of organised politics. These are transitional identities which lack any stable anchorage in our political culture, even though they may initiate a fragmentary cultural politics of their own. This is something of an old-fashioned story, but one whose narrative ingredients are in the process of being refashioned. For at a time when the consuming passions – and privileged autonomies – of youth culture are being stretched to embrace much of childhood as well as a good deal of early adulthood, the State is enforcing a new and enlarged condition of dependency, removing the right to benefits, and making most young people even more powerless than before.

Nowhere is this dependency – and the forms of resistance it engenders – more clearly illustrated than on youth training schemes. One of the salutary messages which this book conveys is

just how difficult it is proving for labour organisations to move
beyond the patriarchal assumptions which have dominated so
much youth policy and research in the past.

Although Robert Hollands's research was originally undertaken
at the Centre for Contemporary Cultural Studies in Birmingham,
it represents in many ways as big a break from earlier CCCS work
in this field as it does from the mainstream tradition of empirical
youth studies. To begin with, the great divide between school-to-
work-transition studies and youth cultural analysis focusing on,
lifestyle is here definitively overcome. Family, schooling, leisure,
are not treated as separate, functionally interdependent sites of
'social reproduction', but as integral elements in cultural bio-
graphy, continually being negotiated through the construction of
identities in and across the full range of structural constraints.
Along with the abandonment of 'functionalism' goes a rejection
of the narrow positivistic concerns which have once more come
to dominate youth sociology. To those who have returned to the
'numbers game', who argue that with declining numbers of school-
leavers coming on to the labour market, youth (un)employment
is no longer the burning issue it was, there is a simple enough
reply, which Robert Hollands here spells out with great cogency.
The training of youth labour has never been simply about match-
ing supply and demand, skills and jobs. That is the vocationalist
fallacy *par excellence*. It has always involved a much wider and
deeper process of cultural apprenticeship, and one to which
government policies have given an ever sharper ideological point.
From this perspective the probable absorption of YTS into the
Employment Training programme does not signify that the youth
training problem has been finally solved, only that the state appar-
atus for remaking the working class has become more fully
rationalised.

The numbers game is part of a biopolitical strategy traditionally
devoted to the surveillance and control of youthful populations;
it is one with which a certain kind of sociology has actively collab-
orated, most recently under the aegis of the ESRC. According to
this paradigm young people become a problem only when there
are too many of them, never when there are too few! Against this
it is necessary to demonstrate that the importance of the youth
question has nothing to do with demography or deviancy. It is a
site of discourses and institutions which play a key role in shaping

the society we all live in – condensing certain strategic contradictions which are otherwise hidden or displaced. And yet, paradoxically, these same 'youth' contradictions ensure that 'young people' never constitute a unitary social category. Robert Hollands does not shrink from exploring the theoretical and political difficulties posed by this fact. Indeed it is because he risks his neck, and refuses to retreat into pontifications or become sidetracked into trivial issues, that his book is such a welcome change from so much recent writing on the youth question.

This is not yet another local study of YTS; it is not a *vox pop* survey of life and love on the dole. It provides us with an original look 'from below' at some of the deep-rooted changes which are working their way through young lives to map out the essential contours of British society in the first quarter of the twenty-first century. As such it makes an important contribution to the debates which this series is concerned to pursue.

PHILIP COHEN
Institute of Education
University of London
June 1989

Acknowledgements

Writing and research are always collective endeavours however much they appear as 'individual' products. In writing this book I would first of all like to thank the young people I interviewed, without whom this research could not have been done. The Education Group at the Centre for Contemporary Cultural Studies was extremely helpful in generating collective ideas around youth and the new vocationalism, and a number of members made written comments on draft chapters. Richard Johnson deserves a special mention for his interest, enthusiasm and critical commentary on much that is written here. Helen Carr read through and made comments on the entire manuscript, as well as provided the cover photographs. Other individuals who have made some contribution to the ideas contained in this book include Lolke Van der Heide, Chris Beasley, Midge Miller, Dan Finn, Paul Willis, Chris Griffin, Cynthia Cockburn, John Schaechter and Dennis Warren. Also, I am indebted to Philip Cohen's original and thought provoking work on the youth question. Finally, I must acknowledge the financial assistance of the Commonwealth Scholarship Commission and the Social Sciences and Humanities Research Council of Canada, for providing the 'material conditions' for writing and researching this book.

ROBERT G. HOLLANDS

Key to ethnographic quotations

– Pause in the conversation
. . . Material edited out
[ ] Explanatory information or actions inserted
X Young person purposefully not identified
BH Bob Hollands

List of Trainees Interviewed or Referred to in the Book

Young women
Alice (white, clerical, PTA)*
Ann (white, distribution, PTA)
Andrea (white, retail, college-based)
Cheryl (white, distribution, PTA)
Daljit (Asian, clerical, community-based)
George (white, manufacturing, college-based)
Jackie (white, childcare, college-based)
Jan (white, clothing manufacture, PTA)
Jennifer (Afro-Caribbean, clothing, PTA)
Jill (white, childcare, college-based)
Julie (white, retail, PTA)
Kamni (Asian, clerical, community-based)
Kathy (white, public utilities, employer-led)
Kelly (Afro-Caribbean, clothing, PTA)
Liz (white, retail, PTA)
Lorraine (white, clothing, PTA)
Mandy (Afro-Caribbean, clerical, community-based)
Margaret (Afro-Caribbean, childcare, college-based)
Michelle (white, distribution, PTA)
Shanaz (Asian, clerical, community-based)
Tracy (white, caring, PTA)

Young men
Andy (white, manual labour,** community-based)
Angus (white, retail, PTA)
Art (white, manual labour, college-based)
Baz (white, maintenance, community-based)

Ben (white, horticulture, community-based)
Billy (white, mechanics, community-based)
Calvin (Afro-Caribbean, manual labour, community-based)
Chris (white, manual labour, community-based)
Craig (white, metalwork, community-based)
Dan (white, maintenance and repairs, PTA)
Finchy (white, signwriting, PTA)
Frank (white, manual labour, community-based)
Garnie (Afro-Caribbean, woodwork, community-based)
Inderjit (Asian, clerical, community-based)
John (white, retail, PTA)
Leonard (Afro-Caribbean, woodwork, community-based)
Mark (white, manual labour, community-based)
Mick (white, maintenance, community-based)
Nigel (Afro-Caribbean, clerical, community-based)
Otis (Afro-Caribbean, construction, college-based)
Paul (white, engineering, employer-led)
Peter (white, horticulture, college-based)
Robert (white, maintenance, community-based)
Shabaz (Asian, metalwork, community-based)
Will (white, maintenance, college-based)

* PTA   Private Training Agency

** Manual labour refers to a broad range of training and work experience in numerous manual trades (i.e. painting and decorating, bricklaying, construction, etc.)

1

Introduction: Class, Culture and Youth Training

If the late 1970s and early 1980s were perceived as the age of mass unemployment, with all its attendant problems, then the current period must surely be marked as the 'training era'. The growing importance of special employment measures in displacing unemployment as a social issue is undeniable. However, of equal significance is the fundamental way training schemes have sought to rigorously redefine the working-class labour market and influence the population's experiences and indeed expectations of work. These twin features of government policy have remained constant from the early days of the youth training programmes to the more recent development of the adult scheme Employment Training (ET).

Nowhere is this more true than for working-class youth today. The spectre of youth unemployment which came to haunt this country has been literally exorcised by the vigorous development of post-16 training policies (for example, numbers in youth training have swelled from 70,000 in 1979 to 396,000 by January 1988).[1] School leavers are now virtually compelled to take part in post-school training schemes in place of either unemployment or a full-time job. What has transpired in this 'training revolution'? What have their experiences on schemes been like and what impact has training made in shaping the future working lives and destinations of the young? How has this new social condition influenced traditional working-class youth transitions into work and adulthood?

This ethnographic study examines, in detail, the transitional experiences and identities of a group of working-class youths as they make their way through one of the most established and comprehensive of these schemes – the Youth Training Scheme (YTS).[2] Yet my concern here is not simply limited to describing and presenting young people's training experiences. Instead, the main rationale of this study is to use the YTS as a key focus for exploring and evaluating a much broader historical shift in working-class transitions, identities and lifestyles. In this book, I set out to chart the main elements of young people's responses to vocational training, discuss their wider transitional effects and relations across a number of key social sites, and assess the significance of these changes for the long-term prospects of the labour movement.

There has been a mass of public debate and commentary on the plight of the young unemployed and on State intervention into the labour market. The Manpower Services Commission (MSC),[3] the government quango responsible for creating and administering the YTS, has produced a great deal of material on the need for a national training scheme emphasising the development of 'flexible' and 'transferable' skills amongst school leavers to overcome their 'poor attitudes' and 'lack of motivation' (in simple terms this is basically what is referred to as the 'new vocationalism').[4] Employers and the business community have, with minor reservations, welcomed the scheme as a source of cheap labour, not to mention supporting its underlying 'enterprise culture' emphasis. Even Mrs Thatcher, head of the self-proclaimed *laissez-faire* Conservative government, has referred to this training 'intervention' as one of the most imaginative in the Western world. And while sections within the labour movement have voiced their opposition to certain aspects of the training debate (particularly in relation to ET), their absolute failure to contest the ideological grounds of the new vocationlism and provide an overall alternative form of youth politics, has meant they have, for the most part, been forced to accept the economic and political necessity of current government schemes (CCCS Education Group, 1981; Cohen, 1982; Cohen, 1984; Finn, 1987).

Much of our public knowledge and information about young people and the YTS are drawn from these dominant sources. The 'common-sense' view tells us that schemes are necessary because young people lack basic skills, motivation and experience. And while problems with the YTS remain, its extention to two years, together with proper monitoring, will result in a high quality training programme geared to industry's need for a flexible and highly motivated workforce.

There have, of course, been alternative analyses of the causes of youth unemployment, critical refutations of the MSC's claims about school leavers and differing views on the effectiveness of the YTS. Unemployment in this perspective is understood to spring from a lack of demand for goods and services rather than from high youth wages, powerful and greedy trade unions or the inevitable effects of new technology.[5] Rather than being seen as a consensus-based social programme, current training policy is viewed as a direct creation of government policy designed to lower wage levels, destroy worker's rights and attack the labour movement at one of its weakest points – the young working class. Much of this analysis is pitched at the economic and political level, drawing its conclusions from the MSC and government documents and from political theory.[6]

While retaining some of the strong points raised by this critical body of work, this book forges a slightly different path through these debates. For instance, an attempt is made to throw new light on existing perspectives by giving priority to the actions, views and daily cultural experiences of young working class people on the YTS.[7] By stressing the importance of this active, 'cultural' level, across a range of youthful sites, the analysis seeks to contextualise and give some insight into how the new vocationalism has actually influenced youth identities and transitions into adulthood. This contrasts to both MSC inspired views which see school leavers as culturally deficient and other analyses which, in their haste to understand training schemes simply as a political charade to disguise unemployment, often relegate young people to the status of 'dupes' or 'pawns'. The study also attempts to differentiate itself from much past work in the youth training field through its wider concern and exploration of a variety of youthful sites, institutions and intra-class identities. Finally, the book seeks to understand how such youth differentiation relates to the labour movement's failure to construct a relevant politics amongst the young.

The notion of transition is a key concept in this study. It refers to both the idea of a 'destination' and an 'identity' which co-exist on three interrelated levels. The first level is most specific and refers to the formation of a general transition into work for young people engineered through the new vocationalism. Part I, contains three separate chapters dealing with young people's daily cultural experiences of the YTS and the construction of a general trainee identity. The legitimation of this new transition is examined in relation to young people's movement from school on to schemes and their interaction with off-the job training and work experience. At the same time, it is argued that the whole idea of transition has to be expanded beyond a simple movement into work through training, by locating identity formation within a plethora of institutional sites inhabited by the young and through the changing nature of working-class cultures and the impact of other fundamental social relations (i.e. gender and race).

Part II, therefore, seeks to understand working-class youth transitions as a product of these broader sets of relations, negotiations and locations. The process of examining how a wide variety of youth transitions and identities are currently being formed, are explored in the context of training and the world of work, the domestic and public spheres, non-work activities, white ethnicity and male sexism and through the political realm. Finally, the 'long transition' of the title, refers to a more lengthy historical process whereby the structures of growing up working-class – whilst maintaining some continuities with the past – have undergone a profound transformation and upheaval.

Before turning to the case study, this type of analysis requires some further background explanation concerning its use of concepts and theoretical perspectives.

Key concepts: youth, class and culture

Let us begin with the concept of 'youth' itself. Cohen (1986a) has argued that a series of what he calls 'bio-political' premises have informed views on the youth question up to the present day. These include assumptions that the youthful stage is a natural (purely biological) phase of human development, involving the formation of rebellious attitudes, which in turn requires professional assistance and guidance in the transition into adulthood and maturity. These premises mask the many ways in which youthfulness is a profoundly social, historical and hence highly variable phenomenon (Aries, 1962; Gillis, 1974). These bio-political perspectives have also contributed to theories of adolescence that overlook the main social divisions which characterise the wider society – the effect of gender, race and class.

This study takes a very different view of the youthful stage. It asserts that while there is a social grouping one can label youth, this phenomenon is not based upon any universal phase, but rather is the result of the social construction of a youthful stage held in place by a series of very specific practices and institutional structures. For example, in contemporary capitalist societies the transformation from the world of the child to that of adult (via youthfulness) has very specific goals in mind. Underneath the rhetoric of adulthood, there are more specific identities and transitions that are encouraged such as that of 'worker', 'housewife', 'man' and 'woman'. Within these categories there are more precise identities like 'manual labourer', 'working mother', 'white collar' employee, etc. The point is that transitions into adulthood have very specific social, cultural and indeed economic meanings attached to them. In this sense, the temporary withholding and initial formation of these more specific identities means that youth is a real social category. The generational division of labour and the political disenfranchisement of the young are two obvious examples of this reality.

Youth is also social in that it is intersected by other social relations – principally those of class, race and gender. While the primary focus of this study is on class formation amongst the young, it is also concerned with the impact gender and race have on transitions within the working-class youth population.[8] As such, it seeks to rethink orthodox notions of class through both these other social divisions and within a generational framework. Class is never a homogeneous category, nor is class formation the same for every generation. Instead it is understood here as a changing and dynamic set of conditions and identities which are formed in specific historical circumstances and institutional sites (Giddens, 1973). The young working class, today for example, are not formed in identical ways nor in the same sites as their parents before them.

This last point relates to a more general argument about the applicability of class analysis in understanding contemporary Western societies. The debates about the post-war working class and its expression in the traditional organs of the labour movement have taken a series of zigzag paths, ranging from their literal disappearance and demise (Gorz, 1982; Laclau, 1987) to more traditional defences of orthodox definitions (Meikisins-Wood,

1986). The most fruitful line of enquiry, in my view, are theories of class recomposition (Clarke *et al.*, 1979; Hall, 1985; Cohen, 1972; Williams, 1965). The basis of this perspective is summed up by Clarke (1979, p. 247) in this lengthy, but important passage:

> What we have said so far has been an attempt to point to the variety of processes of class struggle (in economic, political and ideological forms) which have transformed the conditions of existence of the working class in post-war Britain – processes which have acted to reorganise the sphere of production and the sphere of reproduction. In the transformation of those conditions of existence (and the dominant political and ideological representations of them), the basis of the cultural forms within which the working class represent those conditions, or live their experience of them, has been undermined. The change in those material conditions requires the elaboration of new cultural practices and repertoires which are capable of producing (however partial and contradictory) new cultural frameworks in which to live the experiences of being working class . . . Central to this is an awareness that what we are discussing is in no simple sense the overthrow of one working class culture and its replacement by another one. What we can be certain of is that the period with which we are dealing involves a process of cultural transition – a transition which begins not from some homogeneous entity called working class culture, but from a complex, uneven and contradictory ensemble, made up of internal contradictions, a range or repertoire of different 'cultural solutions' – trade unionism, religion, respectability, crime, domesticity, socialist politics, etc. The process of transition involves both continuities and breaks; some elements continue unmodified, others are sustained in new forms and others disappear and are replaced by new cultural forms.

Central to this version of recomposition theory is a recognition of the persistence and stability of certain class processes and the transformation and disappearance of others. Clarke (1979), amongst others, admits that the 'discipline of the wage relation persists through the supposed abolition of the working class'. Yet this is not to argue that forms of wage labour don't change or that this relationship is the only basis of class relations. The fact is that the wage-labour relationship has never been able to explain and give insight into the entire gamut of working-class lives, nor can it alone account for social differentiation within the class. For example, the working-class household has always been a crucial site for reproducing class in its gendered forms (Barrett, 1980; Luxton, 1980; Cohen, 1984). Changing conditions of employment, subemployment, unemployment, the impact of the domestic and consumer spheres and the complex elaboration of new sites and practices in which identity formation can take place, give rise to new experiences and frameworks which categorically shift orthodox notions of class and accompanying forms of political organisation (Hall, 1985).

The specific location of the young within the recomposition perspective is highly relevant to changing definitions of class: As Clarke (1979, p. 241) argues, 'The area of youth is one in which the changed conditions of existence of the working class and the destruction of existing cultural forms have had their most visible consequences in the construction of new cultural forms and practices.' This is not to argue that the wage-labour relationship is unimportant or coincidental to class formation amongst the young. On the contrary, the present study demonstrates that the transition into and experience of work remains a fundamental preoccupation of the whole of the young working class. However, not all youth transitions into wage labour are of a singular nature nor are they experienced in the same ways or through the same sites as their parents. For example, the movement from school to work is now negotiated through a wide range of new skilling regimes on the YTS. Similarly, youth identities in the post-war era have been heavily influenced by a wide variety of developing social sites and mechanisms (i.e. youth culture, non-work, the media, public space, etc).

Finally, a word should be said about the particular use of the term 'culture'. While the dominant usage still tends to equate the term with the 'arts' and activities defined as 'high culture', the concept has quite a different meaning within the cultural studies tradition (Johnson, 1983; Williams, 1965; Williams, 1977). As one well-known, cultural production theorist has put it, the cultural level is the milieu of everyday existence and its commonplace span of shared concerns, activities and struggles. It is also the realm of meanings, objects, artifacts, and systems of symbols which both help to constitute and make some meaning of these things. These meet on the terrain of 'experience' and the ways in which this is ultimately bound up with the structures and contradictions through which social agents must live. This general level of social existence I designate 'the cultural'. (Willis, 1981, p. 201)

Culture, in this sense, has a specific reference to collective action and meaning within the realm of everyday life. The cultural level signals a particular moment in the 'structuration' (Giddens, 1984) or making of social life which lies in between individual variation and the structural edifact of social order.

Class recomposition theorists have already hinted at how one might relate the term culture to the young working class. Working-class culture refers to the manner in which class relations are lived out and experienced. Because this perspective does not view the working class as a unitary category, neither does it understand working-class culture as a homogeneous entity. Members within the class act and make sense of the world from quite different locations and positions of power. While some elements within this culture can be shared and transmitted, class fractions experience these elements very differently. While I want to maintain that the cultural is an important level of analysis, I use the term 'cultural experiences' to denote a moment of agency in social life which is diverse and fragmented rather than universally shared. In fact, in this case study it is clear that while aspects of a past tradition persist, young people are in the process of constructing a series of varied youthful identities within the confines of an older class culture, modern society and, of course, in the wake of the new vocationalism.

Theorising working-class youth transitions

There has been literally a mountain of commentary and publicity surrounding the topic of youth in Britain. It is not my purpose to sift through and review this mammoth body of work here, nor do

I wish to even map out the varied perspectives surrounding the youth question. This latter task has been conducted elsewhere (Cohen, 1986a). Even the more specific topic of working-class youth has received more than its fair share of review and media attention. Instead, I want to examine selected pieces of work which most closely relate to and probe the issues of working-class youth transitions and identities as they concern this present study.

There has been a series of largely ethnographic projects on the movement from school to work which have broader implications for theorising around working-class youth. While there have been unprecedented changes in education and training provision for the 16–19 age group, some of this previous theoretical and ethnographic material is highly relevant to this case study. For example, as Chapter 2 demonstrates, experiences of schooling continue to have an impact on young people's responses to the new vocationalism and to future transitions into work/unemployment. Second, and more importantly, much of this ethnographic work was concerned not just with movements between institutions, but also dealt with the actual construction of identities in relation to wage and domestic labour.

'Learning to Labour' revisited

Perhaps the most celebrated work on youth transitions from school to work is Paul Willis's *Learning to Labour* (1977). In addition to serving as a forerunner to a large body of ethnographic studies of schooling,[9] the work has also provoked a high level of theoretical debate and critique.[10]

For those not familiar with the work, Willis's main question was 'why do working class kids get working class jobs?' In an attempt to avoid a simplistic answer, he rejects both liberal (because working-class kids are seen by significant others – that is teachers – to be slow or non-academic) and reproduction theories (because the system means them to fail in school). Instead, Willis puts forth a theory of cultural production which suggests, based upon his own ethnographic observations, that working-class males actively help to produce themselves as future, semi-skilled manual labourers. In other words, it is the lad's own handling of the situation and their development of a counter-school culture (drawn from the wider class culture) that leads them to value manual labour and delivers them on to the shop floor. This culture included the development of oppositional schooling behaviours, forms amenable to shop floor survival and the inversion of manual labour as superior to mental labour. Working-class lads don't get middle-class jobs partly because they don't want them.

Notwithstanding a series of sometimes powerful critiques of Willis's work (related to its romanticism of class culture and its exclusion of other working-class groups, i.e., young women, non-lads, etc.), I believe it raises three main issues which have implications for the present case study of youth responses to the new vocationalism.

First, it might be argued that *Learning to Labour* confined itself too closely to the strict parameters of the counter-school culture, without adequately exploring the influence of other social sites – particularly the family. The lads' culture is drawn specifically from the institutional character of the school and its parallels with a manual labour culture. Only rarely do we get a glimpse of the lads elsewhere and there is little sustained analysis of how their power position within the working-class household is crucial in forming masculine identities. In this book, I maintain that the domestic sphere is a crucial element in all young people's construction of a variety of transitions into work.

A second issue concerns the massive changes that have transpired since the researching and writing of *Learning to Labour*. While the particular male working-class transition Willis was talking about continues under the new vocationalism, there have been some significant shifts. For instance, while aspects of 'lad culture' persist, they do so against the backdrop of a rapidly declining manual labour sector of the workforce (Massey, 1983; Beechey, 1985). Additionally, the lad's counter-school culture was at least partly based upon the realisation that there were 'real' jobs that could be obtained without educational qualifications. Significant changes in post-16 education and training mean that this group has had to negotiate new institutional structures and curricula developed under contemporary training and skilling regimes. Finally, the ethnographic limits of Willis's work meant that he was unable to give much insight into what kind of future workers the lads might become. The destruction of craft skills, heightened forms of white ethnicity and sexism, and a weakening of informal links between manual labour and trade unions on schemes has meant that the lads as a cultural group may be headed for a more conservative political agenda under the new vocationalism.

The final and perhaps most important issue that Willis's work raises for this study is his concentration on a single cultural transition and how this is used to theorise about other subsections of the youth population. This is the basic weakness of *Learning to Labour*. By activating and emphasising one particular cultural form, Willis has implicitly played down the significance of other transitions and identities within the young working class, failing to grasp the interrelationship between groups. In other words, the stress placed on the lads apparently self-made and autonomous culture blocked out any real interaction between groups of young people themselves and their relations with 'significant others' and to other social sites. Teachers, for example, appear immobilised and other groups of young people are formed only in relation to the lads' seemingly all-powerful culture. The point is that there can be no simple causal explanation of working-class transitions based purely upon the dominance of a single male cultural form. Willis was unable to theorise and conceptualise adequately a diverse youth population because of his focus on a single cultural form, together with a lack of 'insider' knowledge of other subsections of working-class youth. I argue, however, that although male power is significant in influencing other youth transitions, it does not and cannot in itself explain the wide variety of identities and paths carved out in relation to wage and domestic labour. In summary, because the focus and theory of *Learning to Labour* was so tightly wound around lad culture and its self-development within the school counter-culture, it was unable to put forth a model whereby differential identities and transitions into work might develop in alternative sites and locations for different subsections of working-class youth.

Typical girls?

The transitions made by young working-class women are even more difficult to grasp from the viewpoint of a single cultural form and institutional context such as counter-school culture. This criticism is not simply limited to theories of male working-class

culture like that found in *Learning to Labour*. Attempts to theorise the position of young women through feminist variations of
reproduction or discourse theory have also been hampered by
their concentration around a single sphere – such as domestic
labour, the sexual division of labour or women's treatment as
sexual objects – to explain female transitions and identities (Mac-
Donald, 1980; Wolpe, 1978; Lees, 1986). This is not to argue that
these spheres are unimportant. The point is that such analyses
tend to portray young women as completely powerless and often
the relationship between gender and class is left unexplored (i.e.
the transition is the same for all women).

There is, however, a growing body of feminist-inspired work
which has distanced itself from these deterministic paradigms and
has sought to empower young women. In these cases, young
women are viewed as multiple subjects, drawing their identities
from a range of social sites and practices. Some of this work has
tackled traditionally male areas of youth research – for example,
the school to work transition (Griffin, 1985), experiences of wage
labour (Pollert, 1981), training (Cockburn, 1987), leisure studies
(Deem, 1986) and deviancy (Davies, 1984) – and by utilising
aspects of feminist theory have sought to shed new light on prevail-
ing theoretical orthodoxies. Other research has branched out into
more unconventional territory such as dance and fantasy (McRobbie, 1984), cultural consumption (Carter, 1984) and female subcultures (Rothaus, 1984).

Of particular relevance here are studies on young working-class
women's transitions from school to work. An example of this type
of work is Chris Griffin's *Typical Girls?* (1985). Like *Learning to
Labour*, Griffin's approach is also ethnographic. However, her
work poses a direct challenge to orthodox labour market theory,
the school to work literature and the use of 'malestream' counter-
school cultures for explaining the transitions and experiences of
young women. Griffin's analysis centres on the role of the domestic sphere, female heterosexuality and pressure to 'get a man',
to help explain young women's quite different transition from
school. While she does stress some of the general features which
oppress all young women, the title 'Typical Girls?' expresses a
diversity of identities within the female population.

While there are obvious points of contact between Griffin's
work and this study, it is useful to point out some of the differ-

ences in emphasis. First, the concentration on the school to work transition initially ties the book somewhat to a position whereby education is assumed to be the primary site of the sexual division of labour. However, this should not imply that the analysis begins and ends here. Griffin quickly discovers from the young women themselves that it is the domestic sphere and the sexual and marriage market-place, not a counter-school culture, which best helps to explain young women's transitions into the job market. The assumption here however, is that gender and the domestic sphere are primarily responsible for contouring young women's transitions into work, rather than seeking out how the combined relationship these and other social sites and relations have on female identity formation. This present study suggests that there are in fact several female transitions carved out in relation to the world of work which draw their differences from a combination of a wide variety of sites and identities (i.e. the home, non-work, politics, variants of the new vocationalism).

The second difference of emphasis between this study and Griffin's work lies in the fact that compulsory post-16 training has had a substantial impact on changing transitions for young working-class women (Wickham, 1982; Cockburn, 1986). This is not to argue, as the MSC would have it, that training schemes have opened up new occupational opportunities for women, rather it has thrown up the possibility of developing new images of women's work for the young working class, and this clearly has an important bearing on the creation of future work/home and even class identities. So, for example, the thrust of the new vocationalism's careerist ideology for young women has shifted perceptions of the traditional domestic apprenticeship and of one's class position in the labour market. New identities formed in relation to lifestyle and politics, although embryonic, are also beginning to evolve. The point is not to play down the centrality of the domestic sphere, but to begin to broaden out the growing importance of other sites in influencing young working-class women's future transitions. These changes have led some contemporary researchers to begin to rethink the youth question.

Rethinking the youth question

Certainly, one of the most theoretically sophisticated attempts at coming to terms with the youth question and working-class transitions is the work of Philip Cohen (1986a). In combination with his mapping out of the main perspectives influencing contemporary theories of youth, he has also conducted a series of very concrete studies in support of his own thesis (Cohen, 1983; 1984). In addition, Cohen's theory is particularly well placed in situating the present study as its main focus centres around the interaction between traditional working-class cultural forms, the labour movement and the impact of the new vocationalism.

Cohen's theory of working-class youth transitions rests on his development of the concept 'reproduction codes'. These codes refer to the way in which class relations are 'lived and symbolically represented' (Cohen, 1986a, p. 56). Through the notion of code, Cohen attempts to construct a theory of working-class youth transitions which constitutes both a notion of identity (or subjectivity) and the idea of a social location (class position). The impact of codes, in differing combinations, throws up quite distinct subject positions and 'grids' which help to connect social origins with future destinations.

Cohen gives this idea a historical dimension when he specifically applies his theory to working-class youth. He argues that until quite recently working-class youth transitions were organised around two codes – those of 'apprenticeship' and 'inheritance.' In other words, the transition into adulthood took the form of a cultural apprenticeship rooted in the inheritance of a patrimony of skills (adult, white and male dominated) transmitted through the family, the shop floor and the wider working-class community. In this way young people's destinies were fixed to their class origins through 'an active mastery of shared techniques and conditions of labour' (Cohen, 1983, pp. 29–30). These transitions also entailed that elements of a certain political tradition were transmitted. For working-class males this apprenticeship was specifically related to their embracing the techniques of manual labour (skill) and politicisation through a masculine shop floor culture. Young working-class women's apprenticeship took on a very different form and was focused around their subordination to men and through the domestic rather than the wage-labour sphere (though not exclusively). These apprenticeships threw up a fairly predictable pattern of identity, politics and social position across whole sectors of public and private life.

In the post-war period, this particular combination of codes (or modes of living out one's class position) changed dramatically for young people. While the reasons behind this transformation are extremely varied (ranging from changes in working-class cultures, community, the occupational structure, the rise of the consciousness industries, changes in production, the opening up of the non-work sphere in identity formation, etc), what is of most significance for understanding the impact the new vocationalism is having on changing youth transitions and politics is the rise of the 'career' code, with its particular stress on individualism. Equally important is the decline of a manual political culture centred around traditional working-class notions of skill.

As Cohen (1982; 1984) argues, while the weight of traditional patterns persist under the surface, both male and female youth transitions have clearly fractured in response to the new vocationalism. Changing definitions of skill have led to a weakening and pulling apart of the apprenticeship and inheritance codes. For some working-class males, the lack of jobs and status gained through the acquisition of craft skills has meant a disavowal of the masculine culture of the shop floor and the search for alternative identities in the non-work sphere, youth issues, politics and in middle-class 'white collar' jobs. For others, the breakdown of this inheritance has led to the adoption of exaggerated masculine and nationalist identities in the context of a declining manual culture. For young working-class women, the weakening of the power of the domestic apprenticeship and the rise of 'careerism' and 'paraprofessionalism' (see Chapter 5) through the new vocationalism has led to a more diverse set of female identities and transitions in relation to work. Other spaces in the non-work and political realm have also led to the beginnings of some 'non-traditional' gender identities.

While there are some difficulties surrounding Cohen's level of abstraction (i.e. I prefer to use the term cultural forms rather than reproduction codes), his work clearly informs the analysis of the ethnographic evidence which follows. His concerns with identity and social positioning, the relationship between class cultures and the new vocationalism and the existence of varied youthful transitions, are all reflected in this case study. Furthermore, Cohen's work is also highly suggestive in showing why the elaboration of new youthful sites of identity formation and changes in traditional transitions have had an adverse effect on the appeal of traditional labour ideology amongst working-class youth. Any renewed youth politics must come out of a recognition of these changes and a serious examination of current working-class youth concerns.

The research: details and social context

This study is based upon two and a half years of fieldwork, examining young people's experiences of the YTS in a large city in the West Midlands. While certain aspects of working-class life and culture and the structure of scheme provision may be specific to this locality, the major elements of the transitions described and analysed are, I would argue, applicable to many other parts of the country. Over the course of the research, a series of in-depth interviews and observations were carried out with approximately[11] forty-six young people as they made their way through the YTS into work, further training or unemployment. The methodology and analysis used belongs to a tradition of cultural ethnography which attempts to situate human meanings and actions in the context of social relations, customary practices and institutional arrangements that characterise the social structure.[12]

During the fieldwork phase, over 200 trainees were contacted and twenty individual schemes were visited. A representative cross-section of schemes was chosen and trainees were selected for interview on the basis of their type of training and work experience, gender and race breakdown, and scheme categorisation. Those selected were initially interviewed and subsequently visited at the scheme, out on placement and sometimes in the home and in other venues (pubs, cafes, on the street, etc.). In addition to this, a number of schemes was chosen for in-depth study and they form the three main case studies reported in Chapter 3. Interviews were also carried out with various scheme managers, work supervisors, off-the-job training tutors, training and careers officers.

The fieldwork took place between November 1983 and April

1986, a period which roughly spans the official launch of the YTS and the introduction of the two-year scheme. The basic structure of the one-year scheme was thirteen weeks off-the-job training and thirty-seven weeks work experience. The two-year scheme, by contrast, contains only twenty weeks total off-the-job training over the two years. While the initial classification of schemes into 'Modes'[13] has now been phased out under the two-year programme and has been dropped here, I continue to refer to schemes as either 'employer-led', 'private training agencies' (see below) or 'community-based'.

Despite some of these superficial changes to the YTS, the main structural features of the scheme remain intact. There is little doubt that the emergence, organisation and design of the YTS bears the underlying purpose of displacing unemployment and shaping orientations towards employment. The scheme's original rationale – 'providing a permanent bridge from school to work' (MSC, 1982a) – has been effectively buried by an avalanche of government leaks and admissions that the YTS is clearly important in reducing unemployment figures, easing wage rigidities and reforming young people's attitudes towards work (Department of Employment, 1985; Labour Research, 1983). Furthermore, the recent move to make the scheme compulsory also removes any doubts over its so-called voluntary nature. The aim has been to use training schemes to shift the blame for unemployment away from structural causes (i.e. government policies, lack of demand) towards individualist explanations (i.e. a lack of employability amongst working-class school leavers).

A second crucial influence in shaping the organisation and structure of the YTS is its attempt to invert the schooling experience. If schools were seen as partly to blame for young people's lack of motivation, then schemes had to appear to provide a more practical and relevant programme for working-class school leavers. This is reflected in the primacy of the work experience component of the scheme, as well as in the practically-based off-the-job training element. Concepts such as 'transferable skills' and 'occupational training families' are not only steeped in the language of new technologies and service sector employment ideologies, but they also hinge on the tacit assumption that industry is moving towards a new era of worker-management relations. It is certain that the YTS aims to make a formidable impact on young people's orientations towards working life.

Finally, the organisation, delivery structure and design of the YTS had to be both flexible and hierarchical – not only to meet the diverse and even contradictory needs of industry (Finn, 1982), but also to appeal to a broad spectrum of working-class youth response to the new transition into work. In order to match these disparate needs and expectations effectively, the actual administration and day-to-day running of schemes are contracted out to a variety of managing agents (MA). These agents can range from private employers and companies training to fullfil the needs of their own workforce, private trainers in the business of making a profit out of training young people, to local authority, charities and voluntary organisation schemes.

The actual structure and implementation of the YTS in a particular locality is influenced by a region's economic situation and its socio-geographic history. In the West Midlands, this is clearly the case. For instance, the YTS was introduced in the depths of recession and consequently only a very small number of genuine employers initially came forward to act as MA's for the scheme. This gap was rapidly filled by the growth of private training agencies (PTAs), whose main incentive was to try to make a profit out of training. Their continued participation in the YTS has continued to influence the quality and type of off-the-job training provision available (see case 1 in Chapter 3).[14] This more specific recognition of different types of schemes is particularly important for understanding how a hierarchical training programme works to deepen and further fracture existing divisions within the youth population.

The actual implementation and take-up of YTS is influenced by the socio-geography and economic situation of a region in other ways. For instance, the West Midlands' economy has been built historically upon a manufacturing base and its reputation as a region of multiple trades. More recently, its economy has been drastically altered by the activities of transnational companies, government policy and a severe crisis within the manufacturing sector.

The region, with its relatively high-wage manual economy of the early 1970s, was one of the hardest hit by the early 1980s' economic recession. While other parts of the country have higher rates of unemployment, these have generally taken root over a longer period of time. The West Midlands' unemployment rate in 1985 was almost three times that of 1979, the depth of the recession being reflected in the fact that it had the longest median duration of unemployment of forty-seven weeks (Labour Market Quarterly, May 1985). The region continues to face an uncertain future, as it has been suggested that uneven growth in the service sector may be unable to compensate for further heavy losses in the manufacturing area.

The city in which the research took place reflects these major trends of the region. Historically, a plethora of trades flourished and various forms of 'metal bashing' still continue to the present day. There is also a high number of family-owned businesses and a significant number of companies in the area employ less than ten people. Until recently, nearly half the workforce was involved in the light and medium manufacturing industries, many of these servicing the larger transnational companies in the region. There is still a strong male cultural disposition towards the manual trades, despite a massive decline in this sector over the last decade.

The crisis in manufacturing, aided by a lack of investment, government policies and the movement of capital and operations to developing countries by transnationals, drastically altered the economic prospects of the city. At the time of research, unemployment stood at over 16 per cent and on a ward basis rose to 42.2% and 39.2 per cent for the two worst hit spots. Hidden within these overall figures are groups who suffer the ravages of unemployment differentially – black people, women, the disabled and, of course, working-class school leavers.

The destinations of fifth-form school leavers in the city is a good indication of the effect unemployment is having on job prospects and the construction of a new transition into work through schemes. Careers Service figures show that less than two out of twenty fifth-form school leavers obtained jobs six months after leaving school. The growing role of training schemes in dealing with this 'social problem' is reflected in the fact that nearly 40 per cent of this group were undergoing training at the time of the research (the majority being on the YTS). The simple fact is that in the current economic climate many young people have little choice but to go on schemes.

This then is the new social and economic world into which

working-class school leavers have been thrust into. Although not of their making, they nevertheless struggle to make some sense of the situation through the use of their own cultural resources and come to construct different paths through this lengthened transition into working life. It is to these responses, cultures and subjectivities that I now turn.

Part I

Cultural Experiences on the Scheme

2

From School to Schemes

Julie is 17 years old. She is of average height, with brown eyes and brown hair. She is dressed smartly in high street fashion which has a touch of conservatism about it. Julie both looks and acts older than her age, as if she has weathered all the major experiences of a young adult. She is pleasant to talk to and her warm, sociable manner soon overshadows her initial nervousness. Julie is a YTS trainee.

Julie lives in a small village on the outskirts of an industrial conurbation in the West Midlands. She describes the village as 'remote', giving it a rural feel. When she is not working – at her scheme placement and a part-time job catering at a pub two nights a week – or going out with her boyfriend, Julie spends time at home doing her own washing, helping with the cooking and cleaning, and tending to the family coal fire.

In her fifth year at school, Julie couldn't wait to leave. Her only pleasant memory is of her schoolmates, some of whom she still sees regularly. Other than friendships, eleven years of British education have given Julie little except a stigma that she is, in her own words, 'thick' and 'educationally no good'. Originally, she wanted to work with the disabled, but upon leaving school this idea slipped away. Instead, she enrolled in a home economics and community care course at a local college, but found the experience reminiscent of school and dropped out after six months. This only fuelled her initial feeling that she was educationally deficient.

Determined not to become unemployed, Julie went straight to the local Careers Office where she was given information on two factory jobs and 'about forty' different training schemes. She admitted, 'I'm not the factory type,' and ended up on a private training agency YTS specialising in clothing manufacture, distribution and retailing. She had no previous experience of working in a shop, but soon found that her practical skills and warm personality were extremely sought after attributes at her work placement.

Julie was placed with a small Asian-owned shop in the nearby city centre which sold clothing, jewellery and accessories. Before long she was running the jewellery department, had performed virtually every job in the shop and was even left on her own in charge of the store. While she liked the work, Julie was hoping to move up to one of the larger, more established high street stores where she would be in charge of her own stall and where the salary and conditions were better. Concerning her present work placement, she said, 'They use me and I use them.' By this she meant that her work sponsor used her as a 'free pair of hands', while she used them to gain experience in the retail sector.

Julie admitted that she was highly sceptical when she went on to a scheme. She was aware of its dubious reputation, but like her educational experience saw this primarily in terms of her own personal inadequacies ('it's not good to be on a YTS'). On a personal level, however, the scheme had, in Julie's eyes, given her the first real break in her life. For example, she had gained respect at work by moving up from being 'just one of the trainees' to head the jewellery section. On the off-the-job training component of her YTS she was one of the managing directors of the scheme's simulated public limited companies. For the first time in her life she could see a linkage between learning something, applying it and moving towards a tangible end, i.e. a job.

The odd thing, however, is that rather than attributing her 'success' to the unfolding of her own personal qualities, instead Julie projects her achievements on to the scheme. It is ironic that while young people blame themselves for being unemployed or on a training scheme, when they succeed they often praise the 'system' for their attainment. Indeed, Julie now contrasts herself with the new group of trainees joining the scheme, all 'cheeky' and 'undisciplined'. She talks about how much she has grown up and matured on the YTS. In gratitude, Julie literally embraces the major element of the new vocationalism – the inculcation of a 'proper' working attitude in exchange for the possibility of a job. In the process she has lost something intangible from her own cultural background. Julie talks about the new trainees as 'still young and goin' against the system', at the same time as she mentions that she would work for less money in a shop that sold a better range of products. Under the new vocationalism, upward mobility and 'impression management' (work image) become the goals of a section of young trainees whose likely destination will be the bottom tier of the service sector hierarchy. The ideal shopworker becomes a simple extension of the goods for sale. Job satisfaction for the new model worker, especially in this feminine version, is measured by the work image one can project and the profit one creates for the company.

Billy is also 17 and he has black hair and dark eyes. He is as tall as a full-grown man although his physique has not quite filled out. Billy has a mischievous grin and an amiable manner and it is hard not to like him. He responds to questions with a deadpan face and answers with a mocking exaggeration. It is sometimes difficult to know when he's serious or when he 'takes the piss'.

Billy epitomises the notion of verbal contradiction. For example, he is both anti-Thatcher and anti-union. He berates the scheme manager for being a 'racist cat' and looks up to Afro-Caribbean males as 'superlads', but then says he can't stand 'Pakies'. There are some good policemen but invariably all of them are referred to as 'pigs'. Billy acts macho although the other lads see him as a bit of a 'wally'. He mentions he doesn't smoke or drink before letting slip that he's on an intermediate treatment programme for 'waggin it at school or nickin' something'. In a discussion, Billy reduces general topics to personal examples and by drawing on traditional aphorisms and maxims (like 'there's good and bad in everyone') his views often appear to be confused and contradictory.

Billy lives in an old working-class area of the city, complete with rows of terraced houses interrupted only by corner shops, off-licences and derelict factories. The unemployment rate in his ward is one of the highest in the city and runs close to 40 per cent. Most of Billy's classmates are either on schemes or on the dole. During his first two years of school, he confessed to being a conformist, or in the sociology of education vernacular an 'ear 'ole'. When he changed schools in his third year he said, 'They changed me' – meaning the school, its teachers and his new mates. This schooling process has been described as the emergence of a particularly male form of counter-school culture which helps to prepare working-class kids for a future of manual labour. In this

context, Billy was full of stories about 'skivin' off', 'waggin' it'
(playing truant) and having a 'laff' with his mates. He also possessed one of the most humorous and enlightening critiques of
the school curriculum of any young person I spoke to.

Billy left school only to become unemployed. Initially, he
enjoyed the break but soon became extremely bored. As he said,
you were either stuck in the house 'watchin' the box' or you were
harassed by the police out in the street. Although wary – friends
had told him the YTS was 'no good' and 'cheap labour' – he went
on to a broad-based community scheme run by the city education
department. For the first three weeks Billy received some general
training in painting and decorating and was given some project-
based work experience 'shovellin' sand and shit in an old barn'.
By the end of the third week, the scheme officer obtained a work
placement for him in a small, owner-run garage which pleased
him immensely. He had taken a keen interest in motor vehicle
studies in school and his dream was to become an auto mechanic.

The one subject Billy was serious about was his placement. He
worked from 8 to 6 o'clock every day (against YTS regulations)
and put in a full day on Saturday for an extra £5 from his boss.
He enjoyed the work, the practical application of skill and he was
well versed in male shop floor culture and humour. His definition
of a good job was hard physical labour, reasonable wages and
having a 'laff' with the lads.

It was because of his placement that Billy was prepared to
tolerate the YTS experience at all. Unlike Julie, Billy never felt
that he was somehow untrained or unprepared for his likely occupational destination. Perhaps part of his assuredness came from
his insertion into the more developed male working-class cultural
forms untilised in school, which effectively inverts the mental–
manual distinction (manual labour being clearly superior). As
such, while he enjoyed his work experience placement, Billy
explicitly rejected the life and social skills emphasis evident in the
off-the-job training element of the YTS. Much of this time was
spent socialising and having a laugh with his mates on the scheme,
while he waited for the possibility of being taken on permanently
by his placement. The YTS, for him, was viewed as a temporary
obstacle to a predetermined destination.

I have begun with these personal profiles for a number of
reasons. First, they help to provide a human dimension to the dry

facts and figures representing the large number of school leavers forced on to government training schemes. They are intended to portray real people struggling to make some kind of sense out of their new transitions into working life.

Second, such life-stories also demonstrate some common cultural responses to the new vocationalism, as well as hinting at the very disparate and differentiated transitions that young people eventually forge into adulthood. These common responses spring out of remnants of an older working-class tradition and from the general construction of a new movement into work through a process I describe as 'traineeship'. This traineeship has interrupted previous working-class transitions into jobs and replaced it with a prolonged expectation of schemes, a training programme built upon a theory of deficiency and the creation of a separate status for young people at work. The more differentiated patterns expressed by Julie and Billy extend beyond their own personal circumstances and represent real social divisions within the working-class youth population. These divisions spring not only from the impact gender (and race) have upon class formation, but also hint at the development of more varied sets of identities and transitions forged by young people in the current period.

This chapter provides a background and context to the more general transition on the YTS which I have labelled traineeship. It does so by outlining the changing relationship between varied working-class cultural responses and the official mechanisms and agencies marking the transition from school to work. Young people are in the midst of a new transition, delineated by an arm of the State, whereby they are no longer school children nor are they fullyfledged workers entitled to proper wages and conditions. And yet, they do not easily succumb to the imposition of a new transition into work. Instead, in negotiating their way through the new vocationalism, young people actively help to produce a variety of identities and transitions into work and adulthood. Experiences of schooling provide one of the main social contexts for how they react to and negotiate their way on to training schemes.

Experiences of schooling[1]

Three main experiences of schooling most often recalled by trainees were: (a) the desire to leave school and move into work; (b)
a resentment of the inapplicability of the education curriculum
and criticism of schooling relations and exams; and (c) making
the best of a bad situation, 'muckin' about' and having a good time
as they reached the end of their compulsory time in education.

A significant majority of young people interviewed were
adament that they wanted to leave school for the world of work,
many at the earliest possible moment:

> **BH:**   Did you leave school early?
> **Jackie:** I left School in May – I was 16 the day I left.
>
> **BH:**   When did you start thinking about leaving school?
> **Ben:**   At the end of the second year – I just used to stay at
>   home, that was the fourth year, sit at home and write
>   poems or go for a walk . . . I eventually stopped going
>   to school during the mock exams.

While leaving school was the wish of the majority, there was a
significant gender dimension to those few who wanted to stay on
in an attempt to pass some exams.[2] For example, there was a
small subgroup of young women who saw exams as an essential
stepping stone to a vocational career (i.e. in nursing, childcare,
working with the handicapped, fashion, etc.). This is not to say
they were academically oriented. However, many realised that
such vocational courses offered by colleges often required some
exam results. The YTS, for this group, was a second option or
fall back choice when they failed to achieve satisfactory exam
results. On the other side, there were very few working-class
males in the sample who specifically mentioned they wished to
stay on at school. The dominant desire of working class youth as
a whole social group, in this study, was to leave school to search
for work.

One of the primary reasons for wanting to leave, in addition to
the status gained by moving into the adult world of work, was
criticism of the school curriculum and a dislike of the social
relations of education. Many working-class school leavers come

out of education deeply wounded by the experience. A sense of failure, frustration and powerlessness over what is taught combined to create quite negative self-images and impressions of school:

Julie: Educationally, I'm no good – on the education side I'm not that good. As thick as two short planks. But um, practically . . .

BH: As what?

Julie: I'm as thick as two short planks. It's a saying. I'm thick. Um, but – I'd say educationally I'm no good, but practically I am good. I'm good with children, I'm good with handicapped, I'm good with everything – and shopwork and everything. But educationally I'm no good. I tried to go to college – I had this feeling that if I went to college to try and get this course then I'd be all right. But it just doesn't happen with me.

BH: Do you think at school they don't appreciate those other things? I mean you were saying.

Julie: You have to be educationally – if yer not educationally good, in this place they just put you in um, elementary classes. And they stick you in there and that's about it. And they help you try and build up your education but . . . yuh know, more help.

BH: Were you glad to leave school then?

Julie: I wasn't, I didn't really mind leavin'. There were no tears or anything [laughs]. I just left on goodwill with everybody.

This personal confession expresses a number of broader processes at work in a class-biased education system. For example, it demonstrates how streaming and the curriculum merge to produce self-blame and evaluations that one is 'thick' or a failure. And while many young people realise that they do indeed possess real practical skills, they also recognise that these are often undervalued in relation to academic knowledge. Finally, Julie's comment hints at how young people's frustrations at school can get translated into positive evaluations of training schemes, which are often seen as relevant, practical and related to the world of work.

Other young people provided equally forceful critiques of the education system and curriculum, particularly as it related to preparing them for life in the 'real' world:

> **Mick:** All these things yuh learn at school – is not really genuine knowledge at all yuh need out in the world – yuh don't need nothin' of that.
>
> **BH:** What was the worst thing about school? Ah, what subjects and things?
>
> **Billy:** English and maths are the worst subjects you can get.
>
> **Chris:** Science . . . you ain't gonna be a scientist, yuh ain't gonna end up a scientist in secondary school are yuh?
>
> **BH:** What about mathematics?
>
> **Billy:** It's useful in some ways . . . but the things they teach yuh, yuh know, logs and all that sort of stuff – simple addings and minusing and timesin' – that's all yuh really need. Yuh don't really need all these er logrhythms [logarithms], Pathagorese, Pathagorus' theories and all – I was at school right, got this K+A=B or somethin' like that. I thought, where did they get these letters from and what do they mean? It really got me lost that did.

If the 'real world' is defined primarily in terms of work, home and community, then school was definitely not the institution in which one expected to gain 'really useful knowledge'. Similarly, within working-class culture, purely theoretical knowledge is often viewed as totally absurd, as Billy's final comment so cogently expresses.

More specific criticisms of the school curriculum revolved around the stress on examinations and the ranking of traditional academic subjects over technical ones. The exam system continues to dominate what is meant by success in schools and differentiates 'intelligent' students from the others:

> **Jan:** Well, the 'O' levels are the higher grade one and the CSEs are the lower one. And I took the 'O' levels which were the higher grade one for more sort of intelligent people. I didn't do very well [laughs].

Furthermore, in many cases there is still a bias towards traditional academic subjects in school and young working-class people are acutely aware that technically based subjects are somehow viewed as inferior. This should not imply that all young people readily accepted this distinction. However, they were not always in a position to challenge the situation or relate this dilemma to the outside world of work:

Ben: It's a vicious circle really 'cos they say yuh gotta work towards qualifications to get a job. Then you see the real world outside and there's no jobs around so you think I'm not doin' this anymore. So you drop out and then you do find out that if you do have qualifications it's an advantage, not much, but it is an advantage. But you can't work towards that advantage 'cos it's too late.

Clearly, the contradictions generated by the real world of work and the limited benefit of qualifications for many working-class jobs created a 'no win' situation for many young people.

If the proponents of the new vocationalism are right about anything, it is their criticism of the continuing élitism of much of the educational system. This should not imply that the insertion of work-based subjects back into schools is only a recent phenomenon or is automatically a positive thing in its own terms. Many educational theorists have argued that vocationalism is slowly coming to dominate the school curriculum (Bates *et al.*, 1984). The problem has been that the rise of the new vocationalism in schools has actually been used to justify and exacerbate the distinction between 'hand' and 'head' labour.

Pupils have had their own criticism of the irrelevance of schooling for many working-class jobs before the MSC made its assault on education and these two views should not be conflated. Working-class youngsters have long seen through the value of compulsory schooling (even liberal teaching methods and career guidance) in helping them make the transition from school to work, and instead have relied on their own cultural forms and family/ community contacts to make the transition.[3] A lack of real jobs for young people in the future may signal a further breakdown in the classroom, characterised by disruptive behaviour and non-cooperation from many students:

Kathy: My brother, he don't even bother in school anymore

'cos he knows that you don't need qualifications to
get on YTS. So he's stopped tryin' – he's not doin'
anything in school – just messin' about.

Proponents of the new vocationalism have sought to build on these
dissatisfactions as justification for a work-based school curriculum.
However, they fail to see that young people will similarly reject
aspects of vocationalism unless a direct link to real jobs can be
demonstrated and many will continue to rely on their own cultural
milieu for support, rather than accept patronising life and social
skills educational models.

In addition to their distain of the school curriculum, there was
a generally negative evaluation of the social relations of schooling.
In other words, the desire to leave school was based partly around
wanting to shed the child-like image of school and enter into the
adult world of work:

BH: Did you notice a big difference in the way people treat
you on YTS from school? I mean is YTS like school at
all?

Julie: From school – from school to college you don't know
what's, what's goin' on in the world. You don't, it
sounds terrible, but you don't. And when you come on
this [YTS] you find out that you've got to look after
yourself – that you've got this backing, you've got like
at work, you can, if anything goes wrong you can fall
back on this and they push yuh back up and yuh get
on your way. But yuh know after this you haven't got
anybody to push you back up on a pedestal, you know.

Besides not teaching one about the real world, school relations
were also viewed as 'immature':

Nigel: Well, when I was at school, I really didn't think much
of school. I mean, any young person could say that, I
didn't think much of school. I couldn't see the point
of gettin' up every morning and coming into this building and jus' sit down – and um, school was um, a very
immature place to be really. I don't think anybody in
school could actually say, when I was in the fifth form,

that you were mature. Because you go home and you come back and you're the same person you were the day before. And um, very childlike manner at times.

While this immaturity is often projected on to school leavers themselves, clearly the problem lies with the whole institutional structure of education. For example, many young people felt that teachers had no confidence in them and hence treated them as children. The irony is that working-class pupils may be labelled childish precisely for developing coping behaviours necessary to endure compulsory schooling, which they rightly perceive as blocking their transition into adulthood.

Compulsory schooling up to the age of 16 means that many working-class pupils have little option but to make the best of a bad situation. The third recollection trainees had of school, then, related to an endless array of stories of 'muckin' about,' having fun with mates, winding up teachers and generally making do until their sixteenth birthday.

Disillusionment with formal education often took a few years to set in. Many remembered their initial entry into school as one of general conformity, followed by a transitional period whereby the last few years were viewed as a 'waste of time'. Related research on working-class transitions from school to work shows that although an overall pattern exists, there are crucial gender differences – with the male peer group structure being perhaps more organic to this transformation (Willis, 1977; Griffin, 1985). Billy's story, for instance, demonstrates a shift from trying to be a 'posh' student to his coming out as one of the 'lads':

Billy: [laughs] I used to be an upper class twat. When I went to Broadhurst they changed me.
Mick: Yuh haven't changed much.
Billy: I 'ave, I used to go to Knightsbridge, that was an upper class school . . . Knightsbridge – when I was there, there was all these top notchers and everything, yuh know, ha, ha, ha [thumbs his nose].

The pattern for working-class girls takes on quite a different form. As Griffin (ibid.) argues, best friendships rather than collective group structures characterise female school relations. Additionally, female transitions involve preparing for marriage and the domestic sphere, and forms of deviance amongst working-class girls are often not as visible as that of the lads. This does not mean that young women as a social group were any less disruptive than young men, or equally unsatisfied with the social relations of schooling. In fact, even Julie, who had largely conformed to the ideology of the YTS, admitted she was a bit of a 'troublemaker' in school:

> **BH:** Did you muck around in school?
>
> **Julie:** Yea, a bit yea [laughs] – quite a bit. I was in the lower class anyway so it didn't make any difference to me. I could bunk off and go to the toilets [laughs].

Clearly there were varied gender reasons for disliking school and different oppositional strategies were adopted.

While schooling relations are an important social context for understanding how some youngsters relate to the various skilling regimes on the YTS, they are not the sole factor in determining school leavers' expectations of training schemes. Also crucial in preparing young people's acceptance of schemes is the massive disjuncture between their expectations upon leaving school and the brutal realities of the youth labour market.

Leaving school: expectations and realities

While the main option for the majority of working-class youths was to leave school in search of work, a small number also mentioned college or apprenticeships. Whatever 'choice' was eventually settled on, there was often an unbridgeable gap between what many of these young people expected and what real opportunities existed in the labour market. One of the key elements of the new transitions is the substitution of training schemes for the expectation of work – aided, in part by the sheer monotony of unemployment.

Of course, there were some young people who left school because of lost opportunities and unforeseen events. These circumstances included having to change schools in mid-year, personal problems, a dislike of teachers and 'messing up' one's exams:

> **Shabaz:** I wanted to go back to Broadhurst because ah, all the people I was with then, I had, they all got good marks in the exams and I was all right in school. I didn't take any exams though [at the new school] – I didn't get the chance.

In most cases these missed opportunities were seen in strictly personal terms and in the context of individual failure:

> **Kathy:** I just messed up in school, it was my own fault. You can't get in the police force if you haven't got qualifications. It was my own fault really, I should have done more work at school.

It is far too easy to substitute a middle-class model of choices and options about staying on at school – but for many working-class youngsters life simply didn't work that way. While only a minority actually wanted to stay on, circumstances meant that even these few were often forced to leave early.

There was also a small group of young people interviewed who saw college as a possible option in a shrinking job market. Getting a place on a college course was again no simple choice. Many courses required some kind of entry qualification and there was always the problem of money:

> **Liz:** I was going to go to college full time, but I couldn't get any help. I couldn't get a grant or anything . . . You don't get any help at all from anywhere. The only place where you get decent grants is when you go to university. I went to find out about it when I got interviewed to do this part-time course I'm doing [in fashion]. I was after a full-time place at the college to do a BTEC diploma course. And I went to the grants office to find out if I could actually get a grant and I found that I could get something like £6 a week at the most, if I got a grant at all.

Some young people who started out on college courses, before going on to the YTS, mentioned that they weren't really ready for the experience:

> **Nigel:** When I was at college, I was doing part time and I tended to slack off very much and not do much work . . . I used to spend a lot of time in the canteen actually doing nothing, just wasting time. And my attitude was very carefree indeed. I didn't really put my mind to my work.

So a lack of experience, support, money and qualifications often closed off the college option for many working-class school leavers. Some of this group joined college-based schemes and used the YTS to simulate the college experience.

For the majority, however, college was not seen as a viable option. It was perceived as an extension of formal schooling and was to be avoided at all costs. Those who were effectively forced to undertake a part of their YTS off-the-job training in a local college often mentioned that they saw it as 'a doss' or 'school-like.' Absenteeism in these situations was high.

The vast majority of early leavers left school with the expectation of finding employment. However, their initial enthusiasm and optimism about obtaining work soon faded when the task proved to be much more difficult than they originally anticipated:

> **Mandy:** I'd rather get a job, that's what I thought . . . thought I'd look around for a bit and look for things. Now I'm on YTS.

> **Dan:** I didn't particularly want to go on a scheme, but I knew I had to do something. So, I hadn't really thought beforehand what – I thought I'd get a job as well, but that soon proved to be wrong [laughs].

In fact, six months after leaving school that year, only 9.2 per cent of fifth formers in the city were in employment. Hidden within this overall figure is the influence other factors such as race, gender and disability had upon obtaining work. For example, only 3.6 per cent of Afro-Caribbean, 4.3 per cent of Asians, 8 per cent of women and 18 out of 583 disabled fifth formers found employment over this same period.[4] The apprenticeship route into a trade had virtually collapsed. However much young school leavers expected and wanted to find a job, the reality of the youth labour market prevented them from doing so.

A final option, if it can be considered an option at all, was to become unemployed (go on the 'dole'). Legislation in force at the time meant that young people refusing a scheme could lose up to 40 per cent of their social security payment. Recent changes in benefit entitlement effectively means the YTS is now compulsory (i.e. no payment will be made to refusers or those who leave the scheme to become unemployed). At the time of this research, there was a trend whereby early school leavers had to wait for a period before they qualified for benefit. They often viewed this initial period as a break from school and work, but many soon found they became extremely bored and fed up with having little or no money. Schoolday perceptions of the dole as a 'bit of a lark' were quickly altered:

Baz: I thought, oh, great, get outta school – on the dole now. Everybody thinks, Oh god, lets all go on the dole, doss around, just get money for dossin' around . . . yuh go out and, it's more or less boring.

Liz: I didn't want to be on the dole particularly, you know. I wasn't thinking oh this is great I'm not doin' anything, I don't have to bother gettin' up for work or anything like that.

Billy: When you first go on the dole it's great . . .
Mick: No you don't.
Billy: Yuh know, gettin' paid for dossin' about. But once yuh get used to it, it's really bad, it gets on yer nerves, it's boring and all. I've only bin on it a month or two.
Chris: I'm tellin' yuh, yuh lose, you lose the habit of gettin' up in the morning. It's crap, I tell yuh.

None of the young people I spoke to voluntarily chose to go on the dole. Most had left school with the intention of finding a job and this remained an important goal for them throughout the scheme. It was a combination of a strong desire to work and grow up and the dull experience of unemployment which led many working-class youths back to the Careers Office, only to be offered a training scheme substitute. More and more youngsters are now moving straight from school on to schemes. Part of the reason is 'compulsion' (i.e. no benefit) as well as a recognition that there are very few jobs about. It is also impossible to ignore the hyped up advertising campaigns conducted by the MSC or the importance of the Careers Service in promoting training schemes. Increasingly, the transition into work for many school leavers is now predicated upon the expectation of being placed on the YTS.

'Choosing' a scheme: informal knowledges and the role of the Careers Service

In order to provide a more complete and realistic picture of how young people actually choose a particular type of training scheme, it is useful to compare and contrast young people's informal knowledges of the YTS with the information provided through the Careers Service. While Careers affords the main official mechanism for being placed on schemes young people's own focal concerns and knowledges, drawn from the wider working-class community, are not incidental to this process. What is significant here is the changing relationship and balance of forces between the official agencies and the informal culture.

With virtually no chance of finding a job and with the sour taste of unemployment in their mouths, many of these young people turned to the Careers Service for help and advice. The vast majority of school leavers interviewed gained information and were put in touch with their scheme through their local Careers Office. Some also received advice from careers teachers in schools. Interviews with Careers Officers in the area made it clear that the new vocationalism had literally transformed their entire job description. Advice about schemes, rather than jobs, has become the norm.

Earlier, I argued that many working-class school leavers became acutely aware that their chances of obtaining employment were slim. For some, this realisation began in school:

Mick: Everyone was sayin', everyone didn't think we'd get a

job. Everyone thought we'd go straight on the dole . . .
Yuh had a career lesson, listen, yuh had a career
lesson, instead of talkin' about jobs, they talk about
how to sign on the dole.

In other cases, expectations of training schemes in place of work
were also planted in school:

Finchy: Well, when I was, when I, yea, when I was at school
that was all they [careers teachers] told me I could
have, like. They didn't mention the job side, it was
what training scheme do you want to go on when you
leave school, right?

This was also the kind of advice many young people received
when they visited their local Careers Office:

BH: Were they realistic about your chances of getting
work, do you think?

Shanaz: They just try and tell us to go on a training scheme.
You have to go on a training scheme now, you don't
have any choice.

Only one trainee recalled that Careers actually mentioned a job.
The role of Careers in helping to prepare young school leavers to
accept the YTS, in place of work, cannot be overestimated.

In discussions about the role of the Careers Service, some young
people volunteered additional information as to how they were
treated while speaking to officers about their future prospects:

Dan: Their attitude was ah – it was the first year of YTS and
it was the first term of people actually going on to YTS.
And their attitude was 'at long last we've got something
we can give to them to get them out of the way quickly'.
And ah, like they just were good, glad to get rid of you
as soon as possible and get on to the next person and
get rid of them.

A good number of trainees mentioned that they felt Careers
people saw the YTS as an easy answer to their problems. Schemes

were talked about enthusiastically as new career opportunities, rather than as a substitute for work and a proper wage.

While Careers may have been the main venue for finding out about and getting an interview with a particular scheme, all young people had prior knowledges, alternative sources of information and culturally based dispositions towards training schemes. Much of this information was based upon appraisals of the Youth Opportunities Programme (YOP) which predated the YTS and was heavily criticised, not least by the participants themselves. These often less than favourable evaluations circulated within families, schools and neighbourhoods and came from older brothers, sisters, parents and friends:

Margaret: It's terrible this trainin' scheme wage – my dad calls it slave labour.

Mick: That's what the YOP was, that's why they scrapped the YOP. 'Cos yuh didn't go to the training centre, yuh just went straight to the firm – they'd just use yuh as slave, slave labour.

Mandy: I couldn't be bothered to go on one. All I heard was that they were bad. And ah, I met a friend that was down here on this scheme and she told me to come along.

Angus: They were sayin' like it's a bad thing – people at school were sayin' cheap an' all that.

The possession of this type of information made many young people wary of the YTS. Conversations with friends sometimes helped them to distinguish between and choose the best available scheme. Although parental opinion was important, many families did not have details about the scheme when it was first launched and, anyway, there were few alternatives to boost the family wage. Certainly, one view was that all schemes were 'slave labour'. Other parents saw the scheme virtually as a regular job and welcomed the extra income. Information gleaned at school, from teachers and other pupils, was also taken into account and influenced school leavers' views of the YTS.

With the aid of professional Career counselling, one might initially expect that a young person's choice of scheme and type of training would reflect his or her interest in a particular occupational area. While this was sometimes the case, there were often multiple and conflicting factors which contoured this decision. One of the key factors influencing young people's choice was their orientation towards work and how susceptible they were to officers' suggestions. Some young people were predisposed towards abstract and more generalised forms of manual labour and were usually directed towards broad-based training schemes offering a wide range of work experience. In other words, they possessed a very real cultural knowledge that many contemporary working-class jobs do not require a specialist skill or in-depth training. On the other hand, there was a number of young people who became influenced by certain officers' portrayal of the YTS as a career stepping-stone. They genuinely believed that schemes could be used to work one's way up in a profession and develop a career (this usually, although not always, occurred in the service sector). These general intra-class orientations – what one might refer to as 'destinations' and 'careers' – will surface later on in the analysis and will receive a more detailed discussion. Suffice it to say here that the Careers Service emphasis on the YTS as a genuine 'career opportunity' is attractive to a section of the young working class.

A second element of class culture, which often overshadowed any straightforward choice of scheme, was locality. The location of a scheme in relation to the family household was an important consideration for many young people. Garnie, who desperately wanted to pursue training and possibly a career in electronics, gave up the idea because of the scheme location:

BH: Did you just come to one scheme?

Garnie: No, this scheme I came to because I don't wanna go to no scheme that's in the Isle of Wight or somethin' like that . . . you know? I prefer to just get out of my bed and just walk down this road here and come here. I don't want to go, he wanted to send me to Ashton . . . I told him no I don't wanna go out there, it's too far.

BH: So it was the location of the scheme that was . . .

> **Garnie:**   Yea, it was electronics he said, but it was too far though.

Despite the fact that most school leavers were given a number of schemes to visit, many picked one near their area, even if it did not suit their first occupational choice. Very few actually visited more than one YTS programme and there was no way to compare what different schemes were really offering.[5] Part of the reason why a training scheme is chosen on the basis of locality, I would argue, is a continuing working-class preference for familiarity, neighbourhood and easy access to the family household (Clarke, 1979).

Finally, the choice of a scheme offering training in a particular occupational area did not automatically guarantee work experience in that field. Once accepted on to a scheme, obtaining one's initial choice also depended upon whether an appropriate work placement could be found or one's interest in a certain field matched one's aptitude. This often led to some bizarre training swaps:

> **Dan:**   Well I went on to the scheme originally to do computer programming, or if I couldn't do that computer operating and that. There was no question about my ability to do that. When I went to my interview or the chat and they said 'fine, fine, we'll accept you' and ah – I did computing at school and I was quite good at it. So when it actually came to them findin' us a job they said 'well, we've had a bit of a problem tryin' to find you, tryin' to find computer placements. They're not as easy to find as we expected. So is there anything else you'd like to do?' So I ended up doing plumbing [laughs] and I wasn't very good at all.

There were quite a number of training and career changes in the movement from school to the YTS. Young women often switched from one type of traditionally female labour to another (i.e. hairdressing to office work). Many young lads who requested specific craft training in a particular field were given a broad-based training in the construction field instead. Getting on to a proper scheme and receiving training and work experience in one's chosen field upon leaving school was more a matter of luck and chance than a planned decision.

In summary, the ultimate decision to get on to a scheme must be seen in the larger context of working-class attitudes towards formal education, a lack of jobs and school leavers' aversion to the dole. The process of being accepted for a specific scheme was the product of a combination of official mechanisms (Careers), informal working-class knowledges (cultural forms drawn from family, friends, school networks), and the pull of locality and community. As the new vocationalism slowly takes hold and schemes become the norm, some of these older mechanisms used to find out about training and work may further diminish. In their place a new transition, substituting schemes for jobs and professional advice for local class knowledges, is evolving. At the moment, however, most of these training choices appear to resemble a great training lottery, rather than a service sensitive to the needs, cultures and desires of working-class youth.

3

Off-the-Job Training and Lifeskilling

The Youth Training Scheme aims to provide school leavers with an integrated programme of work experience, training and education. Organisationally, it can be broken down into two main components – work experience and off-the-job training. This chapter focuses in on working-class youth experiences of a variety of types of off-the-job training, particularly as they relate to different lifeskilling regimes. While attention is given to the often conflicting relationship between these experiences, official MSC pronouncements and the actual day-to-day operation of different types of schemes, the primary point of view expressed will be that of the trainees themselves.

Officially, off-the-job training existed as one of the eight design elements under the one-year scheme.[1] Its importance is further confirmed by its elevation as one of the two main scheme inputs for the two-year YTS.[2] This is despite the fact that off-the-job training has actually been held to twenty weeks over two years, in contrast to thirteen week for the old one-year scheme. The existence of a training element was meant to distinguish the YTS from its predecessor YOP and to eliminate criticisms of schemes as 'cheap labour' (Allum and Quigley, 1983). Off-the-job training may be provided by the Managing Agent (the body responsible for organising and administering a particular scheme) or contracted out to an FE college, training institute, skill centre or to private training agencies on a block or day release basis. As such, its organisation and content varies tremendously.

In this study many Managing Agents decided to load the majority of scheme inputs into the off-the-job component. This usually included the induction period, assessment, guidance, recording/review sessions, instruction in the 'core' areas (literacy, numeracy, manual dexterity, computer literacy and information

44

technology), as well as discussions about the world of work, the world outside employment, personal effectiveness and basic skills (MSC, 1983a; 1983b).

Most importantly, however, are the various ways off-the-job training reflect different lifeskilling regimes or life and social skill models. Although life and social skills training is not officially laid down in the design framework, many researchers argue that it undergirds the entire YTS curriculum (Linell, 1983; Davies, 1979; Green, 1983; Finn, 1983). The importance of a deficit model of lifeskilling (that is, working-class kids lack the qualities necessary for employment) is confirmed by the persistence of 'personal effectiveness' as one of the four main training outcomes of the two-year scheme.

Of crucial importance, then, is the way different lifeskilling regimes are used to 'handle' and work on different subsections of the youth population. As Cohen (1982, p. 46) argues:

> lifeskilling ideology revamps the domestic apprenticeship served by working class girls in the home (and the traditional features of boy labour) by taking them under middle-class codes of vocation and career. The very things that most working class school leavers already know how to do . . . are given the honorary status of mental labour under the middle class cultural code and appear as special skills and expertises these kids lack.

However, as will become clear, this revamping is no simple or easy task, nor is it undertaken through any monolithic method. There are very different types of schemes on the YTS and young people react differently to varied forms of discipline, pedagogy and off-the-job training methods. Before delving into three separate case studies of young people's day-to-day interactions with different forms and types of off-the-job training, I look briefly at the role of the induction period in breaking down prior working-class knowledges of schemes and constructing individualised curriculum models.

'Gettin' on': the induction period and introduction to the YTS

The induction period is considered to be a key element of the YTS and is designed to make trainees aware of 'domestic procedures . . . health and safety arrangements' and 'their own role and responsibilities in the Programme' (MSC, 1983b, p. 4). A related FEU document *Supporting YTS* (1983, p. 7), is more explicit about the purpose of a proper induction period: 'The process of induction has always been seen as an important basis of communication and orientation facilitating smooth transition of individuals to company and group activities, enabling *appropriate adjustments to take place*' (my emphasis). While this period could be an important first step in examining the purpose and politics behind the YTS,[3] instead I would argue that it is here where many of the negative orientations and informal working-class knowledges about schemes are challenged.

There is no specified time limit for induction although most schemes set aside a period of 1–2 weeks, with at least a major proportion of this taking place at the beginning of the training programme. Short periods of induction are also deemed necessary by the MSC each time a trainee moves to a different stage or area of work within a scheme. The exact length and quality of the initial induction week varies drastically. Some schemes have been reported to have skipped over this period altogether, while others have been accused of overextending induction weeks to meet the mandatory number of days of off-the-job training (YTS Monitoring Unit, 1985).

The vast majority of scheme providers looked at in this research saw some value in providing a slick and professional presentation of their training programme. The content of induction also varied, although again MSC guidelines request that all schemes must familiarise trainees with the purpose of the YTS and their role within it. Other elements, thought to be important here, include introduction to work experience and training opportunities, information on health and safety and a basic knowledge of scheme administration (allowances, attendance, rules, etc.). Many schemes also used induction to conduct initial assessments, aptitude tests and counselling sessions to determine work interests. These activities were designed to create the impression that the YTS offered a 'personalised' training and work programme. Finally, some schemes brought in outside speakers (i.e. bank managers, policemen, business people, careers officers) and/or planned visits or day trips to local amenities to facilitate social interaction and integration amongst trainees.

The majority of young people interviewed saw the induction period primarily as a familiarisation and information exercise. Yet, clearly there was more to it than that. Induction had other functions such as morale-boosting, cooptation and social integration. The FEU document quoted earlier, makes one of the key problems encountered in this initial period quite explicit: 'In the case of vocational preparation, however, a more complex situation exists: vocational preparation has as yet no assured status and few obvious opportunities for progression . . . To many therefore YTS will be regarded as a poor substitute to employment' (FEU, 1983, p. 7). The document goes on to say that young people 'will need to undergo a re-orientation of attitudes sufficient to encourage them to participate in post-school learning in a positive way' (p. 8). Wherever possible, this cooperation should be brought about by the process of 'negotiation'.

An illustrative example of this process is self-evident in the following discussion with a trainee about the induction period:

Nigel: Everything there [points to a wall chart] we been through and has been explained over and over again and um – it should last for three days but we did it in a day. And everything we went through there we agreed with yea – definitely. And um – it helps you to know what, what procedures to go through if you've any difficulties. You can look back in your notes and see, oh, you can, you should do that, you should do this, not do this 'cos its wrong. And um, it helps you and your employer, your supervisor get on well.

Clearly, some schemes were concerned with changing orientations towards the YTS through the use of participatory and cooperative forms of negotiation.

In addition to this, the induction period also sought to gain consensus for the scheme by assuming that young people somehow were lacking basic skills. Various schemes visited included introductory life and social skills sessions on 'literacy assessment', 'personal hygiene and appearance', or activities like map reading, going to a museum and opening a bank account. The assumption was, of course, that young people were somehow deficient in these basic skills and therefore the YTS was serving some useful purpose. One trainee recalls his induction in the following way:

> **Dan:** The first thing we did I remember was they got two bricks and put, balanced a plank on them and there's about fifteen of us who had to stand on the plank and arrange ourselves in alphabetical order without fallin' off. And you know, its obvious that 16 and 17 year olds weren't findin' that sort of thing very interesting – didn't see the relevance of it for gettin' a job. The trainees knew it was just tokenistic education and didn't really count for anything.

Part of the purpose of the induction, then, was to convince trainees that somehow they were deficient in the skills necessary to obtain a job and that the scheme could help them to overcome these obstacles. However, as the above quote clearly shows, this kind of approach rarely convinced many young people that they were somehow lacking skills necessary for employment.

Induction, according to some trainees, did serve other functions. For example, there were opportunities to meet other young people and it was always possible to use the situation to have a laugh about an activity. For some young people, the social events organised during the first week were the only feature of induction they could recall:

> **Mandy:** Well, we went to the airport [laughs] – yea, somethin' silly like that. What else did we do? We just like, ah – there was one time we actually had to find our way around the city using like these books and you had to tell the driver which way to turn and all that. So that was fun, ah – I can't remember the rest.

So while many young people actually used the first week to make friends and have some fun, at the same time they were also beginning the long process of becoming integrated into the scheme. In fact, encouraging social interaction amongst trainees was one mode of eliciting their cooperation and acceptance of the scheme.

Individualising the YTS and using various forms of social integration were two methods used to gain young people's initial consent over being on a scheme. The complete lack of discussion surrounding the economic and political reasons for training schemes helped to set up very individualised analyses for being on the YTS. Individual assessments, counselling, and the provision of a personalised training plan to meet each trainee's needs were also crucial aspects of many schemes.

A second method of shifting trainee opinions on training schemes was to stress their identification with and social integration into a particular scheme. The leaflet, 'You and the Youth Training Scheme' states: 'You have an important part to play in making your programme a success. The more enthusiastic and interested you are, the more you will get out of it.' YTS was thus to be seen as 'your' programme and 'your' particular scheme. Even Ben, who had a fairly well-developed political analysis of youth training, was drawn towards a personalised version of YTS in relation to his scheme (Crossroads) in the following written statement:

> Those people who do believe in the concept of YTS, who do believe that young people deserve the chance to 'get on' and who are prepared to work for it, are fighting an uphill battle. Crossroads has quite a few of those people and it is *them* that has made the scheme what it is . . . It is the *people* at Crossroads with their conviction, experience and belief in a future for young people which has made it one of the best schemes in the city. [his emphasis]

I want to take this whole argument one step further and assert that the underlying ideology of the induction period is designed to break down young people's informal knowledges about training schemes and construct, in their place, an individualist model of deficiency on the one hand and opportunity on the other. In other words, the new vocationalism seeks to rob common sense working-class knowledges about the world of work, by recodifying them in the life and social skills language of the professionals and policy-makers in the training industry. Self-image becomes more important than technical skills. Similarly, the induction period is the start of the introduction to an individualist version of success, failure and personal choice. The philosophy is if you behave, get on, keep your head down, nose clean, shirt pressed and mouth shut, you might just get a job.

The degree to which the new vocationalism succeeds in this direction is heavily dependent upon a number of factors. For instance, the resilience of informal knowledges and resistant behaviours persist on schemes and resurface in new forms. Additionally, as young people move through the schemes their daily experiences may in fact evoke what they suspected about the YTS all along. The real content of off-the-job training is what happens in the daily struggle between the varied skilling regimes and the different cultural responses of the young.

Off-the-job training: three case studies

In order to overcome the extreme diversity of off-the-job forms of training and a differentiated youth response, three case studies are reported. They provide in-depth examples of how the new vocationalism attempts to handle and gain consent amongst young people on the YTS through quite different skilling models and pedagogics.

The common thread which cuts across these cases is that the new vocationalism not only attempts to reproduce certain types of labour power through off-the-job training, it also seeks to produce the appropriate social and cultural identities for these different forms. It is not simply the case that schemes automatically slot young people into the bottom end of the labour market hierarchy. The new vocationalism also attempts to evoke a variety of subjective identities necessary for a range of future occupational roles. This process is facilitated through the existence of quite distinct types of schemes, the application of different training pedagogics and the exploitation of internal divisions and choices amongst the working-class youth population. The purpose of the case studies is to evaluate the impact these various training regimes are having on young people's identities and perceptions of their destinations and careers.

The cases intend to reflect the overall structive of the YTS in the locality and represent approximately 80 per cent of approved places. The first case looks at a private training agency's (PTA) attempt to set up a public limited company, the second concerns a group of lads surviving life and social skills on a community scheme, and the third looks at the uses and abuses of progressivism on a college-based YTS.

Case 1: 'Warm and Toasty' plc: entrepreneurial pedagogy on a PTA

Background and context: 'Warm and Toasty' plc was the name given to the simulated public limited company set up as part of the off-the-job training element offered by House of Michael, a private training agent (PTA).[4] The scheme was one of two programmes in the city which specialised in training for the clothing industry (manufacturing, distribution and retailing). It recruited on the basis of interest rather than academic qualifications and local MSC statistics showed that approximately 90 per cent of entrants were female.

Off-the-job training was located both in-house and at a local technical college and was organised on a day-release basis. The decision to set up a simulated plc stemmed from attendance problems when training was exclusively college based. The scheme coordinater explained:

> **Sally:** Most of the time the youngsters rebel because they say 'I've left school, I don't want to go back to school, it's like going to school'. Um, we had, last year, a lot of absenteeism in the college and thought, well, how do you get over this? Apart from going around to their houses in the morning and dragging them in by the scruff of the neck, how do you get them there? So we decided around September of last year – to change slightly and we got the youngsters to form their own company, on a limited company basis. And we put it to them and said 'well its not a project, it is real and it works in pound notes'. Which, you know, did motivate them.

Shares (25p each) were sold to family and friends and the trainees, with the help of the coordinater, were responsible for the planning, production, distribution and sales of a product the group itself decided to manufacture. The college sessions were used to manufacture the product and the in-house sessions involved discussion and consultation over various aspects of production, advertising, packaging and selling.

Initial attempts to organise off-the-job training in this way met with some resistance. There were, for instance, problems of motivation and inexperience. Interestingly enough, one of the main difficulties encountered in the first year of this experiment was a conflict generated between workers and the management of the company. Unfortunately, this realistic work situation was seen as a 'problem' rather than a learning experience by scheme personnel. In an attempt to improve workplace relations, a number of competing companies were set up and all members of management also had to be involved in production as well. This reorganisation implicitly suggested that somehow this 'corporate' spirit of cooperation existed out there in the real world of industry. This, plus a sprinkling of entrepreneurship (i.e. small business ideology), undergirded the entire content of off-the-job training. While this was the theory behind the course, the practical application of the pedagogy and content had differential effects and consequences.

Entrepreneurship,   off-the-job   training   and   trainee differentiation: Warm and Toasty plc had been set up for approximately three months when I attended sessions and interviewed trainees. The group was still in the planning stages, having decided to produce nightshirts and oven mitts – hence the company name. The group make-up was approximately fifteen young people (it varied weekly), divided fairly evenly between those in retailing, manufacture and distribution. All but one were female trainees.

The pedagogy or teaching practice has been labelled 'entrepreneurial'. By this I mean that the content was unashamedly *pro* small business in orientation. The assumption was that anyone could learn to run a business if they developed the right skills and attitude. Following MSC principles of simulating the 'world of work' and 'participatory learning', the course was flexible, open-ended and trainee-centred. While the coordinator provided the focus of discussion, the atmosphere was on trainee participation and group decision-making. The main objectives were to develop practical business skills, share responsibility and work cooperatively as a company unit or 'team'.

It was immediately apparent, however, that there were at least two distinct types of trainees on the course who had markedly different orientations towards the curriculum. The first group, which Sally the coordinater referred to as 'the lasses', largely rejected the company idea (and the YTS in general to some extent) and alternatively attempted to use sessions for social interaction, humour and their own focal concerns. Although some had an interest in obtaining work in the clothing industry, none of them had any illusions about their future destination at the bottom of the work hierarchy. Neither did anyone in this group believe that skills related to running one's own business were, in the slightest way, linked to employment prospects. The second group consisted of a number of trainees who had aspirations of either moving up the retail hierarchy or becoming self-employed in the clothing field. Strangely, the two types of trainees did not reflect a simple manual/service sector split. The majority of 'the lasses' had been on manufacturing as well as retailing work placements. The difference was in their orientation towards work in general and this spilled over into how they reacted to the curriculum.

The lasses were represented by three young women – Jennifer, a talkative and vivacious person, Lorraine, her whispering sidekick and Kelly, who could produce gales of laughter from the group with a single facial expression. John, the only male trainee present, played a key intermediate role by maintaining a dialogue with both the official curriculum and with the disruptions of the lasses. On the other side were a small number of trainees interested in the company idea and they often contributed and attempted to legitimate the sessions by supporting the coordinator. One of these young women, Jan, expressed her opposition to the lasses and support for the company:

Jan: A lot of people take it as a joke. I mean there's a lot in there they just do it for the fun of it, they're not taking it seriously at all. But I mean a lot of us wanna make, really make it work.

Sessions often swayed back and forth between two competing dialogues – one, the official entrepreneurial pedagogy and the other, a more informal class-cultural discourse organised around humour and social interaction.

A number of significant incidents which occurred during the company sessions demonstrate some of the subtle ways trainees sought to appropriate and distort the curriculum. The first example centred around some 'market research' trainees were supposed to have performed for the company the previous week. This involved going to the city centre to visit shops selling comparable products to the company and checking prices, quality and packaging. When Sally, the coordinator, requested the information as a basis for the week's discussion, it was obvious that the lasses had actually used the time to window shop and appropriated the exercise for their own purposes. Previous discussions with the lasses revealed this was not the first time they had neglected company responsibilities.

A second group of incidents, which occurred quite frequently, involved the use of disruption to delegitimise the curriculum. The main venues were laughter, play on words, innuendo and the engagement in activities outside the scope of the formal session. One of the main elements of disruption was to 'take the piss' out of the scheme coordinator through sexual innuendo:

(in a discussion about selling)

Sally: And you've got to push, push and push harder, until you've bothered them so much they'll buy something just to get rid of you.

Kelly: Ah – [laughter].

Sally: What is it?

Kelly: It's 'im [laughs and points at John]. It's 'is face when you were sayin' you've gotta push and push harder [laughter].

John: [smiling] I didn't do nothing!

Sally: I don't want to get into this conversation. I'm too young for all this.

During sessions, magazines were passed around and secretly discussed and combs pulled out of handbags were transformed into objects of distraction. Whispers, glances, snatches of conversation and laughter for no apparent reason all served to provide some

fun for the lasses and weaved some life through what were otherwise boring sessions.

Breaktime provided even more of an opportunity to joke
around, talk and construct an agenda closer to the real world of
young people. One display, which both consolidated the position
of the lasses and exposed the sheer triviality of the company idea
came from Jennifer, whose verbal display about the 'real world'
contextualised how she felt about being on the YTS at all:

> **Jennifer:** I don't know what I'm coming here for – Hey, this
> room, it smells like – smells like ah . . .
> **Lorraine:** What?
> **Jennifer:** It smells like ganga, ah drugs, don't you think?
> **Lorraine:** How would I know [laughs].

Besides affirming her position as one of the lasses, Jennifer's
comment about other teenage concerns served to show the irrelevance many young people felt about receiving small business
training. She, like the other lasses didn't really want to be on the
YTS and clearly rejected any upwardly mobile or self-employment
models. Their work experience and cultural knowledge told them
neither of these paths were their likely destination. Work, for
them, was seen as a temporary hiatus between school and a future
family life and it was to be enjoyed and/or tolerated. Life was
many other things besides working in a factory or retail store.

Support for the company was forthcoming from a number of
trainees predisposed towards an entrepreneurial content. Again,
Jan expresses this position well:

(in a discussion about the company)

> **Jan:** Yea – um, like its really useful this. But before we did
> this it was a bit of, well, useless really at college. No
> one seemed to take it seriously. But now we've got this
> on the road like – makin' a business you're learnin' all
> different sides, whereas at work you're makin' the goods.
> You're learning your background work, your accounting
> work, your money and things like that – it's really useful.

Yet even here there were some subtle differences. Jan's support was motivated by a dream that one day she would set up a clothing firm overseas. She had come on to the scheme to learn all aspects of clothing manufacture, distribution and retail. Julie, another trainee supporting the company idea, however, was more concerned with learning business skills as an aid to moving up the retail store hierarchy. Finally, there was Liz, who, although less committed to the company idea, was interested in clothing design and the business angle of commissioning her work to city stores.

What was crucial in maintaining and even widening these divisions amongst trainees in the entrepreneurial model was the promotion of an image of a successful, upwardly mobile and mature young worker. Certain trainees embodied this transformation by differentiating themselves from inexperienced school leavers who were in the process of just joining the scheme. Julie, who had been on the scheme nearly nine months and who had been offered a job with her work provider, spoke about 'being young once' and 'fighting against the system'. She clearly detached herself from the lasses' disruptive antics and was wholly supportive of the company idea:

> **BH:**　Were you sceptical [of YTS]?
> **Julie:**　Very [laughs].
> **BH:**　Do you think you've changed a lot since you've been on YTS?
> **Julie:**　I think I have. I've matured, I think – I hope.
> **BH:**　What do you mean – I mean did you . . .
> **Julie:**　Lookin' at what they [the other trainees] are now, I come here every Wednesday and I'm with the, the old group is gone, so I'm the oldest one now . . . lookin' at the way they act, I think well I acted like that. I was silly and talked back and was cheeky, didn't wanna do this. But you can see a positive side to it and say, oh, right, it will be useful. But they, they don't wanna know.

From the scheme coordinator's point of view Julie was a success story and she provided a model example of what hard work could achieve. From the trainee's perspective she was also a success in terms of obtaining a full-time job (the reason why many of the lasses were on the scheme). Strangely enough, Julie saw herself in a positive light, not because of her own personal qualities and development, but because the scheme had transformed her into a 'mature' worker. She represented the classic upwardly mobile prototype, grateful for what the system has done for her.

It would, however, be wrong to place those trainees like Julie, Jan and Liz on one side and label them 'conformists' and see the lasses as 'resisters' or 'class rebels'. Even amongst this first group of young women there were different degrees of support for the YTS and varied orientations towards their future employment prospects. Additionally, one could say that while these three young women may have adopted more of a middle-class approach towards their future working life, at the same time, they were also seeking to redefine aspects of the traditional domestic apprenticeship which has always curtailed young working-class women's movement into different types of work. Entrepreneurship may have been just an image, and a limited one at that, but it also provided a partial change of identity away from traditional working-class gender roles.

In contrast, the lasses demonstrated a more class-based opposition to the scheme curriculum and the notion of 'careerism'. Their own experience and orientations towards the YTS were more highly influenced by their expectation of work as a destination, shadowed by their future role in family life. This was reflected in their use of sessions for fun, feminine focal concerns and social interaction. However, while the lasses were the primary source of an alternative agenda to the entrepreneurial curriculum, even they understood that taking things too far might jeopardise the basis of the training exchange. In other words, they realised that it was crucial sometimes to 'play the game' to legitimise their chance for getting a job.

Overall, what was clear, was that this type of curriculum did have strong implications for differentiating young people's identities and orientations towards working life. While certain traditional working-class cultural forms persist and work to subvert and appropriate the entrepreneurial skilling model, other young people were strongly influenced by the images of social mobility and self-employment in this type of training pedagogy.

Case 2: Surviving and subverting life and social skills: working-class lad's 'common-sense' responses to off-the-job training

Background and context: This case study looks at the responses of a group of working-class lads on a scheme run by the city education department. Due to the fact that the scheme was community based, only about 50 per cent of the trainees were gaining work experience with a 'real' employer. The rest received project-based work experience either in-house or out in the local area under the supervision of the scheme staff. Also, because the scheme recruited widely on an open door policy, many of its trainees were disaffected school leavers. Consequently, much of the curriculum stressed the acquisition of basic literacy, life and social skills and work socialisation.

While the scheme breakdown by gender was 55 per cent male and 45 per cent female, my contact was restricted to working with and interviewing groups of lads. This was primarily due to the fact that my participation on the scheme was predicated on working with the most overtly disaffected and disruptive groups. The lads interviewed would have been located at the 'rough' end of the working-class youth spectrum and the scheme was privately known as a dumping ground for unwanted school leavers. A large majority of this group had not learned basic reading and writing skills during their years of compulsory schooling.

Off-the-job training consisted of in-house technical skills training, a stint at a local technical college and a basic literacy and numeracy course. This latter course was put on at a disused old school located in the inner city and trainees were expected to work towards gaining a qualification in City and Guilds 364 (numeracy) and 772 (communications). 'Personal effectiveness' and various life and social skills relating to work and everyday life were built into the course content. Examples of the curriculum included mathematical problem solving, reading and writing exercises and life and social skills such as interviewing techniques, telephone manner, writing job applications, developing leisure interests, as well as various other life activities.

The scheme staff responsible for the literacy and numeracy sessions, while somewhat varied in their approach towards teaching young people, preferred to keep relations informal. Yet, despite attempts to create a different atmosphere, the combination of recruiting disaffected trainees and exposing them to a particular type of curriculum quickly led to the adoption and formalisation of schooling relations and a particularly male type of 'lad culture'.

Lad culture, informal groups and school relations: The most obvious phenomenon observed on this scheme paralleled the formation of informal male groups in schools (Hargreaves, 1967; Willis, 1977). While initial assessments, counselling and profiles were designed to provide an individualised experience of the YTS, the immediate cultural responses of many young men was to band together informally into social groups. The structure of these informal groups in this case study were small grouplets of 3–4 lads, who were linked together into a larger collectivity based upon their common experience of being on the YTS.[5]

This larger group sense allowed for brief moments of solidarity, particularly when having a 'laff' or responding to adult authority. The group, as a whole, was a fairly intimidating lot – laughing, smoking and hanging out in the corridor prior to the start of each session. The phenomenon of 'hanging out' appeared to be part of a well-worn repertoire of working-class male behaviours retained from school. There was an ongoing battle between scheme personnel and trainees for control of the neutral corridor.

The corridor also represented the last barrier to the dreaded life and social skills class. The battle to get the whole group of lads, sometimes grouplet by grouplet, into the workroom was a daily ritual. However much attempts were made to informalise the atmosphere, the room had the indelible mark of a school classroom. And while the tutors dressed informally and were addressed by their first names, most of the lads saw through the charade and clearly understood the real relations of power and authority scheme personnel had over them. These knowledges drew heavily upon their experiences of schooling:

Calvin:	Ya, this place is jus' like school.
BH:	You think this is like school here?
Chris:	Do this, don't do that, do this . . .
BH:	They don't make you do things here?
Andy:	Yea! Yuh get kicked off if ya don't.
Calvin:	They do everything. They mek you go to college.
Andy:	I've been suspended four times.

Calvin: They make you do this City and Guilds . . . If you don't do City and Guilds they don't want ya. They'll kick yuh off the scheme.

Although the specific circumstances and outcomes were now different from school – that is, discipline was now exchanged for the chance of obtaining work rather than the acquisition of knowledge – the fundamental power relations were recognised as much the same. The game for many of these lads was to bend the rules and have a good laugh with mates without jeopardising one's chance for a job.

The importance of the lads 'having a laff' within the formal institutional structure of school has been stressed by Willis (1977), who, in its masculinist version, sees this activity as an important linking element between manual labour and working-class, counter-school culture. Billy confirms that this relationship continues on training schemes, in this conversation:

BH: What do you think about the rest of the lads in here?
Billy: They're a great laff. I don't know whether they'll get a job. They should do – if not for anything else for their laff. You know 'cos they're quite good company – even if they're a docile load a' bleeders. They'll get one I reckon just for their laff.
BH: So that's important then?
Billy: This job would really get boring without kids like that – really boring.
BH: So you wanna have people around you can have a laugh with?
Billy: Um, that is most important, that is I reckon. Next to wages it is, yea . . . A good laff and wages, that's all I want.

These group structures, in addition to providing a means for humour and enjoyment, also served to deflect individual forms of assessment and trainee discipline. For example, work could be avoided by blaming others at your table for making too much noise. In mock tests, many of the lads would openly ask each other about questions and answers. In terms of discipline, it was possible to avoid individual blame through a vague collective loyalty. Some of the lads would arrive an hour late only to use the same collective excuse – 'his mom's sick', 'he had to go to the job centre', 'he missed the bus'. Even if something as serious as a fight broke out, groups would quickly close ranks when a figure of authority came on to the scene. As Chris, a trainee, explained, 'If yuh get in a fight and someone comes over, yuh just say yuh slipped and fell.'

Linkages between groups of trainees resulted in broad rings of collective knowledge and strategies. For instance, it was well known that the assistant scheme manager was overtly racist and that the young woman trainee serving tea in the canteen spat daily into the manager's cup. Events and situations involving disciplinary problems, humorous situations and rumours were passed on verbally and circulated surprisingly quick for this mode of communication. In fact, the lads were clearly adept in at least one area of life and social skills – personal communication. Hence, scheme personnel and the MSC do realise some of the inherent dangers of using group work on the YTS. While forms of group work are considered to be more effective than a traditional schooling approach, the danger of independent and unregulated group activity is well recognised, as this quote from a trainee participation document implies: 'There are one or two situations in which a move the other way is made – where the effort is made to break up existing groups because they are in danger of becoming too independent and undisciplined' (Linell, 1983, p. 10). Fortunately, the nebulous character of the informal group negates any simple imposition of authority and control. On the other hand, reliance on such forms rarely allows for any organised and sustained resistance necessary to challenge the curriculum and change the situation. Such is the illusiveness of male working-class cultural forms generated through the informal group.

The lads' critique of life and social skills training: An understanding of informal groups and the adoption of school-based relations provides a context for the lads' critique of life and social skills training. For example, like compulsory schooling, many of them simply didn't want to be on the City and Guilds course:

Calvin: I didn't want to come on it, did I? My name was on the list so I came down to it . . . I say it's not worth it.

The most obvious forms of outright resistance were 'waggin' it' (not showing up), coming in late and hanging about the corridor.

However, unlike compulsory schooling, there was quite severe penalties imposed on those who outwardly rejected the scheme. There was the real possibility of having one's pay docked or being sacked from the scheme altogether. For the majority of those who actually complied with the attendance requirements, there were fall-back strategies. Non-cooperation was one such response. Going to the cupboard to take out one's work folder was a more or less unspoken crime for any self-respecting lad. Even when the work was passed out, another few precious moments reprieve could be gained by doodling on the folder, reading the paper or talking with mates. The response to the course was clear – it was not about the 'real world of work' but rather was like 'pretending at school':

Craig: Yuh don't need all them Maths and English to get a job. The gaffer wants experience.

Baz: It's a waste of time really, I'd rather be at work learnin' something.

The perceived link between obtaining a qualification on the course and getting a job was understood as highly tenuous.

There is a general argument to be made that the ability to read and write is an essential skill for any kind of social and political development (Hall, 1983). Yet, there was a cultural logic to the lad's resistance to numeracy and literacy. Years of failure at the unmerciful hands of abstract mathematical questions and grammatical exercises and a partly correct feeling that much of the school curriculum wasn't applied to the world of manual work, combined to construct a formidable barrier to formal learning. Each week the tutors faced a battle in trying to get many of the lads even to attempt a single maths question. One episode involved a very tough, masculine working-class lad named Frank who had given in to the tutor's prompting to attempt a mock numeracy exam. In the end he was even more determined never to try another question:

Frank: I ain't never doin' maths again.

Bernie: But you need to know how to add and subtract. For example, what happens if you get a wage slip and they've taken too much tax off? What will you do?

Frank: I'll get someone else to check it.

Bernie: What if there is no one else around?

Frank: I'll take it home and get someone to read it.

Bernie: You can't do that forever.

Tutors often made vain attempts to make such questions appear more practical and useful – such as using mathematical formulae to figure out how much paint was needed for a room. Yet these practical questions seemed, to the lads, to be more of a common-sense problem rather than a mathematical one. Besides, as Billy put it, you could always use any leftover paint for something else.

The main argument levelled against life and social skills by the lads, then, was their common-sense character. Lifeskilling and personal effectiveness have often been criticised as representing individualist solutions to social and political problems. Many of the lads recognised that they were not lacking the necessary skills needed for manual work – indeed their own culture and experience was immersed in the inheritance of such skills (Cohen, 1983; Willis, 1977).

Implicit in these common-sense critiques was a contemptuous recognition by the lads of MSC definitions of skill and the absurd categorisation of everyday activities into special work skills that one supposedly needed to learn:

(in a discussion with his placement officer about City and Guilds)

Baz: Yuh just spend yer time answerin' phones and taping phone calls and that. I use a phone all the time – there's six of 'em at work.

Wendy: Well, maybe there are some trainees there who don't know how to answer a phone properly.

Baz: [sarcastically] I'm sure they know how to answer a phone!

Others talked incredulously about 'learning how to use a phone box' and the disdain of these three lads is barely concealable in their discussion of life and social skills:

Robert: What am I gonna get – right, pass City and Guilds – and what did you do to get your City and Guilds? Oh, I did a 5000 word essay on the yellow pages and how to use them and how to use a tape recorder and things like that. That's gonna get you far isn't it? . . . Yuh have to do a 1000 word essay on owls and things like that.

Baz: The telephone calls and all this – they're talkin' to you like a telephone call – that was how to learn to use a tape recorder.

Robert: How to use a telephone properly.

Craig: How to speak over the telephone properly and all that . . .

Robert: And the instructor sez 'well somebody may never have seen a tape recorder' [everyone laughs].

Baz: It's common sense right, it's in front of you what you've got to do anyway on a telephone.

Robert: Just use yer brain, in' it?

Baz: Common sense.

Overall, it was abundantly clear that such a remedial school-like curriculum could not have been more mismatched for this group of trainees. As such, many of them simply resisted and coped with the life and social skills element. Indeed, the very curricular form, designed to help the lads develop basic literacy, numeracy and social skills necessary for their advancement beyond semi-skilled labour, often worked to reinforce and even strengthen their existing orientations towards the manual sphere. While this particular subgroup of working-class youth is one of the most resistant to lifeskilling ideology, their continued reliance upon masculine cultural forms often led to very conservative and reactionary forms of identity and political views. This apparent irony forms the basis for one of the major contradictions thrown up by the clash between the new vocationalism and young male working-class cultural forms.

Case 3: Personal and social development: differential uses of 'progressivism' on a college-based scheme

Background and context: This scheme was based in a Further Education (FE) establishment in the city, which was known locally as a general studies institution rather than a purely technical college. The college ran its own in-house YTS, in addition to offering a life and social skills package to other schemes in the area through its Personal and Social Development Unit (PSDU). The college-based scheme provided occupational training in a number of fields, from manufacturing to childcare, and recruited trainees with a wide range of academic qualifications and abilities.

The sessions organised by the PSDU were an obligatory part of off-the-job training for all trainees on the scheme and took place at the college in a downstairs lecture room one day per week. Unlike the first two case studies, these classes were made up of both young women and men (approximately 60/40). The philosophy and content of the sessions were jointly influenced by a theory of 'progressivism' and by MSC directives concerning off-the-job training. In a central way, the course reflected some of the fundamental contradictions thrown up by working-class youth responses to the new vocationalism's appropriation of liberal–progressive themes.

For example, the course was trainee-centred and group work, participation and peer/self evaluation was encouraged. The course content was potentially progressive and included analyses of the local labour market and discussions on conditions of employment, relations at work and 'issues and values in society'. An afternoon session on trainee rights and trade unions was also considered to be an important part of the curriculum. However, in order to gain MSC approval as well as cater to the needs of private schemes (who contracted into the PSDU), the course also included various elements central to the new vocationalism. For instance, it claimed to cover 'core skills' – communication, problem solving, adaptability, leadership – as well as other 'learning activities' such as interview techniques and tips for self-employment. The course brochure claimed sessions could 'improve the effectiveness of trainees, particularly in the work situation'. A residential week was also considered to be essential in building up skills of teamwork and leadership. The main contradiction is that it is extremely difficult for any course, however progressive in its methods, to escape individualist or cultural deprivation models in explaining the jobless plight of working-class youngsters.

This central contradiction, enhanced by the varied reactions of a diverse working-class youth population, created real problems for the course tutors who, while opposed to many aspects of the YTS, had decided to work within the system. The two main tutors, Dan and Helen, were active in their trade union and both took a progressive stance towards teaching and working with young people. They were faced, however, with a disparate group of trainees who often exploited the loose structure of the course for their own varying purposes. Often the tutors were put in the position of disciplinarians when the progressive model broke down completely. Disaffected school leavers often saw the course as irrelevant to the real world of work, and career-oriented trainees often failed to see how life and social skills training related to their quest for upward mobility on the job. There are in fact few guarantees inherent in a particular pedagogic style or philosophy without a recognition of the different orientations working-class youths have towards education, training and work.

Orientations towards a college scheme: 'careers' and 'destinations': Trainee responses towards PSDU sessions depended, in part, on their impressions of the college scheme as distinct from, or simply as an extension of, formal schooling. Also crucial is the way broader orientations towards the world of work shape the college experience. It was clear that some young people viewed the college scheme as a viable substitute for training for a specific career, while others understood the experience primarily as a delay in one's likely destination into general manual labour. While this distinction contained a significant gender dimension, there were different orientations towards the college scheme within both groups.

A number of young women had wanted to take a proper college course in childcare or a specialist course in working with the physically/mentally disabled, but were unable to do so because they lacked the necessary qualifications:

Margaret: I wanted to do childcare, right, and they sent me to this other place, but they wouldn't take me 'cos

I never, my grades weren't high enough. But I
didn't have any exams and they thought my grades
wouldn't be high enough. So I went out to this
college and they told me my grades still weren't
high enough and they put me in touch with – when
I came for my interview right, they said um – I
couldn't go on the proper course, if I was interested in goin' onto the YTS. And I said I'll think
about it and then I came back from my interview
and said yea, I'll go and see what it's like.

Two other young women on the course, Jill and Jackie, also
utilised the YTS to simulate a college-based career progression in
the childcare field. They preferred to see the scheme as giving
them a student-like status rather than that of a trainee. In their
own words, they were 'students goin' to college':

BH: Do you like the fact that it's a college scheme?
Jackie: Yea . . . People think yer brainy when you go to
college.
BH: What are the good things about college?
Jackie: You get to know more people.

While there were other social reasons for wanting to attend college, the impression of pursuing a career through a student identity was the most significant aspect for some young people.

The career orientation was not strictly limited to young women.
One young man, who had been offered a place with his work
placement following his YTS, viewed the PSDU course positively
because he saw the whole scheme as providing him with the
opportunity to 'get on'. As such, he was the most cooperative
male in the PSDU sessions and mentioned that he would actually
miss the course following his movement into full-time work.

Others on the course, including some young women, were much
more reticent about the college experience. One young woman in
particular, nicknamed George, was openly hostile and contemptuous of the course and she was eventually kicked off the scheme.
It was clear that some young working-class women saw little connection between 'playing games' and understanding 'group process' and their likely destination into domestic and perhaps wage

labour. Will, another non-conformist, who had been disciplined only the week before, complained that the course was 'just like bein' back at school'. Others extended their criticism of college training (even practically and technically based training outside the PSDU course) as being unrelated to the real world of work:

Otis: All we're doin' is soldering and things. Then we started makin' a metal cannon and that got boring.

Peter: We don't do anything at college.
BH: Aren't you supposed to be studying horticulture?
Peter: Yea, but we don't do nothin' – we just sit around a room and doss.

So, for some, the college-based experience was 'boring', 'a doss', a place where nothing tangible or real was produced. It was viewed as a stop-off point – an obstacle blocking one's destination into the world of either domestic or manual labour. For others, however, it provided an alternative identity of 'studentdom', which aided the new vocationalism's ideology of careerism and paraprofessionalism (see Chapter 5). As we shall see, neither orientation sat particularly well with the two tutor's attempt to assert a liberal-progressive curriculum on such a diverse youth population.

The PSDU course, inversions of liberal-progressive themes: The PSDU course was organised to encourage the maximum participation and discussion amongst trainees around a series of topic areas, exercises, role play and the use of interactive games. Sociability, learning social skills, group process and decision-making were fundamental features of the course and initial meetings were organised around day trips and social events. The majority of sessions, however, took place in the college itself and revolved around a particular topic or activity organised by the tutors.

One of the main weaknesses of a liberal progressive approach is its failure to recognise social division, differentiation and power. I have argued that there were at least two main orientations towards the college scheme which were contoured by both class and gender relations. For those who saw the scheme as a barrier to their inherited destination there were very blunt reactions to the course such as absenteeism, disruption, non-cooperation and a sarcastic mocking of the course objectives. Career-orientated trainees took a slightly different approach. While they were convinced that technical training and on-the-job experience would help lead them to a career, they were much less clear about how personal and social development (unless directly applied to their profession) could enhance their job prospects. In many cases, they too viewed the course as boring and irrelevant (although for different reasons than the other group) and often chose to use sessions for sociability and fun. As such there was no strict conformist/rebel split. At times, both groups allied in opposition to a session and the room became sheer pandemonium. Two activities offered by the course serve to highlight the varied appropriation of liberal-progressive themes by these different types of trainees.

The first event concerned the inversion of progressive themes implicit in a game-playing exercise used to stimulate a discussion of competition and cooperation. The object of the game, as explained by Dan the tutor, was to try to convince other teams to cooperate in choosing a common symbol (X or Y) which would allow everyone to profit from that choice. The combined choice of symbols resulted in different teams gaining points, while others lost. The main aim was to elicit either cooperation or competition and use the game to stimulate a discussion about the merits of each.

The most interesting point about the exercise was not necessarily what path each group took but how the game itself prompted the participation and views of some of the main disaffected pupils on the course. One group in particular included three young people (Will, Art and his girlfriend Andrea) who had been threatened with expulsion from the scheme for bad behaviour only the week before. In an animated way they sought both to mock and control the game by enthusiastically leading the activity. The two lads especially took a dominant lead in pleading with other groups to cooperate only to find that someone had changed their symbol thereby gaining at the expense of others.

Following the outcome of the game, Dan attempted to begin a discussion on the merits/weaknesses of competition and cooperation in real life. Once more these lads sought to dominate and control the discussion for their own purposes. By drawing on and asserting their masculine experiences from the 'real world', they continued to mock the exercise through humour and bravado:

Dan: What did you learn from the game?

Art: Not to trust anyone – [dramatically] you just get stabbed in the back.

Dan: I mean if you were ill and fell down on the street do you think someone would stop and help you?

Art: I've been beaten up in the city centre and people walk right by yuh – they just don't wanna know [laughter].

In an attempt to balance the discussion, Dan called into question these negative attitudes. The lads, however, continued to monopolise the discussion while using the session for their own ends.

Despite this example of male control and power over a progressive theme, it would be a mistake to view even the career-oriented women trainees as passive or inactive in relation to the course curriculum. They possessed their own unique forms of solidarity, disruption and resistance to game-playing, as well as other activities. Often this meant using stereotypical female devices (i.e. laughter, whispering or discussing boyfriends) to disrupt otherwise boring sessions:

(in discussions about PSDU classes)

BH: In the leisure survey did you have to write down like on a sheet or something.

Jill: Yea. I wrote down my boyfriend phoned me then came over to my house and then we went to bed. And it wasn't meant to be like that! And then they [her friends] took it the wrong way – and they won't let me live it down now, they keep bringin' it up [laughs].

BH: What do you think of the things you do on the course?

Jackie: Not much, it's boring.

Jill: Most of it is boring.

Jackie: Last week we did a sponsored silence for an hour and a half and that was difficult to keep quiet – nearly killed me [laughs].

BH: A sponsored silence? Who was that for?

Jackie: A charity. Everyone was sayin' I wouldn't keep quiet [laughs].

So while many of the sessions were in fact quite boring even for those young women who responded positively to training for a career, they in no way passively responded to what was seen as a remedial curriculum. Indeed they often used their femininity to get away with much more than some of the lads. In some cases the whole group came together in a resounding opposition to a topic or activity and literally nothing was accomplished during these sessions.

The second example, which demonstrates how life and social skills training can be appropriated and utilised for different purposes, concerned the residential week. This was considered to be an enlighted and essential component of the PSDU course and was organised by a large well-known holiday camp located in South Wales. Residentials are thought to reflect MSC inspired off-the-job training elements such as the 'world outside work'. Whether consciously intended or not the trip functioned as a morale booster and was an incentive for many trainees to stay on the scheme. Prior to the trip, there was a great deal of excitement and enthusiasm and the residential was a hot topic of conversation months after the trainees returned.[6]

Two main points about the organisation and philosophy of the residential should be stressed. First, while the camp provided an interesting array of facilities and activities for trainees, many of them were notably middle-class forms of recreation (i.e. orienteering, canoeing, morning exercises, jogging as well as swimming lessons, and various competitive games). Second, it was made clear by Helen, one of the course tutors who attended the residential, that the camp was implicitly organised around a competitive theme. Both of these factors stem from assumptions about the 'civilising' nature competitive sport and recreation can play in socialising working-class people (Hargreaves, 1986).

The camp was organised by dividing young people into teams or 'cabins' (shared living accommodation) and competition between groups was used as the basis for the weeks events and activities. Emphasis was placed on leadership, team spirit and the will to win. Stress was also placed on the carry-over value of these traits for the world of work.

The way in which these competitive strategies and middle-class activities were inhabited and appropriated by young people varied substantially. For example, some of the career-oriented trainees were very impressed with the facilities the camp had to offer. They viewed such activities as representing elements of a wider upwardly mobile lifestyle. Other groups deviated from the official programme and instead enjoyed their own focal concerns outside the formal structure of the residential. A number of young people mentioned getting together with different cabins 'after hours' – socialising and drinking alcohol. Early morning jogging sessions could not effectively contain late night partying by certain trainees.

In fact, very few young people were influenced by the residential's competitive ethos. Even those young people who were somewhat career-minded and oriented towards middle-class activities were unsure about the competitive stress and instead opted for enjoyment and companionship rather than winning:

> **BH:**   Was it competitive? Did you think it was too competitive?
>
> **Jackie:**   Yea . . . It wasn't as bad for our cabin. We come last anyway, it didn't bother us – we had a good time. We went to enjoy ourselves, not to like beat everybody.

So there was no automatic take-up, by any group of trainees, of the residential's stress on competition and how such values might relate to the world of work.

These two examples from this scheme show that life and social skills conveyed through liberal-progressive forms are not so easily foisted upon the young working class. Neither MSC directives nor liberal forms guarantee a required response. Trainee responses and appropriations varied tremendously and were influenced by both intra-class ('careers' versus 'destinations') and gender relations. In general, it could be said that any progressive teaching approach, however well intended, which fails to recognise social division, differentiation and power amongst the youth population is clearly inadequate for those who want to work with, not 'on', the subjectivities of working-class youths.

Summary and conclusions

If the initial induction period of off-the-job training provides a model of the origins of building consent amongst the young working class, then the three case studies have sought to demonstrate the variety of lifeskilling regimes applied on the YTS. The general attempt to impose a new kind of training exchange (the acceptance of deficiency, the repackaging of already existing skills and the exchange of discipline for a chance for a job) was examined in a number of diverse forms.

As the case studies demonstrate, the imposition of new skilling regimes is by no means an unproblematic or automatic gesture. Some young people refuse to accept that they are deficient in the skills and cultures necessary for many working-class jobs. As such, they often see through life and social skills training and develop common-sense critiques of the curriculum. Different working-class cultural responses also exploit the loose structure of progressive forms and flaunt entrepreneurial models, as much as they reject formal learning in basic literacy and numeracy.

However, it would be short-sighted not to note those instances in which various forms of lifeskilling and careerism in off-the-job training successfully work on the subjective identities of sections of the youth population. Some do come to believe in either corporate, entrepreneurial or careerist ideologies during their stint on schemes. Additionally, there is a certain self-damnation inherent in some of the resistant male working-class cultures to literacy and numeracy. There should be little doubt that despite the resiliance of particular class cultural forms, there is clearly the beginning of a series of new subjectivities being formed in the off-the-job training element of the YTS.

4

Work Experience and the Trainee Identity

One of the central features of youth labour has always been its subordinate and marginal character (Cohen, 1982). Through its use of work placements and the construction of a trainee status for school leavers, the YTS has legitimated and formalised this historical relation under a new guise. Work experience on the scheme represents a key formative moment in young people's introduction to working life and, I would argue, has implications for the development of future identities in employment.

While there is no singular experience of being a trainee at work, it is clear that one can outline a series of general features marking the monetary, symbolic and legal construction of a new introduction to work through training schemes.[1] In other words, I want to give some weight to what it feels like to be defined and treated as a trainee at work. Particularly important in this respect is how young people respond to these definitions and relations and how they seek to develop work identities appropriate to their situation. Also crucial here is the impact trainee identities have on collective representations of workplace problems and grievances. I begin by looking at young people's distinction between 'real' employers and project-based work experience.

'Real' employers and project-based work experience

Young people's experiences of work on the YTS depend on the type of scheme they find themselves on, their work sponsor's expertise and commitment towards training and their relations with management and other workers. For example, some trainees are placed in work with the managing agent itself, while others on private training agencies may find themselves 'loaned out' to high street shops or family businesses. Similarly, those on apprenticeship schemes may receive a full year of off-the-job training, while others on community-based programmes gain work experience out on project-based placements rather than with an actual employer.

A crucial distinction, expressed by numerous young people on the YTS, was made between work experience gained on employer's premises and that undertaken on project-based placements (at the scheme itself or out in the community). This separation should not imply that all young people favoured one type of work experience over the other. In some cases the distinction was simply the difference between 'shit jobs' and 'govvy schemes' discussed by Coffield *et al.* (1986). Such choices were also influenced by the quality of training offered on-the-job and differing orientations towards work.

For some young people, there was a general feeling that employer-based placements were superior because they offered a much greater chance of obtaining a job:

BH: Do you think there's a chance that they'll maybe take you on at the end?

Margaret: Well, they need more staff and they're extendin' – I don't know.

The recognition of gaining possible full-time employment was not the only motivating factor influencing young people's choices in this matter. There was also the realisation that project-based work was more or less a 'time filler ' – that is, it was not the real world of work. Jackie, for instance, contrasted her in-house work experience with her employer-based placement by stating that the former was 'boring' while the latter gave her 'responsibility' and a 'real sense of value'. In-house work experience was 'just pretending' while being based with an employer was 'real' work for a wage. A young man on a project-based scheme, expresses this position well:

BH: Are you doing what you want on the scheme?

Calvin: No – they're just stupid jobs aren't they? . . . That's

why they put yah on placement – it's a better chance
of gettin' a job at the end . . . Unless you was on
placement, you probably have a chance of bein' taken
on, Bob. When yer at the Centre [project-based
work], they don't take you on at the end.

An additional example of this attitude towards 'real' work is
portrayed in this lengthy but important conversation between two
manual labour lads, Billy and Mick. On their scheme they were
forced to undergo a period of in-house work until an appropriate
placement with an employer could be found. Here they graphically
express their feelings about the two different types of work
experience:

Mick: I wouldn't have stayed this long if, unless I was in a
placement. I wouldn't stay at the Centre [in-house project-based work]. If I wasn't in the placement, the job
I'm in now, I wouldn't stay at the Centre. It's absolutely rubbish. It's crap.

Billy: I'll try for another year at this place [his employer
placement] and try an' learn a bit more. If I can't get
at this place, I'd just jack it in. 'Cos the only thing I
like is mechanics.

Mick: There's a lot a kids just at the Centre. I was there three
weeks and I just couldn't wait to get out.

BH: What are they doing at the Centre, just making things?

Billy: Absolutely nothing! [laughs]

Mick: You go out in a van, might do –

Billy: Shit-shovellin'.

Mick: We had to go to these big horse stables and there was
all this sand and we had to shovel it all out [Billy laughs
hysterically]. It was somethin' like 40 tons.

Billy: [laughing] I'll never forget that.

Mick: It was 40 or 50 tons, wasn't it? It took us two days –
there were fourteen or fifteen of us, wheelbarrows and
everything – gct the shit all out of it.

Billy: [laughing] There was these two Pakis just standin'
around doin' bugger all.

Mick: There was horseshit mixed in with it and everything like.

Billy: And sand and grass and ugh.

Mick: It was the first week I was there. Joined on a Monday, started work there on Tuesday.

BH: What was the purpose of shovelling all this?

Billy: For a disco.

Mick: It was gonna be a big barn disco. They wanted all the sand off the floor.

Billy: They [other trainees] had to go back down, didn't they?

Mick: They had to, we didn't.

Billy: But it was somethin' to do wasn't it? [laughs]

Mick: That was the first two days I started workin' there, so I couldn't stand it no more.

BH: So you were standing at the end of a shovel?

Mick: Yea, end of a shovel, shovellin' away – shovel down to the ground.

Billy: [laughing] It was bad!

Mick: It was about six inches deep.

Billy: Must'a been, at least . . . I was really lucky, I was. I was only down at the Centre for one week. Then I went to college and then –

Mick: Yea, I was down there for four weeks and there's people down there waitin' three or four months.

Billy: There's still some of 'em there.

Mick: Yea, waitin' for a placement. When I went out on placement I found out how much better it is.

Billy: All they do down ah, at the Centre is get there at 8, clock in, wait until about 10 or half gone 10, then go out, do a job, yuh know gardening or something, come back to eat, then go out and do that job again. Then yuh come back, it's really boring that is – for most of the morning yer just dossin'. It's only in the afternoon that yuh get down to some real work and by then yer so tired of dossin' yuh can't do anything, you're all weak.

This conversation reveals far more than just the difference between employer-based and project-based work experience. It speaks particularly to the specific position white male lads occupy in relation to manual labour. For example, it is obvious that these lads embrace tough manual labour if, and only if, it is perceived as 'real work'. Ironically, it is this fixation of masculinity in and through the real work of capitalist production which often masks any critical questioning of many of the exploitative elements of wage labour (Willis, 1979). Second, it is equally clear from Billy's racist remark that this inheritance of manual work is largely viewed as the prerogative of the white male working class. More will be said about each of these issues in later chapters. Suffice it to say here that it forms a particular strand of a more general working-class orientation.

Not all young people viewed employer-based work experience with the same enthusiasm as their colleagues. Kamni, a young woman, had mixed feelings about her work placements and had opted to spend the last few months of her YTS 'in-house' to improve her skills. Following this, she planned to extend her training by enrolling in a 17+ training course run by the city council. She explained her dilemma as follows:

BH: Would you rather do the 17+ course, I mean if you had a choice between that and getting a job what would you do?

Kamni: I think, um, gettin' a permanent job, I'd prefer to do. But the reason why I've taken up this 17+ course is because I want to improve my skills, so I can uh, chase a full-time job better. 'Cos at the moment I'm not satisfied with yuh know, 'cos I feel I want to learn more.

Part of Kamni's hesitation about obtaining a job with an employer was that she had become convinced, while on the YTS, that she lacked skills and wasn't prepared for work. As such she preferred training and work experience in-house, through a scheme, rather than with an employer.

Garnie, a black trainee on a community-based scheme, provided a much more explicit view of employer-based placements:

BH: So you're quite happy with the training but you're pretty suspicious about going out on placement?

Garnie: Yea, I'm not suspicious – I know. It's just that I know right, they're just using us as slavedrivers. Now I'm not gonna work for no man, no employer right and get £35 in my hand or £43. I don't want that, he can take that and buy his chicken or whatever he wants to buy with it. 'Cos I'm not, you ain't gonna find me out there workin' for him at that low price. I know what I'm worth, everybody knows what they're worth. See everybody knows what they're worth and I know what I'm worth and I'm worth more 'an that. You see? And you get out there and you be workin' your bollocks and you come home right, you wouldn't be able to eat your food, you have to jump in your bed, jump in the car again, work your bollocks off. By the end of week comes, right, you've done so much workin' right, you come home with £45 right – they tax yah, insurance after that and listen man, you don't, you just look back to £29, you might as well, yuh know what I mean? It's a waste 'a time. What I got here, yuh know what I mean, I'm satisfied.

Garnie, had in fact, chosen to stay on his community-based scheme because he could work at his own pace, have some control over what he did and what skills he learned, and develop a good working relationship with his supervisors. While his insightful remarks need to be contextualised in terms of his overall 'survivalist' philosophy, his position was representative of one response many black youths adopt in relation to a racist labour market.[2]

Some young blacks, like Garnie, did consciously seek to use the YTS to shield themselves against the discriminatory edges of the labour market. Institutional racism on employer-based schemes and in the wider labour market both exclude job opportunities for black youngsters, as well as confine them to schemes designated to help those with 'special needs' (Pollert, 1985; YETRU, 1987). This is not to say that choices between employer-based and project-based work is categorically defined by race, but that it is a central factor.

Despite the impact both gender and race have on structuring orientations towards work and work experience, there are some general features all young trainees face out on placement. They can be summed up under the general concept of 'traineeship and work experience' explored in the next section.

Traineeship and work experience: legal, monetary and symbolic elements

The creation of a new trainee status on the YTS has, I would argue, three constituent elements – young people's legal position in relation to employee rights, their monetary value in the labour market and the symbolic status afforded to those in training. While these elements have been analytically separated, in practice they are interrelated aspects of a single process.

The fundamental parameter affecting young people's status on the work experience placement is their formal-legal definition as a 'trainee'. Very few young people are in fact made aware of the legal distinction between 'employee' and 'trainee' when on the YTS and many are unclear of where they stand in relation to acts governing the workplace and worker's rights.[3] The Youth Task Group Report (MSC, 1982a) clearly states that young people on the YTS have the status of trainee rather than employee. Legally, this means that young people sign a trainee agreement rather than a contract of employment.

Managing agents and work experience providers do have the option of entering into a contract of employment with YTS participants and MSC officials were hopeful that up to one-third of young people would be classed as employees. However, early figures collected by the charity 'Youthaid' revealed that only 4 per cent of the initial intake of trainees were in fact defined as employees. What this means is that the vast majority of trainees are exempt from the legal rights afforded by a contract of employment. This legal distinction is responsible for the payment of an 'allowance' rather than a 'wage'. As a result, young people on the YTS are unable to bargain collectively for a higher wage for this would lawfully give them the status of employees (ibid.). Their definition as trainees also influenced the level of the allowance, which was set below the rate where trainees and employers would be liable for National Insurance payments. Without a contract of employment, these young people presumably do not have the right to strike, and it is important to note that initially trainees were not adequately covered by either the existing Health and Safety legislation or the Race Relations and Sexual Discrimination Acts, until various pressure groups forced the government to close these loopholes. These rights may, however, be seen to be threatened under the terms of the 1987 Employment Bill.

While young people may be unaware of their legal position as trainees, they were acutely conscious of their status in monetary terms. The level of the allowance was perhaps the single most contentious issue for the majority of trainees on the YTS. The MSC has consistently argued that payment should be considered an allowance rather than a wage: 'Except where employers choose to embody the traineeship agreement in a contract of employment, young people on the scheme would be trainees. As such the appropriate nature of renumeration would be an allowance' (MSC, 1982a, pp. 13–14). From the point of view of many trainees, there was little doubt that the YTS payment was understood largely as a wage and the placement as a job. As such there was generally a high level of dissatisfaction with the weekly payment:

BH: What do you think of the £25 a week for YTS?
Leonard: It's slave labour, slave labour.

Alice: I get a weekly bus pass, so that's £5 a week and I give £10 to me mam. I've got no money to go out. The money hasn't gone up for three years. Inflation's gone up, but they haven't put the money up.

BH: What do you think of the YTS allowance of £25?
Mark: Aw, it's not very good really, not much better than the dole.

Despite these critical appraisals, I would argue that there are three consecutive moments of accommodation in the lowering of wage expectations. First, for many, £25 per week did seem like a reasonable sum of money initially upon leaving school:

Finchy: It wasn't too bad because I'd never really experienced money and things like that and I'd just left school and £25 was quite a lot to be gettin' right? . . . I mean now I got a job right, I realise what absolutely crap money it is. I don't know how I lived on £25 a week! I don't know how I live on the money I make now.

Second, once on the YTS, there is an acute resignation that as a trainee one is not exactly in a position to bargain collectively for a higher allowance:

BH: So you guys think you need more money. How do you think that's going to happen?

Calvin: It won't happen . . . yuh can't do nothin' about it.

Chris: Will you help me find the best way to get off a training scheme!

Finally, over a period of time there was, for some, an acceptance that they were lucky to get an allowance at all for training and the answer was simply to curb one's expectations and get used to living on £25 a week. This was particularly the case for those trainees who came to view the YTS as training for a career or self-employment:

Jan: Because we're lucky to get an allowance at all, because I mean for the government to give it to us, we're not gettin' an allowance off the company we're working for, so we're lucky to get an allowance.

Julie: I can get by fine on the money I make . . . you know what your ah, limit is, and you go by that limit.

The advantage of this threefold preparation for lowering wage expectations is that it spreads across the entire school/YTS/work transition. Initially, £25 a week does seem like a lot of money upon leaving school and once on the YTS there are few avenues available for negotiating a higher payment. Finally, the accommodation to the allowance begins to lower future expectations of wages for work. Many young people felt £40–50 a week was the average wage for their age group, while in fact the figure cited by the Low Pay Unit, at that time, was £63 a week for a 16 year old in employment. This systematic lowering of expectations should not mask the fact that the level of allowance remains of paramount interest to most trainees.

The final element in legitimating a trainee status and identity is the formalisation of some of the symbolic features of youth labour. For example, the level of remuneration on the YTS is not simply capitalism's quantitative method of categorising the value of youth labour – it is also symbolic of how trainees are defined in terms of 'skill', 'ability' and 'experience'. Even those young people who were in the main quite happy with their scheme, and the YTS in general, privately expressed how being a trainee afforded inferior status:

Julie: In England, we don't think YTS is very respectable, not respectable, it's ah, the same as the dole really. It ain't that good. So what I say is like I work in town, I just say I'm a stock controller and a jewellery – I'm a sales assistant. And then I kind of sneak in afterwards that I'm a YTS. Just to lower it down a bit. 'Cos it isn't ah, it isn't a very good thing to be on, if yuh know what I mean – it puts yuh down a bit.

Billy: 'Cos say yuh got a new trainee right, and you was the boss of the place, yuh wouldn't trust a new trainee. No way!

Neither of these comments should imply that young people like Julie and Billy were against the YTS or that they disliked their own particular scheme. It simply shows that many, including those who accept various aspects of the training paradigm, realise deep down that trainees do possess an overall inferior status.

The historical character of youth labour and the symbolic status afforded to it has been discussed in detail by Cohen (1982). The central feature was its 'fetching and carrying' and subordinate character. The new vocationalism, while extending some of these features into the present day labour market, has also sought subtly to displace some of these older apprentice-like transitions through a thorough revamping of training destinations in the direction of a so called 'career'. The disjuncture between image (working one's way up) and reality (doing all the dirty jobs) is at least partly resolved through young people's daily reactions to their situation.

One of the main contradictions trainees had to deal with out on placement was that they were either treated as a subemployee (in their own words, a 'dogsbody' or a 'gofer')[4] or they were used as a full-time worker without the same benefits, rights or remuneration as other employees. The first scenario tended to be in the manufacturing sphere, while the second approach was more common in the service sector. However, there were exceptions to the rule in both areas of the labour market and much depended upon the goodwill and training expertise of work providers. An additional factor was how trainees responded to their status and treatment at work.

The first situation of being treated as a dogsbody on the YTS is well known and forms the basis for the charge that schemes are 'slave labour'. Of course, young workers have always been initiated into work roles by both management and through informal work cultures. The subordination and feminisation of the young male school leaver, the illusion of the 'temporary stay' for the factory girl and the mistreatment of the office junior have all been well documented in the school to work literature (Pollert, 1981; Valli, 1986; Willis, 1977; Downing, 1981; Cohen, 1982). The crucial difference on the YTS is that a good part of this initiation process has in fact been taken on by the State (via the MSC). This is why it is important to distinguish the process of traineeship from that of apprenticeship. While the traditional apprenticeship system was highly exclusive in both gender and racial terms, at least workers and trade unions often had a hand in the work socialisation and some young people had real opportunities for jobs. Under the new vocationalism, young people are defined as deficient, lose their legal status as employees and have no guarantee of a job or career. Although some of the stories recounted below may appear familiar, I want to argue that they possess a new legitimacy about them, backed up by the State:

BH: How did you like your work placement?

Shanaz: I didn't – I was doing all the bad jobs and I had to make the tea and coffee and I didn't like that. I had to clean up all the time – they'd even leave things for me to clean up in the morning. They treated me like a slave . . . If you're a worker you'd be respected. People would bring you a coffee, not you bring them one.

(in discussions about work sponsors and employers)

Billy: They're too old fashioned and they think we should respect 'em and not stand up for ourselves. That's what I reckon they think.

Andy: And they made me mek the tea all the time!
Calvin: That's all they do – you make the tea and sweep up every minute.

Other work sponsors saw the benefit of having a 'free pair of hands' and quickly put trainees to work, adding value to the company. This second scenario utilised young people's desire to become accepted as regular workers and required a slightly more 'progressive' attitude towards employee relations. Not surprisingly, some of these placements were in the service sector. Part of the reason for this quick initiation was that many jobs in these areas did not require a high level of technical knowledge or craft skills:

Liz: If you work in a shop two or three months, you knows what goes on – it's the same.

In many cases the necessary skills involved things like 'appearance', 'time-keeping' and 'customer service'. Many trainees found that after an initial period, they could in fact perform a wide range of tasks necessary for the job. The problem was they were often doing exactly the same duties as other workers without proper remuneration or full employment rights. This situation often provided the basis for allegations of 'cheap labour' on the YTS.

Yet many young people accepted these two different situations – indeed the contradiction between 'being used' and 'working one's way up', was often used to discipline and control trainees. The basic dilemma was that one was either seen as a trainee and given all the dirty jobs, or one became a full-fledged worker with none of the rights or financial rewards. The increased role of State intervention in defining the legal, monetary and symbolic status of the trainee, combined with young people's desire to move into employment, worked to legitimise the idea of 'traineeship'. The exact path a young person took in relation to his or her work status was also heavily influenced by actual workplace relations.

Trainees and workplace relations: sponsors, supervisors and workmates

One of the primary definers of a trainee's status and experience on the job is their work sponsor. Under the YTS, not only are the sponsors representative of 'employers', they are also in charge of carrying out the training programme on-the-job. As previously mentioned, work sponsors ranged from managing agents themselves (usually established private companies) to placements with major high street stores, medium-sized contractors or even small, family-owned businesses. Trainee relations at work then depended not only upon their own cultural orientations towards work but also upon the type of placement found for them. It was clear that some sponsors obviously viewed the YTS simply as a source of 'free' labour, while others saw it as a valuable company recruitment exercise.

This latter approach, while largely characteristic of the service sector, also occurred in various small manual labour placements, such as those in the repair and building field. Such an approach often cut across the sponsor's relationship with all employees – not just trainees. Within this so called 'progressive' school of human management, hierarchy at the workplace was played down and an illusion of equality amongst company employees was also extended to include trainees:

Mandy: Well it depends really, 'cos if I'm havin' a cuppa tea I'll make it – whereas Stan, the boss, if he's doin' it, he'll make me one. So it's like that over there.

Jan: Where I'm working that's, you know, that's happened, they haven't looked down on me or they haven't made me do sort of cleaning because I'm a trainee.

BH: So they treat you equally at work, just like other full-time workers?

Jan: Yea, exactly the same as everybody else.

This was even sometimes the case for those young people who were working for a small privately-owned business:

Mick: Yea, um, there is crappy jobs, it goes with the job, but everyone does it. The first one ah, in the kitchen place, the first one meks the tea. If I'm in first I'll mek the tea, if the gaffers in first he'll make the tea. So that's the way it goes.

The way in which work sponsors projected these images of workplace relations to trainees was simply through treating young people as bona fide workers.[5] As Mick (above) went on to say, 'They give me good jobs as well . . . they got confidence in me.' Julie, for example, was often put in charge of the small shop she trained with. In her words, she 'worked up to the position I am in now, I'm needed there'.

Attempts to integrate YTS participants into the workforce, however, were fraught with contradictions. I have already mentioned how their separate legal, monetary and symbolic status as trainees prevents young people from achieving the recognition of regular employees. Even those trainees who were relatively satisfied with their workplace relations, found that there were indeed barriers to equal treatment. The most obvious contradiction was the vast difference in levels of pay trainees and employees received for doing exactly the same types of jobs:

Mandy: Yea, I do the same work as everyone else – for a lot less money, of course.

Mick: I'm doin exactly the same as them. Exact same thing, there's nothin' I don't do.

BH: So you're doing exactly the same work?

Mick: Yea, but for less money.

Billy: That's the only bad thing about this.

There were other reasons why trainees were not treated exactly the same as regular workers:

Jan: The only – the only sort of drawback is I get expected, like we get three breaks, we have three breaks and because the workers I'm workin' with are on piecework, they get paid for the amount of goods they produce. So they wanna make as much stuff as they can to get the money for it, so I got to make the tea all the time. So I get, that's the only drawback.

Billy: If I learned to drive, I'd be doin' exactly the same work as they're doin'.

So levels of remuneration, combined with age and production-related barriers, worked to differentiate young people on-the-job however much some sponsors tried to integrate them into the workplace.

Other sponsors used the trainee status as a licence for ill-treatment and exploitation of young workers. This often occurred in small, owner-managed firms where the sponsor had no previous experience of training. In many of these cases trainees did not even come into contact with other workers. Some young people overlooked this negative treatment in the hope of gaining possible employment, while others became very anti-YTS. Finchy, who expected some quality training in signwriting, was placed with such a work sponsor:

Finchy: First of all the placement that I was on, it was to a bloke that, who worked for himself and never took anybody on himself – he never ah, trained people or things like that, had no experience in that. He sort of took it as a bit of a joke at first, right, yuh know he had a go about ah, the first week or so. Decided after a week that it wasn't such a good idea and ah – let me sweep the floors and move these big cupboards around. And then he got another trainee. The front of his shop right, he had the whole of his machinery you could see, so he decided to build a new front on it. So we built a new front on it for him. So he promised, he said, 'OK, I'll help you out at the end of the week, I'll give you some more money' right.

BH: So he was going to top you up?

Finchy: So we thought. Fair enough, if he, yuh know gives us £10 or something. So at the end of the week, Friday night, yuh know, we walk in 'ah, our money right?' – and he gives us a pound each. Right, a pound each! And sez, 'cos it was just before we had a week holiday, 'enjoy your holiday lads'. Fuck! We walked out and just started cursin' and kickin' his windows.

Dan, who was placed with a small building contractor, also had a very similar experience:

Dan: I was just digging holes, sweepin' up, makin' the tea . . . all the rest of it. 'Cos if you think about it, he can't really afford to give you training if he's fittin' somebody's bathroom that they're spendin' thousands of pounds on. You know it's unfair, but he shouldn't have accepted me. And he realised that afterwards.

Exploitation of youth labour was also rife in the clerical/secretarial field, with many young women being used to provide free office help in small workplaces and factories. Kamni, who had illusions of secretarial work as glamorous, was placed in a dingy office at a small factory:

Kamni: I was the only girl workin' there . . . Yea and it was a pretty lousy atmosphere and uh, it wasn't really good for me so I tried to get out of the place. I don't think they liked that sort of attitude, so I got the sack eventually.

These experiences of ill-treatment and the lack of contact with other workers sometimes led trainees to quit or change schemes.

The majority of young people were placed with work sponsors who employed at least a handful of regular employees. The relationship between trainees and older workers is one fraught with tension. Employees often view trainees as either secondary workers ('gofers') or a possible threat to full-time jobs. Trainees, while resenting this treatment, nevertheless continue to have strong attachments to the informal work culture. This general tension influenced many young people's relationships with other workers on the job.

So while many viewed 'getting on with others' as a central feature of a good job, there were barriers which often separated trainees from the existing workforce. Many young people, who were given full responsibilities at work, came to resent the fact that other workers were doing the same job but for much higher wages:

> **BH:** Is it all trainees or did you say that there were some regular employees working there?
> **Andy:** Lots next door.
> **BH:** How much do you think they're getting paid per week?
> **Andy:** A lot more 'an we are! Get a hundred – a hundred a week.
>
> **BH:** And would you be doing the same, exactly the same thing as other people working there full time?
> **Julie:** I'm doing more – and for less money!

In some situations there was open hostility between workers and trainees. Paul, who had been placed with a well-established engineering firm, was clearly frustrated with the worker-trainee divide regarding assembly-line production and pay:

> **Paul:** They just sit around readin' the paper half the time. Then they get up and make about twenty pieces and then sit back down again. I can do twice that much – and they get paid more than me.

Ironically, it was the workers themselves, through the union, who had arranged a substantial top-up of Paul's allowance. Similarly, trainees often forget that work experience is to contain a significant training element and should not be a substitute for existing jobs.

Boisterous attempts by trainees to become accepted at work

could often backfire and assertiveness was often mistaken for aggression:

Margaret: They keep saying that I'm cheeky and that, but it's just my way of gettin' to know them, get on with them yuh know.

While some young people may have been able to handle themselves in these situations, there were many trainees who did not possess the confidence to deal with older workers on their own terms. Some trainees specifically mentioned that one aspect of a good job was working with people your own age. There was also evidence that some young people resented older workers' monopoly of the labour market:

Robert: I'll tell yuh what should happen – they should retire and give us lot a chance.

The most significant aspect of this on-the-job 'traineeship', however, is the way in which many young people's introduction into work is increasingly being regulated by the State (i.e. the MSC) and employers (i.e. sponsors, managing agents), at the expense of some of the formal and informal elements of working-class life and organisation (i.e. trade unions). In the next section, I want to make the case that the institutional separation of trainees from employees and the dominance of State and private interests in defining young people's experiences of employment are beginning to undermine a whole political culture which has traditionally supported working-class struggles at work.

'Problems' at work: collective representation and the trainee identity

The creation of a 'trainee' as opposed to an 'employee' identity on the YTS has important implications for how young people are encouraged to deal with workplace problems and grievances. By legally separating trainees from the rest of the workforce and lengthening their transition into work, the new vocationalism has

made a specific impact on traditional modes of worker representation and employee rights.

For example, in making a clear legal distinction between a
trainee agreement and a contract of employment, the YTS ensures
that many young workers don't in fact have the same rights to
challenge certain conditions and problems at work (wage increases
being an obvious one). More important than even this legal distinction, is the fact that very few trainee's experience the benefits
of collective representation and action while on schemes. In other
words, many of the workplace issues central to trade unionism are
increasingly being taken over by scheme management, programme
review teams and in some cases trainee councils. Reference is
made below to three personal examples drawn from literally hundreds of workplace problems.[6] All these cases demonstrate the
blunting effect the YTS has on dealing with legitimate grievances
through appropriate bodies and democratic channels.

Dan was one of the first group of young people actually to go
on to a YTS in the area. He joined a private training agency
scheme largely because it purported to offer broad-based training
and he was interested in computer programming. Unfortunately,
no placement could be found in this area and Dan was placed
with a small building contractor who had little time or experience
in training young workers. While he spent most of the time doing
'gofer' jobs, there were times when he was given responsibility
for a task and was left to get on with it. One such job clearly
stuck out in his mind:

> **Dan:**   And another time he [his work sponsor] left me in the
> house chiselling a hole in the wall for a waste pipe to
> go through. And I wasn't very good at it. And so he
> came back and said, 'Oh, you haven't finished this yet,
> I'd better do it.' So he started chiselling away and I
> went off for my dinner. I came back and he'd chiselled
> right back to the mains, electric mains, right, and he'd
> blown a massive hole in the chisel and like he'd left me
> – if I'd been chiselling I'd probably have killed myself.

In addition to working unsupervised with dangerous equipment,
Dan was also asked to work with asbestos without any protective
equipment. The final irony was that he had to equip himself with

proper work boots and protective equipment in order to do a number of jobs safely.

Alice was also on a private training scheme which placed her in a small firm as a secretarial worker. During her placement she was constantly harassed by a male full-time cleaner:

Alice: There was a bloke there called, ah, Harry, he used to sweep the floors like, dustin', the odd job and that. He never used to do nothing, he'd just sit there. I think there was something wrong with him. And he broke my radio right and I wasn't there 'cos I went back to the scheme then for my trainin' and when I come back and found my radio broken he never came and apologised. I said, 'Yuh broke my radio.' Well then he called me a slug and threatened to break my neck and everytime he'd see me he'd start nudgin' or pushin' or somethin'. So I told the gaffer and he said, 'I'll have a word with him', but he was his favourite. So I went back and told my mum and she said, 'Has he threatened to hit you?' and I said yea, so she said, 'Go into the scheme and tell them, right?' So I was leavin anyhow, so I went into the scheme manager's office and told her and that's when she really turned against me. 'Cos she liked the gaffer there.

Alice subsequently left the scheme because of the incident, only to be offered another YTS.

The last example of a workplace problem involved a black youth named Otis who was on a college-based scheme. He was sent by the college placement officer to a small construction company for an interview, only to be turned away because of the sponsor's racism:

Otis: The placement officer sent me down to this place but the gaffer said he couldn't take me on because of me colour. He said it didn't matter to him, but some of his customers might not like it. So I went back and told her and she wrote a few things down.

BH: Did she report them to anyone like the Commission for Racial Equality [CRE]?

Otis: Naw, she didn't do nothing.

Otis ended up doing project-based work experience on the scheme and the incident was not taken up by the placement officer or the managing agent.

Although all three of these cases represent very different issues and circumstances, they all have one thing in common – not one of the grievances was referred to a representative organisation for investigation. Dan was not only left unsupervised with a potentially dangerous piece of machinery, his work sponsor consistently refused to provide appropriate protective equipment. At the time, Dan and other trainees were not fully covered under the Health and Safety at Work Act (coverage only came later after pressure by various trade union and labour groups). Alice's complaint about harassment could also have been taken up by a trade union or appropriate body. Instead, it was dismissed in a private conversation between her and the scheme manageress. Finally, the very serious case of workplace discrimination, involving Otis, clearly would appear to contravene the Race Relations Act and should have been referred to an appropriate body like the CRE for investigation. In all cases, the mechanisms for dealing properly with workplace grievances were subverted through 'in-house' scheme channels. In this way, very few complaints are actually brought to the attention of the MSC or the public at large.

It would be wrong to suggest that the intervention of the MSC into industrial relations and workplace disputes is in any way a conspiratorial phenomenon. In effect, the problem stems as much from trade union inactivity and ineffectiveness as from the government's ulterior motives. Trade union participation on MSC programmes was predicated on their involvement with schemes and contact with trainees. Yet the very structure of the YTS has effectively militated against any real trade union imput at the workplace level. For example, despite a local agreement in the area which makes trade union education mandatory during the induction period, less than 10 per cent of schemes visited had such an imput (both were community based). None of the trainees on private training agencies had been in contact with trade union officials and local research reveals that a staggering 87 per cent of PTA schemes themselves appeared to be non-unionised (YTS Monitoring Unit, 1985).[7] The complacency of the trade union movement concerning these problems is staggering, considering what can only be called a growing distrust of collective organisations and solutions amongst young workers.

The failure of trade unions to penetrate either work placements or the off-the-job training element of the scheme, combined with the internal handling of problems by scheme management, means that very few young people are aware they could join a union or understood the role they might play in handling workplace issues:

> **BH:** What other things do they do in induction besides health and safety? Did they ever have trade unions come in at all?
>
> **Shabaz:** No – no, they were tellin' us about trade unions but they sez you really don't have to join – so no one bothered like.

Even those few young people who were predisposed to the idea of collective representation found that many trade unions were unreliable and did not appear interested in representing trainees:

> **BH:** You actually joined a union when you were on a scheme. I mean how did that work out?
>
> **Dan:** It was basically a complete waste of time. The union didn't want to know about us. 'Cos I joined it in a bit of a rush. I was a bit worried that the management on my scheme were gonna try and get rid of me or something 'cos I was causing a bit of trouble for them. So I thought I'd better join a union and defend myself. So I sent off the money and the sheet of paper and things and that was the last I heard. They never sent me a card or anything. They don't particularly want to touch YTS 'cos it's a lot of hard work for them tryin' to defend people on schemes. But at the same time they gotta start. Trainees gotta force 'em into it.

Schemes where trade unions were active often reflected those sectors which have traditionally been heavily unionised (i.e. manufacturing, maintenance and construction). There were some expectations amongst young people in these sectors (usually

males) that trade unions might have a role in protecting workers'
jobs and fighting for decent wages:

> **Baz:**   Once ya get older an' that, then you expect a bigger
> rise – that's why its better to join a union.
>
> **Robert:** Yea, join a union right, 'cos they got a bit of security
> right?
>
> **Baz:**   'Cos when I was at college, I was talkin' to some of
> the other kids there who was workin' properly and
> they turned around and go, 'You in a union?' 'Cos
> when you leave or if yuh stay like, the union will
> find, will try and find you a job. By rights, they have
> to find, make the gaffer keep you on there till you
> can find another job.

However, contact with unions in the manufacturing sector in no
way guaranteed support for the idea of collective representation.
There are equally conservative images of trade unions within a
manual labour culture:

> **Billy:**   If I had my way I'd have all unions abolished. I know
> that sounds stupid 'cos in some way they are helpful to
> us, but in most – that's why this country is down in the
> dumps now – wastin' money on unions and that and
> stupid people like Margaret Thatcher and that.

Despite some reservations, at least a section of young males came
to expect protection and security from trade unions. Not a single
young woman mentioned trade unionism in relation to her work
experience or problems at work. Many unions in the service occupations did not appear to be reaching young people training in
these areas.

The vast majority of trainees had developed negative images
of trade unions during school and through the media (Glasgow
University Media Group, 1982). Fear of reprisal and lack of confidence was one reason why young people shunned the idea:

> **Finchy:** For example, in a place there right, there was this
> kid on a training scheme right, and he's lost it now,
> they kicked him off when his trainin' scheme finished.

He thought they were gonna kick him off and I said, 'Why don't you join the T & G right? He said, 'Oh, no, no, no', and I said, 'Well, why not?' and he said, 'Oh, I don't want to get involved in that sort of thing' right? People are afraid, right? Youth more than anybody.

Other's saw unions on the losing end and this negative image often put them off the idea. Images of strikes, greed, disruption and trouble surrounded and dominated many young people's views and perceptions.

The most significant point, however, is the way in which the YTS itself is implicated in severing young people's links with collective strategies and organisation:

Kamni: I don't intend to join the union so . . . yuh know, a trade union has nothing really to do with YTS . . . But I'm not really interested in trade unions, not really, like I say I wouldn't join a trade union. Yuh know, I think hearin' about it is OK, but not really socialising with it.

Garnie: Unions lose, that's what I believe. They don't win, they lose. They can win to a certain extent, but they lose to a certain extent. They don't win against the government ' cos they're the one's in power . . . I don't agree with a union on this scheme because I think unions are a waste of time. People get in a union 'cos they are very weak-minded, they need backin'. I don't believe in that, I don't believe in back-up. I believe in dealin' with a person by myself you see. You see, union –

BH: But isn't the trainee organisation a bit like a union?

Garnie: Oh, yea, but we don't make decisions about, ah, work or anything like that you see. We usually do it for the buildin', like the canteen, for repairs – we don't usually get into personal affairs or anything like that 'cos they'd be calling for the manager, see?

What is so significant about both these conversations is how trade unions appear to be irrelevant to training schemes. Kamni expresses the fact that trade unions really have little to do with the YTS and trainees' concerns. Meanwhile, Garnie views trade unions as 'losers' and for the 'weak-minded'. He also demonstrates how trainee councils (of which he was leader) have pre-empted union representation, while effectively side-stepping many of the real issues surrounding young workers' rights.

The exemption of trainees from employment rights, the failure of trade unions to recruit and make themselves relevant and the construction of individualist problem-solving models on the YTS, all contribute to threaten the long-term viability of collective representation at work. It should be no surprise to find that the majority of new transitions and identities on the YTS are largely anti-union and anti-labourist. This issue will receive further analysis and commentary in the concluding chapter.

In summary, this chapter has concentrated on the generalised experience of being defined as a trainee and has sought to demonstrate how such an identity is constructed legally, monetarily and symbolically. Furthermore, I have sought to show how workplace relations with management and fellow workers also contribute towards the process of traineeship 'on-the-job'. Of particular importance is how the new vocationalism, by separating and lengthening youth transitions into work, has laid the groundwork for reproducing not only a general and malleable labour force, but has also affected how young people come to view their future working life in terms of collective representation and rights. Of course, youth labour is required in many different forms and the traineeship pattern explored here and in Chapter 3 forms only a basis for the construction of a variety of different orientations towards wage labour and adulthood. Part II attempts to deal with these more diverse and specific identities and transitions in more detail, explore their relation to other sites and wider cultural forms and link them to the current problems and future prospects of the labour movement.

Part II

Wider Cultural Forms, Sites and Identities

5

Youth Differentiation, Training and the World of Work

In Part I, I have consciously emphasised the more immediate cultural experiences and responses of working-class youth on training schemes. In doing so, I have demonstrated that all young people are facing a new set of structures which have fundamentally altered the old school to work transition. Yet even here it is clear that subsections of the young working class vary substantially in how they deal with 'life on the scheme'. In order to come to terms with the more specific transitions formed under the new vocationalism, it is crucial to move beyond the confines of the scheme itself and explore the impact wider cultural forms, social relations and other institutional sites have on training identities.

Part II provides the ethnographic material for understanding how a series of distinct working-class transitions and identities are formed and implicitly explores the political implications of this differentiation. It does so by examining the combined role the YTS, broader cultural forms and other social sites and relations have on the production of a diverse youth population. Youth experiences and concerns in the world of work, leisure (or non-work), the working-class household and community, identities based around white ethnicity and sexism and political views on umemployment, training and the economy are all crucial elements of contemporary youthful identities. By widening the focus of the study I am also explicitly arguing that any coherent political analysis and policy surrounding the training/employment debate must begin to understand how the young working-class is differentially formed in relation to a wide variety of social sites and processes.

This chapter examines how the YTS specifically acts to differentiate youth responses to the world of work. While the centrality of employment and the experience of wage labour remains important to the whole of the youth population, the process I referred to as 'traineeship' remains too crude an indicator of the varied range of work subjectivities on offer under the new vocationalism.

Of course, the experience of work for the working-class has always been variable. One need only to think of the distinctions between skilled and unskilled, manual and non-manual labour, the divide between men's and women's jobs and the relationship between older and younger workers. Despite these internal differences, the transition into work for the majority of young working-class people has, until quite recently, taken very particular forms. As Cohen (1984) has suggested, this transition literally took the form of an apprenticeship – an inheritance of concrete skills transmitted through the family, the shop floor and through the working-class community. This apprenticeship, while transmitting a very particular type of shop floor politics, took on very rigid forms for young men and women and contained definite patriarchal and racial elements (Cohen, 1983).

In the post-war period, while elements and vestiges of these apprenticeships persist, there has been a considerable weakening of these traditional transitions. While the reasons behind this are complex, what is of immediate concern here is the way the new vocationalism has exploited the exclusive and limiting nature of these cultural apprenticeships and challenged them through the elaboration of new skilling regimes and a restructuring of the working-class labour market.

One of the most significant features of the new vocationalism, then, is the way in which it purports to break down the older, more limited, transitions into employment, while at the same time offering new opportunities for working-class youth in the world of work.[1] The MSC, for example, has consistently maintained that it is committed to equal opportunities on the YTS and breaking down the exclusive nature of the old apprenticeship system. Furthermore, young people are given the distinct impression that the YTS can offer them a way into new careers and occupations. In summary, the new vocationalism has sought to produce the image that it is a viable and, indeed, a progressive alternative to traditional working-class routes into work.

Underneath this rhetoric, there is a wealth of evidence suggesting that training schemes are merely reproducing many of the social characteristics of the wider labour market. This is particularly evident in terms of the sexual and racial division of labour.[2]

However, very little research has attempted to come to terms with the intra-class divisions created by the YTS, or to contrast the images of work and opportunity available to trainees during their early experiences of employment on schemes with the actual reality of their job and career prospects. This chapter aims to make a contribution to an analysis of the construction of new and varied working-class transitions into work through training. I begin by assessing the impact the new vocationalism has made in altering traditional working-class patterns of work, particularly as they relate to the social processes of masculinity and femininity.

Beyond beauty and the beast: the new vocationalism and working-class youth experiences of work

Cohen (1982, 1983, 1984) has argued that until recently growing up working-class has meant being apprenticed to a special kind of 'inheritance'. In this cultural apprenticeship, young people's destinies were closely fixed to their class origins (Cohen, 1983). For working-class males this apprenticeship was specifically related to their transition into manual labour and their politicisation through a peculiarly masculine shop floor culture. Young working-class women's apprenticeship took on a quite different form and involved a process of feminine maturation into eligible domestic labourers. Although not exclusively, domestic rather than wage labour was the main focus of this latter apprenticeship.

Contemporary research by Griffin (1985) indicates that this pattern continues to influence working-class schoolgirl's images and ideas about the labour market and what constitutes a 'good job'. She specifically mentions the distinction made by young women between office work (portrayed as glamorous and clean) and factory jobs (seen as dirty, boring and repetitive). Griffin (1982, p. 6) traces the roots of this division back to young women's particular position in relation to the sexual, marriage and labour market:

I want to suggest that women are simultaneously positioned in the labour market and the sexual marketplace. The former includes the traditional sociological view of the labour market and the full range of potential jobs for women – and men. The latter refers to the ways in which women are judged as potential lovers (paid and unpaid) and as potential objects of male gaze and sexual consumption – as 'fair game' . . . The sexual market overlaps with what has been called the marriage market for women . . . in which women are judged as potential wives and mothers, working for, and emotionally and sexually servicing, men and their families.

While these factors have a specific influence on young working-class women, Griffin goes on to argue that this triple marketplace impacts on the entire structure and culture of women's work and their position in the labour market.

Similarly, traditional working-class male orientations towards work cannot be fully understood outside the processes and ideologies of masculinity and male working-class culture. Tolson (1977, pp. 12–13) argues that masculinity in contemporary society is completely intertwined and bound up with the institution of work: 'In Western, industrialised, capitalist societies, definitions of masculinity are bound up with definitions of work. Whether in terms of physical strength or mechanical expertise, or in terms of ambition and competitiveness, the qualities needed by the successful worker are closely related to those of the successful man.'

The specific relationship between working-class masculinity and the capitalist labour process has been examined in more detail by Willis (1977, 1979). His argument relies on the general premise that despite the fact that much labour under capitalism is emptied of any real significance, workers seek to impose meaningful frameworks in an attempt to humanise the work environment. In the case of working-class men and their jobs, this imposition takes a certain form. One aspect of this culture is the development of a specifically masculine orientation towards a confrontation with physical labour and production. It is within this construction of meaning and identity, which revolves around performing hard, dirty and often unpleasant labour, that there develops both a shop floor politics and an exaggerated style of working-class masculinity. The carrying out of labour power in production, despite being performed for someone else under difficult conditions, is viewed as an engagement with the 'real world' and is expressed as masculine style.

How do these broader cultural patterns relate to young people's orientations towards and experiences of work on the YTS? In what way has the new vocationalism sought to deal with these processes and how has it attempted to alter images of the working-class youth labour market for both young women and men?

'Glam', domestic and factory transitions for young women

In the case of young working-class women on schemes, it is clear that the traditional domestic apprenticeship pattern continues under the surface of job 'choice' and training opportunities. Local Careers Service figures reveal that 83 per cent of female trainees were receiving training in only four occupational areas (clerical, retailing, catering, personal services). However, it is equally obvious that the new vocationalism has sought to redefine some of the more traditional forms of female labour and create the illusion of increased career opportunities for young women. Crucial to this process is the way in which a particular type of labour was imagined or perceived by a young woman, as well as how it was promoted under the new types of skilling regimes on the YTS.

Transitions into work, for the majority of young women on the YTS, were perceived on a continuum ranging from careers in 'glam' (glamorous) jobs, paraprofessional/domestic work to factory jobs. Young women's definition of glam jobs included office work, some types of shop work (i.e. high fashion jewellery, clothes, cosmetics), hairdressing, fashion design and beauty therapy. Paraprofessional and domestic orientations, while representing different poles of opinion, related to similar fields like childcare, care of the elderly or disabled, catering and service jobs. Finally, factory transitions included work on assembly line production, distribution and warehouse jobs.

Schemes offering training in what are considered to be glam jobs, or at least 'clean' occupations, are highly sought after by female trainees. Secretarial and retail schemes attract a significant proportion of young women and training places in hairdressing and beauty therapy are highly competitive. Of course, not all work placements in these fields were considered to be particularly glamorous. It was more the image of an occupation's potential and anyway there was a clear distinction between a respectable job and factory work:

BH: And you mentioned, did they offer, were one of the
        slips a job?
Julie: About two and they were in a factory.
BH: And you didn't fancy that?
Julie: No – I'm not the factory type, sorry to say.

While present work experience placements on the YTS were not
always necessarily seen as glamorous jobs, some trainees had
moved up the work hierarchy and were given the impression in
off-the-job training sessions that these occupations were definitely
the beginning of a career.

Office work was also viewed, if not experienced, by some young
women as a possible glam job, particularly through the illusion of
moving up the office hierarchy and becoming the boss's personal
secretary. Even for those YTS trainees starting at the bottom, it
was seen as a good job in terms of 'standards':

Kamni: Yea, I think I'd like to have a really good job as
        secretary or an office junior. You know, I think that
        would be up to my standards – Yea, I think that's it,
        I think that would, ah, be the main thing I'm aimin'
        for in life.

The other main attraction about office work was that it was considered to be a clean work environment. This meant not only
should the office be neat and tidy, it also drew on young women's
expectations about appearance and dressing up for work. One
young woman, was highly distressed when her office placement
didn't live up to this image:

BH: But what was the reason why you didn't like it?
Alice: It was really scruffy, dirty, yuh couldn't wear nice clo-
        thes, you'd get oil all over the place – it's horrible.

Glam jobs and the impressions that they hold for young working-class women were often supported by the off-the-job training
element and pedagogy, despite poor quality work experience
placements. The impression of job mobility and possibly self-
employment and trainee's insertion in a feminine work culture of
sexuality was enough to attract and convince a significant pro-

portion of young women that they could achieve a career through
the YTS.

Paraprofessional and domestic orientations were most prevalent
in jobs such as working with children or the elderly, as well as
catering and cleaning work. Ursula Huws (1982) has described
many of these occupations as 'doing other people's housework'.
However, within this general categorisation of jobs, it is clear that
the new vocational emphasis is on paraprofessionalising strands
of this type of work. By this I mean preparing people primarily
for the social aspects of a job, at the expense of technical knowledge and formal qualifications necessary for real career advancement within a field. Off-the-job training of this type was usually
administered through 'personal and social development' courses
and 'personal effectiveness' sessions. For domestic jobs (like the
childcare example below), this often involved polishing up already
existing 'feminine' knowledge and offering a minimum of technical
training:

BH: So do you think you're getting good training at
         your work placement?
Margaret: They don't train yuh exactly, yuh just pick it up.
         You know, they say 'can you change nappies?' and
         what they do, you just ah, watch'em and do it –
         what they're doin'.

Other young women in the domestic field obviously did not view
their training in professional terms. Tracy, who initially did not
request training in the caring area, definitely viewed her placement
as 'doing someone else's housework'. Her disillusionment with
training in the caring field later led her to leave the YTS and
become involved in youth rights, as well as various forms of class
and gender politics. Despite this anomoly, it is clear that for many
young women there are important links between these transitions
and one's future role in the domestic and marriage marketplace
(Griffin, 1982).

The third main orientation, already mentioned in relation to
office jobs, is factory transitions. While many women choose to
avoid training in factory jobs, a small number I interviewed were
on placements in clothing manufacture and warehouse distribution. Jan, who was completely atypical of this grouping, was

training as a machinist in a clothing manufacture firm. Her orientation was very much one of the budding entrepreneur learning about the work from the bottom up – an idea clearly supported by the small business training offered by her PTA scheme. Three other young women had chosen to receive training in the distribution field and all of them were at the same placement at a factory-like warehouse filling orders, transporting and packaging various goods. Although the work was strenuous, they appeared to enjoy the type of job and the sociable working atmosphere, as one of the women testifies:

Michelle: I work in a big warehouse, filling orders and things. It's quite hard work but I really like my mates and the other people working there – were always havin' a laugh about somethin'.

None of these young women distinguished between 'clean' jobs and factory work and from their own accounts they all enjoyed the informal factory culture. Related research (Pollert, 1981) has shown that young working-class women's perception of manual work as a 'temporary stay' often results in a double burden of wage and domestic labour in later years.

These three main orientations towards work constructed through training schemes do not exhaust the full range of identities amongst young women. I have already mentioned the subtle distinction between young women who see the caring field through the quite distinct lens of a paraprofessional career and those who view it as 'doing other people's housework'. Similarly, there were also variations in how self-employment was viewed. Liz, for example, saw her working future very much as a part-time 'youth culture enterpriser' – selling her own unorthodox clothing designs and styles to stores on a commissioned basis. Leisure and style rather than traditional values of thrift and hard work influenced her vision of self-employment (see also Chapter 7). Finally, a minority of those young women who became highly disillusioned with their experience of the YTS turned towards youth rights and issues campaigns, rather than clinging to shattered images of the feminine labour market.

These subjective responses to the new vocationalism are instrumental features of a series of wider changes in working-class women's transitions into work and adulthood. Before turning to a more specific examination of how these identities manifest themselves in different aspects of work for young women, I turn briefly to look at how the new vocationalism has sought to shift young men's images of work.

Masculinity, manual labour and the YTS: the lads are all here, or are they?

How do theories of masculinity and traditional male working-class transitions relate to young men's expectations of work through their experience of the YTS? First, it is undeniable that the changing nature of labour power under capitalism has irrevocably altered many traditional male occupations, particularly in the craft and manufacturing sector. Second, it is equally clear that young working-class men now face a set of new structures in making the transition into work through the YTS. Under these rapidly changing circumstances no decisive pattern has yet emerged. For some of the lads these developments have merely served to strengthen aspects of traditional male orientations, while for others there are the beginnings of alternative routes and identities not quite so strongly rooted in the tradition of wage labour and masculine style.

It must be stressed that despite the changing nature of industry and production, masculine attitudes to manual labour amongst young working-class men remain out of proportion to the number of jobs still requiring great physical exertion. This is not to say that this kind of work doesn't still exist, but rather that there is an exaggerated stress on the physical nature of wage labour for many of the lads on the YTS. One trainee, whose desire to become a butcher led to some early work experience in this field, prior to his movement on to a painting and decorating scheme, exemplifies this perspective in his description of the job:

Chris: I wanna be a butcher.
BH: Is that a long day?
Chris: Its a, it is a long day – yea. Yuh start about 6 o'clock and about 6 o'clock yuh finish and then yuh go to the pub until about 9 o'clock – 'cos if yuh worked that hard he, the gaffer, takes yuh out.

Work identities and future expectations of work for many of these lads were predicted on the value they saw in hard physical labour. Nearly two-thirds of male trainees in the locality were training in the manufacturing or construction sectors, despite a massive downturn in employment prospects in these areas.

The maintenance of this masculine adherence to manual work was largely responsible for some of the young men's distinction between 'real' and 'project-based' work on the YTS. The male version of this distinction is connected up with the recognition that project-based work experience is not comparable to the confrontation with the real work of capitalist production. It was in this latter sphere that one's labour really mattered and it was at work that one learned about the real world. The YTS, because it sometimes served to block the realisation of one's masculine status, actually appeared to heighten at least some of the lad's desire to engage in any type of manual work, however exploitative in nature.

There is an important qualification to this general pattern. Manual labour for many of the lads was viewed in a favourable light only if it was connected to some recognisable skill or craft knowledge. The strong desire to become accepted as a bona-fide worker was balanced off against the promise that the YTS was supposed to deliver some form of skills training.

While the orientation to manual work described above was clearly the dominant pattern, there was a number of other important trends. These have crucial implications for developing new theories of masculine class culture and attachments to different types of labour. For example, vocational training in the administration and retail fields for some young men is increasingly being constructed as a practical start up th corporate hierarchy. Angus, who was receiving work experience from a high street men's clothing shop, saw his training as the first step up the company ladder. Nigel, who was training in the administration and clerical sector, also saw his future in these terms:

BH: Do you know what you'd like to go on to do next after YTS?

Nigel: Definitely management, definitely. Actually, I would like a job, to have the experience after working in an office and seeing the pressures you go through, the ups and downs – build you up in yourself so you get a bit

stronger inside. But definitely management of some
sort. My future plans really would actually be to go
self-employed. In what, I don't know.

It is clear that the YTS has created the image of a particularly
male working-class route into white collar jobs and possibly self
employment amongst some youngsters.

There were also other exceptions to the manual labour pattern.
Dan, who initially went on to the scheme to do computer programming, ended up on placements doing manual labour, work he
described as 'something I'm not very good at'. Finchy chose to
train in a skilled trade (signwriting), not because he had any deep
desire for that kind of work, but rather because he felt it was a
type of craft labour less susceptible to exploitation by employers.
Similarly, manual labour on the YTS for many black youths, like
Garnie for instance, was only acceptable if it contained real skill
training. Finally, Ben, who was on a horticultural scheme, had
wanted to get some training in the conservation field because he
liked the solitude and the socially useful nature of that type of
work. His orientation towards work was much more vocational
(in the true sense of the word), and he was interested in labour
in so far as it was socially relevant.

It is crucial to keep in mind these traditional and emergent
patterns for both young men and women, constructed as they
are out of the changing nature of older working-class cultural
apprenticeships and the effects of the new vocationalism. The
manner in which they influence various aspects of working life
begins with a look at differential orientations to the wage.

The wage: differential expectations and orientations

One of the central facets of contemporary work in capitalist
society is the exchange of labour power for a wage. While this is
a reality for the whole of the working class, I want to argue that
the new vocationalism, in addition to lowering expectations, helps
to throw up a variety of different orientations towards the wage.

The payment of an allowance on the YTS, rather than a wage,
has had some significant effects on class orientations towards the
wage. The general impact has been an overall lowering of expec-

tations, with young women being in an additionally weak position in judging the worth of their labour. With the casualisation and part-time nature of much of women's work, female trainees often have no real standard from which to judge the allowance. There were also crucial differences between young women who saw themselves as training for a career, in which case the allowance seemed fair, and those who viewed their placement as a proper job, thereby requiring a proper wage.

Generally, wage expectations for working-class males declined in a similar fashion, with one important exception. For those lads training in the manual trades, there was some kind of benchmark available in the wages of a skilled male worker:

BH: How much do you think a 19 years old should make?
Baz: It all depends, doesn't it?
BH: It depends on the job, I guess?
Robert: What job he's in and what e's doin'.
Baz: If he's trained or . . .
BH: What about a mechanic or someone like that?
Robert: If he's a qualified mechanic he should be pickin' up £70–80 a week.
Baz: Round the hundred mark.
Robert: Maybe even more.

Even though these figures represent an underestimation in terms of what skilled workers actually do earn, it demonstrates how such wage rates for men can be passed on to young male workers and be utilised for comparative purposes.

Orientations towards the wage were also significantly affected by how young people viewed their work experience and how they saw their future working life. For young working-class women these orientations were closely linked to the main transitions outlined earlier. For example, Michelle, one of the factory workers, was very instrumental in her orientation about working for a wage, and what kind of things the wage brought with it. Julie, on the other hand, viewed the pay as secondary to the quality of the job, particularly as it related to moving up the retail hierarchy:

BH: What about the money, is that important in a job?
Julie: It is, yuh can't say that it isn't, but it is important. I

> could live on, say if somebody said, 'Oh, I'll give you
> a job at £80', and it would be a rubbish job or else give
> you a job on a, a job for £60 and good clothes to sell
> and everything, I'd sooner have that. I'd take a little
> less.

While these different perspectives on the wage are at least partly accounted for by young women's predispositions towards factory and careerist transitions, I would argue that they all viewed it partly in terms of the freedom and pleasure it brought to them in the sphere of consumption. However, unlike some of their male counterparts, young women were not in the same position to use the wage to assert their independence and power within the family household (for example, see Chapter 6).

The meaning of the wage for many working-class males is closely tied to masculine orientations towards manual labour. These orientations are more closely linked to what the wage packet symbolises rather than its exact material worth. However, the substitution of an allowance for a proper wage can result in a peculiarly masculine version of the 'fetishisation' of the wage packet. I would argue that the lack of a proper wage for some working-class lads is compensated for through their overexaggeration of the importance of the allowance in contributing to the family wage. Although none of these lads was in fact the family 'bread-winner', many of them symbolically played out a version of this role in relation to the family household. The payment of household keep was viewed as sufficient to maintain male status in the family, it acted to release the lads from contributing to domestic chores and was used to buy additional time for leisure activities outside the home.

This main orientation does not exhaust the full range of male responses. For Ben, pay was not nearly as important as doing a socially useful job and his later involvement in voluntary work testifies to his commitment to such a perspective. For those males, like Nigel and Angus, who saw the YTS as a stepping stone to a business career, the wage (or in these case 'the salary') was also seen as secondary to such things as career prospects, independence and promotional opportunities. Finally, a unique philosophical approach to wage labour was expressed by Garnie, a black youth training in woodwork:

Garnie: I believe that everyone should work for their labour right and get their labour. But its like say, everybody is workin' for their labour are not gettin' their labour, they're gettin' a quarter of their labour whereas they should get the whole lot of their labour, right?

These examples show that despite the continuance of a dominant male orientation towards wage labour, there is a series of alternative positions developing. Different orientations towards the wage for young working-class women are also evolving out of their engagement with different forms of female labour and the influence the new vocationalism has had in redefining the feminine youth labour market.

Work placements and work cultures

I have so far argued that the new vocationalism has challenged previous working-class transitions into work and in doing so has influenced images of youth labour and created different orientations towards the wage. In this section, I want to show further how different transitions and identities are interlinked with young people's insertion into quite distinct work cultures while on the YTS.

For some young women, particularly those involved in glam and paraprofessional jobs, a key criterion for judging work was that it should be interesting. This usually meant work that was varied, challenging and allowed for the development of a range of skills and competencies. While this was very rarely the situation on scheme placements, many of these young women accepted their current inferior status as a temporary measure:

Liz: Oh, its not too, I mean working in a shop is really boring which is what I'm doing. You know, it's really boring, but I mean I don't think you expect much from it. You're just getting some experience.

If it was so obvious to these young women that many of the jobs they were currently doing on the YTS were neither challenging nor interesting, why did some continue to believe in the ideology of glam jobs and careerism? I want to argue that the new vocationalism has capitalised on particular images surrounding particular female labour forms and have used these to construct the impression that the YTS is in fact the initial stage of a career. Trainees are told that it is necessary for them to take on unpleasant jobs before moving up the occupational ladder. Jan, who was working as machinist in a clothing factory, truly believed that learning from the 'bottom up' was essential for running her own clothing business in the future. In jobs such as office work (Downing, 1981), hairdressing (Attwood and Hatton, 1983; Cohen, 1984) and certain types of retailing work, there exist illusory structures signalling opportunity and promotion, as the following quote testifies:

Julie: I've built up my own little thing. I'm in charge of the shop sometimes for a half hour at a time. I'm in charge of me own jewellery, when I started I didn't have that. So I've worked up to the position I'm in now. I'm needed there.

BH: Is that the kind of work that you might want to continue?

Julie: There's no future in – I've learnt now lookin' at it, there's no future in shop work unless you're in one of the big shops.

The experience of mobility (however small), combined with the illusion of a glam job tomorrow, worked to secure some kind of consent around young women's acceptance of mediocre jobs while on the YTS.

Of course, not all young women experienced placements which held out the promise of interesting work and promotion. While paraprofessional transitions were also infused with this ideology, work placements in domestic type jobs were often so far removed from the image of having professional status that there was little chance of such an identity taking root. One woman described her nursing home work placement as 'carrying bodies up and down stairs and cleaning up food and shit'. For those unsure of their exact status, there was at least the carry-over value of domestic jobs in the marriage marketplace. As Jackie, who was in a nursery placement, stated, '. . . at least this will come in handy when I get married and have children'.

Young women training in manufacturing and given factory placements neither expected nor desired promotional opportunities and creative work. Previous research has shown that instrumental orientations towards work and the wage, humour and getting on with people on the job (sociability) are the main elements of a working-class female factory culture (Griffin, 1985; Pollert, 1981). These elements are clearly expressed by these two young women (the former's placement was in a warehouse, while the latter worked in a microfilm lab):

> **Cheryl:** You don't expect much workin' in a warehouse – it's pretty boring really. But I really enjoy the people that work there – a couple of my mates from the scheme work there and we have a good time together.

> **Mandy:** They're [the people at work] really nice over there . . . Yea, we have a laugh when the boss is out and all that, yea [laughs].

While this workplace camaraderie was sometimes restricted to older and often male shop floor workers (Cheryl mentioned that some of the male workers kidded them that warehouse work was a 'man's job'), there were examples where the culture appeared to embrace the majority of the workforce. On a tour of his hospital maintenance work placement, Baz warned me that some of the women are 'worse 'en us'. On my arrival I was quickly introduced into a shared workplace humour by two young women cleaning surgical instruments:

> **Woman 1:** What's pink and likes oral sex?
> **BH:** I don't know.
> **Woman 2:** [Sticks her tongue out and everyone laughs].

While there are obvious gender differences and patriarchal hierarchies in shop floor culture (see Willis, 1979; Pollert, 1981), it is also clear that there are some common class experiences and forms utilised.

On the whole, the work culture of glam transitions was based upon the façade of social mobility and the promise of interesting future work. Factory transitions and identities, on the other hand, were characterised by an informal work culture stressing the values of humour and sociability. The domestic/paraprofessional split represents an emerging form combining aspects of both these other two patterns, with the common denominator being its link to the household sphere.

The dominant work culture for a large section of working-class lads is their adaptation into a shop floor environment. This peculiarly male form of shop floor culture and its relation to male school counterculture has been extensively researched by Willis (1976; 1977). Also crucial in this transition is the way in which young male workers must negotiate their new-found status as trainees.

The vast majority of these lads had little trouble in adjusting to the dictates of wage labour. In other words, they already possessed knowledge about the world of work and had developed cultural forms which helped to prepare them for the transition on to the shop floor. The main difficulty they faced out on placement was how to deal with their status as a trainee. There is a profound sense of practical knowledge and experience on the shop floor and young male workers must quickly learn how to relate to both supervisors and fellow workers. As Willis (1979) has argued, competency for the unskilled and semi-skilled worker has always entailed a kind of 'cheek', a 'trial and error' method of getting through a task using physical strength and bravado as much as ingenuity and knowledge. This phenomenon, is particularly important for the young trainee:

> **Billy:** I reckon that it would be better for the trainee, yuh know, once's he's trained, to work by himself from then on. 'Cos at the place I work at, right, this bloke's OK but if, sometimes I got the chief mechanic lookin' over my shoulder yuh know. And I got a particular way of doin' things and he, he reckons it's wrong the way I do things, but they work out but he just doesn't see that.

With deskilling in the labour process (Braverman, 1974) and with the redefinition of skill itself through vocationalisation, this notion of competency becomes even more significant for young people in becoming accepted as bona fide workers.

The above comment also hints at a more general social relationship which has historically existed between young trainees and older workers in the manual trades. As Cohen (1983) argues, the traditional male apprenticeship at work involved the transmission of skills, techniques and a particular politics based around the shop floor and the labour process. In order to learn these techniques and conditions, the young worker was placed in an inferior and subordinate relationship to his elders and was expected to inherit these skills in a predetermined sequence. In addition to the transmission of skills, this process of what might be called the 'feminisation' of young male workers, was also designed to mark the passage into the masculine political culture of manual work (Cohen, 1986a). The use of often cruel practical jokes and the initiation of the young upstart as the factory 'skivvy' were key elements in this transition. Another element of this process was initiation into worker's societies or trade unions.

The impact of the YTS on these processes is really quite contradictory. While it functions to produce and extend an inferior status at work, in another way sensitivity to charges of exploitation on schemes may afford some sort of protection for some trainees. On the issue of unionisation, it is clear that the trainee status has had an adverse effect on the transmission of collective solutions to workplace problems. So while elements of this cultural apprenticeship persist, other aspects have become unhinged and disengaged.

With the decline of the manufacturing sector and the attempt within the new vocationalism to redefine the nature of skill itself, it is important to recognise cases whereby alternative apprenticeships are being constructed. As Cohen (1982, p. 44) has suggested, 'they [male youths] were beginning to recognise and revalue precisely the "feminine" characteristics of youth labour, but as a means of dissociating themselves from their working class place'. For example, some lads refused to be drawn into a work culture which, in extolling the virtues of being 'manly', often meant carrying out very dangerous work practices. Others saw the manual labour they performed on the YTS in exploitative rather than masculine terms, particularly when it was thought to be unskilled.

There were other work ideologies, embellished by the new

vocationalism, which offered alternative identities to the dominant cultural apprenticeship revolving around masculinity and manual labour. One perceived alternative was an upwardly mobile movement towards the white collar sector, management or self-employment. The ideology and attraction of this type of work culture is aptly expressed by Nigel:

> Nigel: That's the best way to start, start at the bottom and work your way up to the top of the ladder. The problem with young people today is they want to go right to the top of the ladder.
>
> BH: What attracts you to a management job?
>
> Nigel: The um – I would say the wealth of it. I feel the total independence of it really. If you're a sole trader you're proving something to yourself in the sense that you can do something for yourself and be happy with it.

Nigel saw the YTS as giving him practical experience 'from the bottom up', which would someday lead him to either a management position or possibly self-employment. In making a separation between management (men's work) and clerical jobs (women's work), the non-manual male is able to construct his own version of masculinity and work.

Another alternative route was typified by Ben. While he admitted he enjoyed working with his hands, he mentioned that it had to involve some 'brain work' and purpose as well. Ben's interest in certain types of jobs was motivated by a truly vocational orientation – that is, work is approached as a 'calling' and must involve some broader social purpose and utility. The following quote demonstrates this vocational emphasis:

> Ben: Since I first began thinkin' about having a job, I wanted to be a scientist all the time, when I was young. And then as I got towards middle school, I began to get interested in the outdoors. I wanted to make a career in the outdoors, you know a lumberjack sort 'a thing. And now – funnily YTS has provided me with an opportunity, which I shouldn't have really, doing union work and trainee rights – that sort of thing. That's where I'll probably be going . . . but I wish I wasn't [laughs].

Ben's comment demonstrates his predisposition towards doing socially relevant work. Nearly all the jobs mentioned here, particularly conservation and youth rights work, point towards a slightly different way of thinking about one's class destination. While many of the lads in the manual trades saw their movement on to the shop floor as an inevitable destination and others saw themselves moving up the company ladder, Ben viewed his future through the lens of a true vocational calling.

Work and future family commitments

Present conceptions of work are also crucially connected up with future projections of how a job may or may not be combined with family commitments. While these linkages take on quite distinct forms for young working-class women and men, there are also significant differences within the broader category of gender.

Orientations towards work for many young working-class women are closely tied to contradictory feelings about combining a job with their role as future mothers and wives. It has been suggested that young women's insertion into an informal culture of femininity prepares them as much, if not more, for the marriage market-place as it does for the labour market. For professional women workers this phenomenon is commonly referred to as the 'dual career', but for most working-class women it is more aptly described as the 'double burden' (Pollert, 1981). This latter description, however, has been complicated by young women's engagement in, and orientation towards, different types of jobs currently being redefined under the new vocational emphasis.

For example, Pollert (ibid.), in her study of women factory workers, has argued that young women respond to their lack of cultural preparation for the labour market by viewing work as a 'temporary stay', until they move into a domestic career through marriage. As Pollert's work demonstrates, the temporary stay often continues for working-class women, with marriage and children only bringing on a double burden of wage and domestic labour. In a similar fashion, domestic jobs may also be seen as useful experience and training for young women before they move into marriage and household commitments (perhaps combined with low paid part-time work).

Glam jobs, and paraprofessional orientations, with their implicit assumptions of social mobility, promotion and career emphasis, may have some affect on how young women see themselves moving in and out of the labour market. Julie, a representative of this perspective, expressed contradictory feelings about career and household choices. When asked, 'do you see yourself doing this same kind of job in the future?', she felt that she would have to work hard 'all me life'. Yet, in the same breath, Julie mentioned that she would probably stay home for five or six years to raise children and 'to have a steady home', before returning to work. Jan, who also saw her future in terms of self-employment, was also torn between work and family:

Jan: I'd probably say no, nothing could stop me from doing it, I'd have, my career would be first. But when it comes to it, I suppose marriage and everything, I suppose that would come first. I don't know. I can't answer that one.

The effect that marriage and childbearing might have on the future working lives of young working-class men is perceived quite differently than it is for their female counterparts. For instance, there is no comparable assumption that getting married and raising a family will compete or conflict with work. Indeed, men's jobs are built on the notion of separate work and family commitments and it is largely assumed that men can rely on female domestic and reproductive labour to deal with this latter life sphere.

The main effect training schemes are having on many young men's future family expectations are the fear of low wages and postponement of being able to provide for a wife and child. In other words, schemes were threatening the 'family wage':

Chris: Imagine gettin' married on a training scheme [laughter]. I'd be embarrassin' [changes his voice to impersonate a woman]. 'Are you goin' to work?' . . . Just say yuh got married on a scheme . . . I'd be embarrassin' yuh know . . . She reckons you got a full-time job, you pretend yuh got a full-time job . . . bring home your pay for the week, but yuh spent it all on booze [laughter from everyone].

This comment hints at a kind of 'hypermasculinity' – a form of self-deprecation at work, combined with a knowledge that male power still reigns supreme in the household. If a young lad wasn't 'man enough' to bring home a proper wage packet, he could always resort to another masculine activity to reaffirm his status and position of dominance. Many of these lads realised that schemes could be the beginning of a future of low paid jobs and it was in this context that the YTS was linked to a concern over obtaining a proper family wage.

Of course, the lack of a decent wage and the status it confers on a young working-class male could be turned on its head. In other words, a future of low pay and work on training schemes actually removed the pressure from some young men to consider their future as the primary wage earner. Garnie, for example, preferred the scheme to 'real work' because he had control over his labour, despite the fact that his girlfriend earned more money at her full-time job. Ben later took on interesting voluntary work rather than search for a boring manual labour job. Some young men used training schemes to go into areas other than manual labour and still others used this space in between school and work to develop alternative identities in relation to home, politics and leisure.

Generally, work and future family commitments for the majority of working-class males were viewed as separate spheres and they expected women to handle domestic and childrearing chores. Part of this belief was sustained by their current position of power within the family household. For young women, there appears to be a mixture of traditional and emerging views, which are at least partly influenced by their insertion into different forms of female labour constructed out of their interaction with the new vocationalism. The role of the domestic sphere is looked at in more detail in the following chapter, specifically through the impact domestic labour has on youthful identities in work and elsewhere.

6

At Home and Out on the Street: Domestic Labour and Public Space

In this chapter I examine two basic sites involved in the production of youth identities – the home and the street – and show how they are affected by and, in turn, influence the experiences of the young working class as they make the transition to adulthood through training schemes. The YTS, because it signals the initial move into waged work and involves the acquisition of a 'substitute' wage, has an important bearing on both family and public life. Similarly, what happens to young people at home and on the street are also crucial elements of an overall politics of youth.

The common-sense terms of 'home' and 'the street' have been supplemented by the concepts of 'domestic labour' and 'public space'. The reason is simply to note that the former terms are, for the most part, ideological concepts. Home, for example, conjures up the image of somewhere cosy – a place where one rests, recuperates and recreates, while the term 'the street' implies a sphere which is accessible to and used by everyone. Because of these images, neither of these spheres has, to any significant degree, been related very well to the youth training debate, nor have they formed part of an overall political strategy emanating from the labour movement.

In contrast, I prefer to emphasise the political dimensions these sites have for young people by utilising the concepts of domestic labour and public space. I use domestic labour not as a substitute for all aspects of home life, but to refer to a central component of the domestic sphere which reflects a strict division of labour within the working-class household. The relationship between experiences of domestic labour and young people's wider social identities are crucial for understanding how differential transitions into work and adulthood are constructed. By 'a' public space I am specifically referring to how a particular part of the urban

123

environment (the street) is structured, defined and inhabited differentially by groups in society, depending on the combined effect of age, class, gender and racial characteristics. The impact these spheres have on young people's transitions into adult and working life necessitates that they become part of the political debate on youth, employment and training.

Domestic labour, YTS and household relations

Domestic labour, while including housework, is not synonymous with it. It also encompasses childcare responsibilities, the financial and organisational management of the household and all the emotional and sexual nurturing required by children and partners. As Fox (1980, p. 9) argues, 'domestic labour is basic to society: it involves the reproduction of daily life itself'. Contemporary research shows that just housework alone takes the average 'British family' nearly four hours of labour per day.[1] The vast majority of this work is undertaken by women.

In our society domestic labour is not only viewed as women's work, it is sometimes exclusively seen as a female responsibility. Even when women are employed in the labour force (either full or part time), a disproportionate amount of household labour falls to them. Because domestic labour is not viewed as wage labour and hence does not constitute paid work, it is often seen as unimportant or goes unrecognised. Studies on the lifecycle and domestic work show that between the ages of 15 and 40 housework for women increases from 50 to 300 minutes a day as wage labour decreases (but by no means disappears) from 550 to 300 minutes a day (Gershuny *et al*, 1986). Domestic labour then is one of the main activities undertaken in the home, and the bulk of this work is usually performed by women.

One of the difficulties in evaluating the domestic tasks undertaken in the typical British family is that there is no such entity. Of the young people I interviewed, only a minority were living in the archetypal nuclear family (father working full-time, mother at home). A significant number of trainees lived with only one parent.[2] Only three trainees did not live at home and two of these were staying with relatives. One young women, Tracy, had moved into her own flat part way through her scheme. This wide variety of household arrangements calls into question the whole concept of the nuclear family and it also demonstrates the importance of the YTS allowance for some families. Young people, particularly those with a single parent, often mentioned that they felt compelled to stay on the scheme because their contribution was a necessary component of the family income.

Despite differences in family structure, there existed a common pattern of payment and negotiation of the weekly household contribution from the YTS allowance. The key individual for nearly all trainees in working out the balance of payments (including the amount of contribution plus the domestic work required) was the mother. The amount of 'keep' given was comparable for both females and males (the average being £5 per week), although this amount varied substantially. This seemingly natural exchange, however, masks the unequal distribution of power within the family unit and does not take into account differential amounts of domestic work required on top of the monetary contribution. The employment situation and role of siblings was also crucial and had a distinct bearing on this arrangement.

In order to come to terms adequately with both gender and differential class experiences of domestic labour while on the YTS, it is important to consider such factors as the different power positions young women and men occupy in the home, experiences of housework while at school and on the dole, family structure and the influence different work orientations have on the domestic sphere.

Two important social contexts for evaluating the impact the YTS has on changing domestic commitments are young people's experiences of domestic work while at school and on the dole. Research undertaken on the youth population (aged 16–24) in the West Midlands found that while a higher percentage of unemployed males engage in household tasks than their employed counterparts, they did far less than employed women and drastically less than unemployed women (Willis, 1985). Griffin's (1985, p. 37) work on female school students also showed that overall only 8 per cent of fathers and 0 per cent of brothers did any domestic work, compared with 45 per cent of young women, 75 per cent of mothers and 19 per cent of sisters. The group most likely to have domestic responsibilities were working-class girls (51 per cent of white working-class girls and 52 per cent of black working-class girls).

These patterns were largely reproduced in my interviews with some of the manual labour lads in connection with their experiences of domestic labour while unemployed:

> **Robert:** If somebody's home on the dole they'll help out. Like I used to be home on the dole but I never helped out, oh no, not me – I did from time to time – that is when I got up.
>
> **BH:** What kind of things would you do?
>
> **Robert:** The hooverin'.
>
> **BH:** So you'd do that – would you make dinner?
>
> **Robert:** I could make dinner but I never intend to.

While some of these lads mentioned that they did bits of housework, there was nothing really substantial. Chris, who was unemployed for six months, did no domestic labour and Andy expected his mother to look after both him and the household chores when he was on the dole.

The main impact the movement into work and the YTS had for these lads was to provide a mechanism for them to escape what little domestic duties they were required to do while in school or on the dole. Masculine orientations towards work and the wage (or allowance) provided the rationale for expecting a quantity of domestic labour from mothers:

> **BH:** Since you've been on the training scheme, have you had to do anything different at home than when you're not working? Like do –
>
> **Billy:** I haven't 'ad to do housework.
>
> **BH:** You didn't have to when you were unemployed?
>
> **Billy:** I didn't have to, but I helped – now we got an excuse, I go to work, why should I go to work and come back and do anything?
>
> **Mick:** Yea, she [his mother] didn't see yuh workin' before, she didn't give a hell about yuh – make yer own dinner. Now that you're goin' to work, it's on the table.

These comments are striking not simply because they suggest that the movement into work should absolve one from undertaking domestic labour, but more importantly because it implicitly signals a recognition that male wage labour (even on the YTS) 'deserves' and 'requires' additional household labour in order for it to be reproduced. The peculiarly masculine monetary contribution to the household symbolises not only a portion of the wage labour performed, it is also used to buy an expected quantity of domestic labour and hence time for additional leisure activities.

There were some exceptions to this dominant pattern. Ben, who was from a one-parent family, mentioned that because of this 'everyone has always had to pull together a bit'. His experience of domestic work while on the dole and on the YTS was significantly different from many of the lads:

Ben: When I was unemployed, yuh know, I used to do the housework everyday – 'cos I had nothin' else to do. Now I'm on YTS I don't help as much, if, on a Saturday or if I have a day off, I'll try and do the housework . . . Generally the hooverin' and the washing and that sort of thing. Now she still expects me to do something, which she should do, but it's less, it tends to be less now.

Due to the fact that he was a vegetarian, Ben also did a lot of his own cooking. Other types of family arrangements also resulted in a slightly different male pattern. Whilst Garnie lived with his aunt, he insisted upon a separate living arrangement (for reasons of independence) and he did all his own shopping, cooking, cleaning and washing. Angus, whose mother and father both worked, said he would cook his own tea 'if nobody's there'. However, the main chores he was expected to perform around the house were typical 'men's jobs' (cutting grass, trimming hedges, etc.).

Young women's movement into work through schemes does not so readily allow them to negotiate a similar deal whereby a payment of a portion of the allowance could be used to release them from domestic responsibilities. While they paid in approximately the same amount of money to the family household, many were expected to continue to contribute to the domestic side. Most found that their new work status only marginally lessened what was expected of them around the house:

BH: Like what sort of jobs do you have to do?

Kamni: Ah housework, the odd washing up and ah [laughs], yuh know, cooking, cleaning, all that. But yuh know, since I've gone to work I don't do half as much as I used to.

This situation was partly dependent upon the number and gender of one's siblings, young women's indentification with mothers and whether father and/or brothers were involved in domestic labour.

Regarding siblings, if a female YTS trainee had an older sister who was working, she might conceivably be burdened with extra chores, while if she had a younger sister, she in turn might be able to offload some of her household duties upon joining a scheme. This was definitely not the case with brothers:

Jackie: I do more than my sister does – she just started a job as a hairdresser.
BH: Do you have anybody else? [to Jill]
Jill: Yea, my brother.
BH: And what does he do?
Jill: Nothing [laughs].

BH: What about your younger brother, does he help out?
Jan: No [laughs], not at all. He's never in. He's at the age where he wants to be out all the time. So, he's never there, he's just there for meals.

The double irony is that while some young women complain about doing more housework than their sisters, brothers actually create the need for extra domestic labour from household members. Additionally, only two trainees stated that their father contributed to the household duties. Father's participation in domestic labour often tends to occur around infrequent 'special occasions', rather than being directed towards the mundane but absolutely necessary daily domestic chores.

Mothers generally performed the bulk of domestic labour undertaken in the household. This was even the case when they were also working full time in the labour market. Young women may have been expected to contribute disproportionately to the housework, but many did so out of the recognition that their mothers were often left alone to do most of the work:

Shanaz: Well, if you were unemployed and just sitting around all day while your mother did the housework, you'd feel sorry for her doing everything.

Identification with mothers by some young women may reflect their own sense of unfairness concerning the different levels of domestic responsibilities males and females have in the working-class household. This identification sometimes took the form of an emotional closeness between mother and daughter which extended far beyond simply helping with the housework:[3]

BH: Do you do quite a lot of housework at home as well?

Alice: I help my mom yes, there's only me and me mum. My parents got divorced so I help me mom a lot now . . . It's like when me mum was ill and she had to go to the hospital all over Christmas, so I wanted to take a few days off around Christmas . . . So, I went to the scheme and said I wasn't comin' into work 'cos me mum was ill. And then I went back to the scheme and they called me in to the office and they said 'Them three days yuh had off, yer takin' em as yer holidays'. I couldn't have left her, I mean she was really ill. Yer not gonna walk out the door and just leave yer mum.

This remark also demonstrates that domestic labour involves far more than just housework – under certain circumstances it can become a full-time job. The main point is that not only were young women expected to engage in a certain amount of domestic labour, but that some felt an additional sense of responsibility for helping out mothers in a sphere plagued by a highly unequal division of labour.

The pull of this domestic apprenticeship, however, did not mean that all young working-class women automatically followed their mothers' footsteps 'to the kitchen sink' (Cohen, 1984). There were in fact a number of different orientations shown towards the domestic sphere which closely mirrored young women's approaches towards work and a career. For example, the group most heavily involved in household tasks were those young women possessing factory and domestic work orientations:

BH: Do you have to do a lot?

Mandy: Yes [laughs], just hoover and make sure the place is tidy and clean – sometimes cook and ah, go shopping Saturday . . . but usually we go on Friday so I don't have to buy much.

Jackie: When I have to go out my mum says leave it [the housework] and she'll do it. When I'm supposed to go out I'll do it anyway.

Mandy went on to mention that she in fact did far less housework now than what was expected of her prior to being on the YTS. In her case domestic tasks were rearranged at the weekend in order to accommodate her working week.

While this group of young women was still closely tied to a 'double burden', those possessing careerist orientations exhibited quite different commitments to the domestic sphere. Julie said she did far less than was expected of her when at school because, in her own words, 'I'm too tired now and get out of it.' Jan, who had visions of being her 'own boss', displayed a much lower level of activity around the home than did many of the other young women involved in factory work:

BH: Do you help out a lot at home in terms of –

Jan: No, not really [laughs]. Ah, when I do, I do my fair share but – I suppose I'm selfish in a way but – you know, I don't give any keep. I don't do much at home, I don't cook or anything. I can't cook. I do the odd washing up and vaccuuming or whatever.

Finally, Liz revealed that she did very little at home because she had come to an arrangement with her parents whereby they were literally 'partitioned off'. In other words, she was responsible for getting her own meals and virtually lived in her own room when she was at home. Liz's particular leisure lifestyle, however, meant that she spent very little time in the domestic household.

The main finding concerning the relationship between the YTS and the family household is the unequal division of labour according to gender. The dominant effect schemes had was to further release young men from any engagement in the domestic sphere, although there were some exceptions to this general pattern. The majority of young women were in no such position to use the movement into work to release them from household duties. Nevertheless, there were important differences within subgroups of young working-class women which were linked to work orientations and leisure lifestyles. Clearly, the link between work, the YTS and household relations needs and deserves to be placed on the political agenda.

Out on the street: experiences and constructions of a public space

Experiences and constructions of public space are also political issues which closely relate to the formation of different youth identities. By 'a' public space, I am referring to a particular social site of working-class youth identity formation – the street.

Images of the street, whether it be Coronation Street, the local neighbourhood or public space in city centres, all attempt to construct the illusion that everyone has equal access and control of the outside environment. Many social groups, however, are either excluded from, or strictly controlled in their use of, public space. Youth is one such group which has only partial control and conditional access to this particular public sphere.

Yet youth is already a highly differentiated social group. For example, young women's access to the street is highly conditioned by expectations of male companionship and notions about 'nice girls don't walk alone'. Genuine fears of harassment, rape, violence and trouble have always prevented women's open access to this public arena. These fears are not so easily separable from other social constructions of street activity such as 'mugging' (Hall *et al.*, 1978). The creation of moral panics in the public sphere has clear ageist, racial and class dimensions. The impact that these and other factors, such as unemployment and the lack of money on training schemes, have on young people's experiences and constructions of public space requires a political analysis.

Of course, differential access and use of public space by young working-class men and women has a long history (Robins and Cohen, 1978; Mungham, 1982). Part of the explanation lies in women's confinement to the domestic sphere and men's domination of the public arena (including work, politics and the street).

Young women's movement into work through training schemes does little to open up their access to the public realm. The limiting nature of the substitute wage, the pull of the domestic sphere and male domination of the street all combine to confine many women to the home (except, of course, when they are accompanied by men in the public domain). Young men, on the other hand, utilise their movement into work (via the YTS) and their power position within the family household to release themselves from domestic work, thereby gaining increased access to the public sphere. For instance, compare the following two quotations:

> **BH:**　　Do you go to the city centre much?
> **Ann:**　　Me, I'm like a hermit at home.

> **BH:**　　Do you do stuff [domestic labour] at home now?
> **Robert:**　No, I never am at home.
> **BH:**　　What about you Baz?
> **Robert:**　He's never at home either –
> **Baz:**　　I don't either.
> **Robert:**　. . . prancin' around town.

This does not mean that all young women are totally home-bound and all young males are out on the street. Young women do have access to the street and city centre but usually only under certain conditions and constraints. Their access to the city centre during the daytime was limited largely to the weekend (because they were working full-time on the YTS). The main uses mentioned by young women included window shopping/shopping, domestic chores and meeting friends. Use of the city centre in the evening was much more highly constrained. For it is here that the phenomenon of mugging and trouble elides with the very real threat of harassment, rape and violence. Even though none of the women I interviewed admitted to being attacked, many had heard about such incidents:

> **Mandy:**　I've never been mugged – but a friend of mine has. Um, yuh know, mind you he was silly – he was, he started talking to the person. That's a bit stupid.
> **BH:**　　So would you go down to the city centre on your own in the evening?

Mandy: Um, let me see – well it depends on what part of the city centre you're going to. Um, I might do but – you can't trust people really. I don't usually go by myself.

One young women mentioned 'yuh hear quite a few stories in the paper' and another said she found the city centre unsafe because 'it's really the coloureds'. This is not to say that young women's fears for their safety are unjustified, but simply to make the point that the mugging phenomenon is a social construction with clear media, not to mention racist, dimensions (Hall *et al.*, 1978).

If fear of harassment and violence in the city centre was partly relayed through social constructions in the media, it was also reinforced by boyfriends, fathers and even through young women's own 'self-policing':

(discussions about going to the city centre at night)

Jackie: I'd only go if my boyfriend's with me. I wouldn't go on my own.

BH: Do you think it's unsafe?

Jackie: Yea, he wouldn't let me go on my own. He'd go mad at me if I did – 'cos it's unsafe in the daytime.

Julie: Depends on what part you go to – I mean it's not as if you're gonna get shot or anything, but there's a red light area. It doesn't matter, it's further down from the town. It's fine really, there's nothin' wrong with the town . . .

BH: Would you go on your own?

Julie: But I wouldn't go on me own. A girl, it's not, it's funny if a girl goes on her own. It's not a thing to do really – not at night.

Neither of these remarks expose the root cause of why women in particular feel unsafe out on the street at night. Instead, many young women rely on the protective attitudes of boyfriends and forms of self-policing based on male opinions that 'nice girls' don't go out at night alone.

There was one interesting exception to this general pattern which had its basis in a particular subcultural style. Liz, who described her style as 'weirdo' (a post-punk fashion), didn't see the city centre as a problem because of the way young people massed together when they attended 'alternative' nights at a local club in town:

> Liz: When we come out of a club it's, you know, between two and half-past two in the morning, but there's always crowds of people. Like we come out, everybody's going in the same direction so you can guarantee there's going to be someone you know somewhere. I think for a lot of people perhaps it is dangerous, but in my case it isn't. Because well, you know, everybody walks in a tribe, you get this massive, great group of people walking up where the bus stops. And you can guarantee that's it's going to be packed until about three o'clock. I don't think it is, I mean perhaps when you get off the bus at the other end it is, but the city centre isn't I don't think.

For Liz, the group structure and solidarity created through a common subcultural style provides a shield of protection and security for her and other female friends using the city centre late at night. She was, however, aware of the fact that the centre was dangerous for other young women and that even she was vulnerable outside the group. The majority of young women are constrained from utilising this public space outside the confines of femininity (i.e. shopping/domestic labour, accompanied by boyfriends, etc.) and hence the capacity for developing alternative public identities in this sphere is highly limited.

Public identities for a large majority of working-class males, while constrained in other ways, are maintained if not heightened while on the YTS. Possessing some control over one's local environment can, and does, in fact compensate for one's inferior position at work (Robins and Cohen, 1978; Willis, 1984). While the YTS effectively got them off the street during the daytime, they maintained their monopoly of this sphere in the evenings and at the weekend. The lads' payment into the family was used to release them from domestic work and the confines of the working-class household. Once released, though, it was obvious that in the context of the substitute wage there was an acute shortage of things to do out on the street. Corrigan (1976) has written about the peculiarly working-class masculine leisure practice of simply 'doing nothing', and related research undertaken in the West Midlands demonstrates that 'hanging out' increases dramatically for unemployed males (Willis, 1985). Due to a lack of disposable income on the YTS, this was also a major activity engaged in by male trainees:

Shabaz: Most of the nights we do stay just around our area, just walk around you know and, ah, on Saturday sometimes at night we go up town.

BH: What is there to do in your neighbourhood?
Leonard: Nothin' really – just hang out.

The irony is that while many of the lads hang out in their neighbourhood or city centre because of a lack of money, it is often the way they deal with their boredom which works to curtail young women's equal access to this sphere. Young men's domination of the street and the things they get up to can mean trouble and harrassment for young women who do venture out.

Not all working-class males use this public sphere to compensate for their lack of status at work or inability to afford alternative leisure pursuits. Ben, for example, chose to become more home-bound during his stint on the YTS. He preferred to deal with the limiting nature of the substitute wage not by taking to the street to assert his identity, but by engaging in a number of solitary leisure pursuits undertaken in the family home. Some of the more upwardly mobile male trainees also chose to save up and spend their allowance on more 'rational' leisure pursuits, and Nigel in particular was openly disdainful of young people hanging around the street.

To say that the majority of young lads on the YTS continue the practice of monopolising public space does not imply that their domination is either wholly deliberate or in any way complete. Young men's use of the street exists in a definite subordinate relationship to the police and to the private ownership of much of the inner city. For example, under the blinding illusion that city centres are indeed a public arena lies the reality that much of this area is privately owned and policed accordingly. This subordination is most clearly revealed when young men's experiences of public space are related to such factors as unemployment, subcultural style (both class-based) and institutional racism.

Unemployment is an important social context in structuring many of these young men's experiences of the policing of inner cities and city centres. Many of them had been temporarily unemployed upon leaving school and had felt unfairly treated by both the police and shopkeepers:

> **Billy:** It's a waste of time really 'cos all yuh can do on the dole is go to town and doss. Yuh can't spend no money at all . . . Me and my mates went around town once, there was about four of us goin' around reading somethin', yuh know from motorbikes or somethin' like that and er – we got ever so filthy looks from the people. After, the police followed us all over town, they must sense it.

So while many of the white lads rehearsed private versions of the 'moral panic' argument about the city centre, blaming 'Skinheads' or gangs of black youths as the source of the problem, they themselves experienced being stereotyped as troublemakers when on the dole.

Youth subcultural styles also influenced relations with the authorities:

> (in a discussion about the police)
>
> **Billy:** They mostly bother the coloureds – skinheads and punks and disgraceful people like that. I reckon that the young yobos called, yuh know, like he looks, looks a bit like a yobo right? [points to Mick, a rocker] . . . Anyway, yuh see this yobo walkin' up town all innocent, right? The policeman, he thinks 'Ah, he's a yobo, I'll nick 'im'.
> **Chris:** Nick 'im for what?
> **Billy:** I don't know, they did it to me . . . They just cuff you like that, right, bung you up against the wall and say yer under arrest . . . Suspicion of a – loiterin' with intent to . . .
> **Mick:** Keep yuh in a detention centre for so many hours.

Billy: Yer stuck in a detention cell, right, yer mum's worried sick and when she comes to pick you up, smack, smack around the 'ead.

Chris: The coppers are laughin' at yuh.

Billy: You've done nothin', yer just walkin' up town.

While being on the dole was in itself sufficient grounds for a confrontation, having a visible subcultural style or looking like a 'yobo' was a sure recipe for being hassled and possibly searched and detained. Many of the lads did have experiential knowledge about being confronted by the authorities, and incidents involving the police appeared to occur on a fairly regular basis in the city centre.

The experience of white youth, however, paled in significance in comparison to the policing of black youth in the inner city areas (Gilroy, 1981–2; Cashmore and Troyna, 1982). Due to the fact that the mugging discourse has a strong racist current, young black males often find themselves under constant surveillance in urban areas. In fact, one might say that this public sphere is indeed one of the main arenas of struggle over black youthful identities. Being black and just trying to walk down the street with a group of mates was cause for suspicion. The reality of institutional racism in this sphere might partly explain the compromising position adopted below by Garnie towards the police, although what is even more significant is his internalisation of a white racist discourse. In his own words, he preferred to 'walk alone' in order to stay out of trouble:

Garnie: There's plenty of times I walk past 'em and I say hello. You have manners to them and you get far. There's some guys that believe they can rule the law and they can't rule the law 'cos the law is higher than you, man. That's when you give the police any cheek, right, I don't blame 'em for takin' you inside and kickin' your ribs and that's it. You know, I don't blame 'em. You see 'em on the street and you say hello. Yuh shouldn't walk in gangs as if you're a Zulu tribe or somethin' like that, when they march downtown. Yuh know what I mean, you should walk by yourself man, be reasonable.

While perhaps some of this is understandable in terms of his own 'survivalist' philosophy (his comments might hint at a kind of pragmatism, an understanding of the sheer power of institutional racism), it is surely the case that Garnie has forfeited his right to use the street in a certain manner by internalising racist constructions of the public arena. Many black (and white) youths, however, prefer to fight back and resist attempts to control their use of public space, and there is evidence that there is a growing distrust of the men who police the inner city.

I have argued that the movement into work via the YTS does little to change class, race and gender meanings and experiences of this public space. Young women, for example, are still highly constrained from using the street to construct alternative identities outside work and the home. While the lads continue to dominate this sphere, the effect of the substitute wage limits their use and anyway they too exist in a subordinate relationship to the policing of this public space. Furthermore, I want to suggest that working-class male public activities are rarely understood in terms of their inner cultural meanings or within a social and political framework. There is at present no popular coherent alternative to the hooligan ideology perpetuated by the conservative theorists' attack on the 'permissive society'. In a short addendum, I briefly outline the basic elements of an alternative analysis in relation to some of the symbolic meanings and social consequences of an actual incident – the lads' involvement in a street fight.

Addendum: 'gettin' battered': the meaning of a street fight

In any type of ethnography which claims to capture something of the everyday lives of a group of people, there is probably at least one event which interrupts and restructures aspects of the research in a fundamental way. Here I want to pursue the topic of male working-class use of public space by focusing on three lads' involvement in a fight in the city centre.[4] I want to utilise this episode to theorise around the symbolic meanings attached to white male's constructions of public space in the context of masculinity/territoriality, racism and subcultural identities and divisions.

On the day of the altercation, or the 'panic' as it came to be known, I visited the city centre with three white lads (Billy, Chris and Mick) on a leisure facilities field trip approved by the scheme. On route, the discussion ranged from places to visit to subcultural styles. It was clear from previous conversations that masculinity, territoriality and racial differences were important components of subcultural affiliation. My fieldnotes that day speculated on the importance of subcultures and how far identities in this sphere might work to transform social differentiation into real differences and divisions amongst male working-class youth. Minutes after leaving the lads, they were confronted by a group of 8–10 black youths described as 'Rude boys' and Chris was beaten up twice. Mick had been punched in the face for attempting to stop the fight and Billy, who had quickly weighed up the odds, ran off immediately.

This single event prompted a reinterpretation of my views on white working-class male youth's use of public space. It was only after the altercation that I began to notice the number of past references to fighting and aggressive behaviour amongst the lads. Mock fighting and physical posturing were an everyday part of life both on the scheme and in other spheres. There existed in fact a whole vocabulary of words describing fighting and getting beaten up ('battered'):

Mick: There's a load of words for gettin' beaten up – there's gettin' panned, that's another word . . .
Chris: Gettin' decked.
Mick: Battered.
Chris: Gettin' splattered . . .
Mick: And then you're getting chased, there's lots of words for that . . . gettin' legged.
Billy: We got legged [laughter from everyone].

Aggressive and often violent language – 'beat 'em up', 'castrate 'em', 'kick 'is head in' – was peppered through everyday conversations and surfaced frequently, for many lads, on the scheme and on the street.

By making this point, I do not wish to slip into the moral panic paradigm. The underlying problem with what might be called the 'hooligan ideology', perpetuated by the Right and the popular press, is that it begins and finishes its analysis with the most obvious and external features of human behaviour. It has literally nothing to say about the historical origins (Pearson, 1983), cultural meanings and 'non-serious' elements of these types of human action. Furthermore, such right-wing constructions fail to put any kind of so-called 'deviant' behaviour into a social, cultural or political context. What is so odd about the hooligan ideology is that two of its main elements – the affirmation of working-class masculine identities and its peculiarly white ethnic character – are rarely mentioned or addressed. The moral majority solution of 'bringing back the birch' is itself steeped in a parallel masculine discourse reminiscent of the upper-class school headmaster.

Alternatively, one can begin to theorise seriously about male public activities in a social, political and cultural context, taking into account the inner meanings, symbolic representations and actual outcomes of these actions. In this case, the main social context of the fight, I would argue, is its linkage to a wider culture of working-class masculinity. It is also centrally connected to white working-class youth's adoption of white ethnic identities and their preoccupation with locality and territoriality.

A fundamental element of male working-class culture is the importance of strength and physical prowess. One of the main avenues in which this culture was forged and expressed was through manual labour and industrial production. Some researchers have argued that blockages of this traditional outlet (with unemployment and possibly work substitution schemes) could result in heightened forms of masculinity in other social sites (such as the home and street, Willis, 1984). Whatever the case, it is clear that fighting in public is yet another example of the affirmation of masculine identities. It contains the obvious elements of physicality and engagement with the real world (even if that world is the receiving end of a hard fist). For these lads, it wasn't so much winning a fight as it was just being part of it. For Chris, getting beaten up or 'battered' was a source of pride – he had survived and lived to tell the tale.

There were other more specific versions of masculinity tied up in the fight which were connected to male subcultural identities. Billy insisted that they went after Chris because he was a 'Mod' and 'Mods and Rudies don't get on'. He had run off not just because they were outnumbered but because it wasn't 'his fight'. Mick had stepped in, not out of any loyalty to Chris, but simply to maintain his image as a Rocker. He argued that Rockers don't normally have to fight to prove their toughness, but this was an exceptional case. Subcultural identities, then, are closely bound up with more specific forms of masculinity.

A final element connecting subcultures with working-class masculinity and territoriality is its linkages with forms of white ethnicity. The rude boys were black and the fight only served to reinforce racist ideas already held by the white lads. In a conversation after the fight, Chris mentioned that tension and conflict existed between Mods and Rudies because 'half the rude boys are black'. The altercation merely re-emphasised and congealed the white lad's racist preconceptions of black youth. The 'gang' was described as 'dirty fighters' and 'greasy opponents' and Mick's comment about 'this one git come out of the pack and nabbed me one' constructs the group as animal-like and inhuman. Chris pledged that he would soon return to the city centre with a group of his local mates for revenge. The overall outcome was to reconfirm white working-class ethnicity, territoriality and masculinity in the public arena.

So far, I have laid most of the emphasis on the more negative and serious side of this episode. The fight was a serious matter and there were clear negative outcomes in terms of reaffirming masculine and ethnic identities. Despite this, there was also a 'non-serious', almost play-like element to the altercation. The event was recounted over and over again, embellished by ever increasing bizarre details. In this sense it was just something that happened, an interesting event in an otherwise boring life.

The contradictory and complex nature of even a single event such as this demonstrates the sheer shallowness of the hooligan ideology. It is important to build alternative theoretical explanations of male public behaviour which situates such actions in a social context and explores both its non-serious as well as real negative social outcomes. So-called 'deviant' male behaviours must be located within the wider masculinist and racist cultures they spring from. Such explanations must also be untangled from their anti-working-class bias which masks the real issues and constraints blocking young people's full participation in and access to the public realm.

7

Non-work Activity and the Substitute Wage: The Limits of Leisure

Leisure is a notoriously elusive concept. As such, this chapter is concerned with exploring the actual and conceptual limits of the term for understanding more fully working-class youth identities in the context of the new vocationalism. In place of leisure I prefer to use a range of terms such as lifestyle, identity, consumption and subcultures to explore the differential experiences, practices and meanings adopted by trainees in the non-work sphere.

Conventional notions of leisure as 'freedom from constraint' and 'free' choice mask how non-work activities are linked to both the domestic sphere and the wage-labour relationship. For example, a dominant assumption has been to define leisure as the opposite of work. In this scenario work is viewed as unmitigated toil while leisure is understood as freedom from the dictates of social regulation. This perspective contributes to the view that leisure is somehow separate from the political and social relations which characterise and structure everyday life (for a critique see Hollands, 1988). Similarly, by contrasting 'real work' (i.e. wage labour) with 'free time', the whole relationship between domestic labour and leisure is viewed unproblematically.[1]

The false notion of leisure as an autonomous sphere has important implications when applied to the youth studies field. This perspective informed and indeed has been aided by post-war studies of the 'affluent teenager' (Abrams, 1959) and the supposed demise of class forms of consumption (discussed and critiqued in Hall and Jefferson, 1976). In this framework, youth culture became cut off from the main social divisions and relations characterising contemporary society and was seen instead as a self-generating phenomenon. Leisure, as consumption, became the generator for theories of youth as a 'new class' in itself (i.e. the 'generation gap').

142

While this perspective persists, there has been a growing trend to develop more radical theories of the relationship between youth and leisure. One of the most influential attempts to redress the interrelationship between youth, leisure and class was the Centre for Contemporary Cultural Studies' (CCCS) collective work contained in *Resistance Through Rituals* (Hall and Jefferson, 1976). In addition to its critical survey of the field, this work attempted to define the relationship between youth culture, class and politics through its theory and case studies of post-war 'youth subcultures'. It should be acknowledged here that *Resistance* was heavily indebted to Phil Cohen's (1972) earlier study on subcultural conflict and changes in the post-war working-class community.[2]

In the CCCS perspective, youth subcultures were viewed as variations on a general class culture, related both to their 'parent culture' and to a dominant culture. These subcultures were seen to exhibit distinctive shapes and were focused around certain activities, values and artefacts (for example, dress, hairstyle, music, etc.) and styles (i.e. Mods, Rockers, Skinheads, Teds, etc.). The general theory was that subcultures represented specific generational solutions to young people's class problems. They won political space for the young and were crucial to their everyday identities. However, they were also seen as problematic in the sense that they were unable to solve the basic class-based sets of contradictions which provided the social context to young people's experiences.

The impact that the subcultural perspective has had on youth and leisure studies has been substantial. For instance, it decisively challenged previous classless theories of youth culture and it sought to dispel élitist myths about 'mass' consumption amongst the youth population. Furthermore, it gave youthful cultural forms a political dimension which was lacking in the affluent teenager model. Emphasis was placed on the class basis of subcultural solutions and upon the creative appropriation of commodities and lifestyles by working-class youth. Additionally, it superseded the more descriptive and empirical strands of leisure studies concerned with 'who does what activity?', by stressing the importance of meaning, form, style and culture for comprehending youth identities in the non-work sphere.

There are, however, a range of criticisms that can be levelled against the subcultural perspective advanced in *Resistance* and related work. In the context of what I propose in this chapter, there are three main problems. First, there is the limiting emphasis on the most visible and spectacular post-war youth subcultures. These, the authors themselves admit 'may be less significant than what most young people do most of the time' (Hall and Jefferson, 1976, p. 16). Second, the trajectory of such an approach deflected attention away from the economic, domestic and occupational aspects of youth subcultures originally formulated by Cohen (1972) to an almost exclusive concern with 'reading' the signification of various artefacts and symbolic styles (Hebdige, 1979). This led to an overreliance on theorising youth practices almost wholly within the realm of leisure and culture. And finally, the emphasis on spectacular male subcultures and the move away from the whole social context of youth experiences, particularly in the kinship and domestic area, left the perspective open to feminist critiques (McRobbie, 1980). Young working-class women were either banished to the margins of subcultural analysis or were located exclusively within a 'bedroom' leisure culture.

In this chapter, I attempt to move beyond some of the limiting features of the 'affluent teenager' and 'leisure as freedom from constraint' paradigms. And while building upon some of the advances made by the subcultural perspective, I hope to provide an analysis which avoids some of its inherent shortcomings. For example, the most central social context for understanding most young people's contemporary non-work activities and practices is the absolutely massive impact unemployment and the substitute wage on training schemes has had on working-class life.

A return to some of Cohen's (1972) original formations around the economic, domestic and occupational determinants of lifestyles also inform the perspective taken in the present study. For example, his theory about the fragmentation of the working-class youth response points far beyond a concern with spectacular subcultural styles. While subcultures remain important for a minority of working-class youth, there is now evidence of a far more diffuse pattern of consumption and lifestyle orientation. The impact that domestic, sexual and household relations have on restricting non-work identities for many young people (particularly women) is also taken into account here. Finally, also important are the ways in which new work and occupational identities, thrown up by the new vocationalism, are linked up to broader lifestyle and consumption patterns.

Rethinking leisure: household relations and the substitute wage

The need to rethink conventional definitions of leisure for working-class youth on training schemes stems from two main factors. First, the organisation of household relations, particularly with respect to domestic labour, provides an important social context for understanding how different non-work activities are both enabled and constrained. Second, the limitations the substitute wage, paid on the YTS, has on spending and consumption patterns is undeniable.

In the previous chapter, I discussed how the payment of 'keep' for a section of working-class males acted to release them from domestic commitments, while freeing time for what we conventionally recognise as leisure. Many young women, on the other hand, who contributed similarly to the family household, were often required to supplement their payment with an additional amount of domestic labour.

This link between household relations and non-work identities has two implications. First, the home as a site of leisure can be experienced very differently by groups of young men and women. While some young people may spend more of their non-work time at home, this does not necessarily mean that they have more free time in this sphere. The different amounts of domestic labour undertaken mean that there are large variations in the amount of non-work time available to young people. Second, the surplus payment of domestic labour required from some young women means that they have less time to spend outside the family household. This, combined with additional factors restricting young women's access to the public sphere, means that leisure as 'freedom from constraint' is a highly suspect concept.

The second factor, which necessitates a more rigorous rethinking of the concept of leisure for all young trainees, is the influence the substitute wage on the YTS has on non-work identities, activities and consumption patterns. The vast majority of young people I interviewed contributed between £5 and £10 per week towards the family household and then spent approximately another £5 on bus fares (while claiming back £3 from the scheme). This left them with anywhere between £10 and £18 per week to spend on themselves (the allowance was £25 at this time). The brutal reality of this situation is that it is virtually impossible to afford leisure in a commodified and commercialised society, where nearly all activities and objects cost money:

> **Margaret:** It's not a lot considering clothes prices are going up and yuh know yuh need a lot more now to get something really nice . . . I haven't saved nothin'. I wanted to save, ah, when I first started the trainin' scheme, but I couldn't afford it 'cos Christmas came up and birthdays come up and I just couldn't manage it, couldn't do it. I haven't saved anything so far.

> **BH:** What things can't you do because you only get £25 a week?
> **Mick:** Yuh can't buy clothes that yuh want 'cos . . .
> **Billy:** Yuh can't take yer bird out.
> **Mick:** Yuh haven't got one anyway.
> **Billy:** I do now.
> **Chris:** It's more or less the clothes really.
> **Mick:** You'd be broke as soon as yuh buy one thing a week.
> **Chris:** A pair a jeans is suicidal – a good pair of trousers, yuh know, a really good pair a trousers cost about £15 quid.
> **Mick:** Yuh can't go anywhere.

> **Jan:** I'm very interested in travelling. We used to travel a lot over the weekend in a caravan but, I mean, we don't do that anymore. But I can't afford to go anywhere now, you know it's, you can't afford to travel at all.

This range of comments demonstrates how the substitute wage can and does restrict young working-class people from fully engaging in consuming a range of commodities and activities. The ability to purchase appropriate clothes both for work and for pleasure, having money to go out and possessing the means to travel are all curtailed by the scheme wage. For those not sheltered by the family wage, leisure was even more of a remote possibility:

Garnie: Twenty-six pound a week, man, listen man, that can't even buy you a pound a sugar, much less chicken . . . Listen man, I go to Quicksave and it is one of cheapest places and I spend a good £15 on food. Listen man, by the time you look in your back pocket, you gotta pay your rent, you gotta fix yourself up, you gotta buy clothes, listen man, there's no money left . . . All the money they give us right, we give them back at the end of the week.

For some young people, items necessary for the reproduction of daily life itself had to take precedence over affording any non-work activities or luxury commodities.

The inability to participate fully in this sphere of human life has implications not only for previous theories of youth affluence and consumption, it also has a crucial impact on making a smooth transition into adulthood. The movement into work (via the YTS) is not the only element necessary to mark the acquisition of adult status. While many young people come to feel themselves to be adults at work, they were unable to buy into the adult world outside the job. While adulthood means different things for young men and women, there was a general feeling that the substitute wage somehow blocked the ability to achieve adult status in the non-work sphere:

Baz: Years ago, yuh know, yuh got a bit a money. Now yer gettin' older yuh want things, but yuh can't, yuh can't save on £25 a week.

Most young people begrudged the limits imposed upon them by the substitute wage throughout their stint on the YTS. A few, however, particularly those who viewed the scheme in careerist terms, began to accommodate to this situation:

BH: Are there things that you'd like to do that you find you just can't?

Julie: Well, go out and buy nice expensive clothes and blouses
and God knows what else, but it's just not, you know
what yer, ah, limit is and you go by that limit.

In these cases it was the philosophy rather than the practice which
is significant. In fact, Julie was very much into an upwardly mobile
consumerist lifestyle – she just accepted that she couldn't afford
it while on the YTS. The constant promise of 'jam tomorrow' is
an important element of the new vocationalism. The YTS is not
simply about reducing wage expectations in the work sphere, it
also involves compensations in the non-work sphere as well.

Spending patterns, consumption and identity

Despite their acute lack of disposable income, young people's
desire to engage in the consumer market-place remains intact
throughout the YTS. Interaction with the consumption sphere is
a crucial site in the development of differential youth identities
and in the construction of varied transitions into adult life (Cohen,
1983; Hall and Jefferson, 1976; Hebdige, 1979). These identities
include not only gender and racial influences but are also linked
quite closely to intra-class orientations towards the work sphere
and subcultural styles.

An important factor in differentiating youth orientations
towards consumption and consumer choice is how the substitute
wage is used in terms of spending patterns. Some young persons
attempted to save up a bit of money from their weekly allowance
while others preferred to 'blow it' on a good night out and scrimp
through the week until their next pay cheque arrived. The choice
of either of these options depended, at least in part, on how one
viewed the YTS wage or allowance.

One of the cruel and underhand arguments prompted by the
government, the MSC and even some scheme managers, is that
young people have not only priced themselves out of the market
but they are irresponsible with money anyway. When I asked
young people about their saving and spending patterns this was
clearly not the case for the vast majority. In fact, some were
actually trying to put away a bit of money out of the £10–18 per
week:

Jackie: I put £5 away every week. I put it in but I can't get it out [laughs]. My dad won't let me take any money out and I wouldn't be able to take it out without his permission or until I'm 18. So I can't cheat.

With help from parents (who were actually subsidising the YTS allowance), a number of young people were able to save a small amount each week. This saving pattern was particularly acute amongst those trainees who viewed themselves as upwardly mobile. In many cases they were saving up for a certain article of clothing, a trip or some commodity beyond their immediate financial reach. Most trainees, however, found it impossible to save money while on the scheme.

For those unable to save there were two options. One was to buy goods from a catalogue by hire purchase and pay off a small amount each week. Others saw the allowance as such a pittance that they preferred to spend their entire weekly wage on a single item or a good night out (neither of which was difficult). Liz mentioned that although she often couldn't really afford to go out, she went anyway by borrowing and scraping a few pounds here and there. For some of the lads, this spending pattern took on a particularly masculine gloss, such as going out drinking:

BH: What are you going to spend your £50 [two weeks' pay] on over the holidays?

Andy: I'm just gonna drink it.

However, when asked what they would do with a higher wage, many of these same lads actually mentioned saving up or spending the money on items which were clearly connected to how they saw their own specific future transition into adulthood:

BH: What would you do with that £60 a week [my suggestion of a youth wage], if that was made into a law?

Leonard: Save it up I guess, buy a car – a house maybe – a stereo.

BH: What types of things would you do if say it [the allowance] was £60 a week?

| **Mick:** | Save up whatever yuh want. |
| **Chris:** | Buy a car, get a motorbike or somethin' – a car. Or yuh could save up and buy yer own house when yer older, get a flat, get married. |

While some of these consumer items are accompaniments to conventional masculine images and identities, it is equally clear that these lads are also concerned about their future needs. Suggestions about 'savin' up', 'buyin' a house' and 'gettin' married', while hardly transformative, put into context remarks about irresponsibility. These notions are partly related to male working-class knowledge about the instability of the unskilled end of the capitalist labour market and their desire to benefit from the patriarchal household.

In the context of these spending patterns and the constraining effect of the substitute wage, what were the major items young people did consume and how were they related to wider youth identities? Clothing was the major item of consumption mentioned by the majority of young people I spoke to. Smart attire was necessary for 'going out' and it was also a crucial prerequisite for many trainees working in the administrative/clerical and retailing fields. Clothes for young women had a special significance. Many of them, particularly those with glam orientations, were expected to look presentable in the office or shop. Almost all young women, however, spoke about the importance of having something to wear to go out. A nice pair of jeans, a skirt or blouse often represented two weeks' wages. Despite this, clothing was considered to be worth saving up for and it was the main item of consumption mentioned by young women.

Some young women found it was much cheaper to design and make their own clothes. Jan, who worked in a sewing factory and dreamt about running her own clothing business, spent over 50 per cent of her scheme allowance on material:

> **Jan:** I buy all the material to make my own clothes . . . That's ah, out of my allowance, I put £15 towards materials to make clothes.

Liz, who was also on a clothing scheme, designed and made her own clothes as well. Because of her particular subcultural style and dress she often bought second-hand things and revamped them:

> **Liz:** I make clothes or I do my best to renovate clothes – go around jumble sales, the rag market, find things that you can do things with.

Clothing for Liz was much more than a simple representation of femininity or the 'office look'. Clothes symbolically represented her own style and subcultural affiliation. Personal style for Liz worked to structure the entire context of her engagement in non-work activities, including going out, and it also influenced her particular orientation towards work itself (I've referred to this orientation previously as representative of a 'youth culture enterpriser' type). For example, she viewed her working future in neither glam nor factory terms, but preferred rather to break down the distinction between work and non-work, labour and pleasure. Her ideal future was to commission her own alternative clothing designs on a part-time basis, thus leaving space and time for other non-work activities and going out (thereby generating new ideas for clothing designs).

Clothes also had a certain significance for young men. This was especially the case for going out 'on the town' and it was considered essential in the maintenance of social relations with young women. The substitute wage on the YTS did little to enhance some of the lad's social appearances:

(in a discussion about girlfriends and clothes)

> **Chris:** She's always better clothed yuh know and yuh look like a tramp. Yuh know what I mean?
> **Billy:** She's into fashion and you're like a tramp . . .
> **Chris:** Yuh gotta wear a suit if yuh go anywhere nice . . .
> **Billy:** And we can't afford suits!

Dress for working-class males in the non-work sphere was also tied in with subcultural affiliations, although this encompassed only a small minority of the lads. Subcultural styles appear to be far more diffuse and ill-defined than in the past (Hebdige, 1979), although there was a number of so called 'revivals' as well as continuities in fashion. A lack of money for some, like Mick who saw himself as a Rocker, was solved through the purchase of a second-hand leather jacket and a single pair of jeans which he wore faithfully every day. For others, like Chris who was into Mod fashion, buying smart clothes was a sheer impossibility on scheme wages. Billy described himself as 'straight' and stated that the advantage of this was 'yuh can wear what yuh want'. Regardless of their desires, it was clear that while some held on to a subcultural orientation, many could simply not afford to participate fully in a particular style.

Many of these same lads were also into a manual worker culture and style. Part of the process of being incorporated into the informal shop floor culture was to look like a proper worker. This often meant having a certain type of work-boot (which could also be worn outside work), quality overalls and a decent donkey jacket. Looking like a real worker was, for some, as important off the job as it was at work. Clothing also played a particularly important role in the male culture of business and the while collar sector. Nigel, who was in the office administration field, and Angus, who worked in retail, both strained their budgets to look smart at work and on the scheme.

Other commodities bought by young women included fashion accessories such as magazines and jewellery, records and tapes and video rentals. It would be a grave mistake to generalise about the importance of these items in relation to a general feminine culture (Carter, 1984). In fact, the consumption of these commodities is unintelligible outside the inner meanings and appropriations made by quite different subsections of the female youth population. In the absence of any comparable studies, I would argue that there were substantial differences in the choice of particular commodities amongst upwardly mobile and subcultural types and those young women who could be said to possess factory or domestic orientations. For example, while both Liz and Jennifer (a trainee in the manufacturing sphere) bought magazines, the former read *The Face* because it was related to her lifestyle, while the latter and her friends bought *Miz* (a more conventional young women's magazine). Real differences were also evident in the choice of non-work activities and how they are shaped and refashioned around lifestyle.

A similar division existed between the manual labour lads and the upwardly mobile working-class males in the sphere of consumption. The main consumer goods the lads spent their money on included gambling, cigarettes, records, drink, hobbies and in some cases the purchase of second-hand motorbikes. A proportion of these goods and activities involved 'blowing' a week's wages. Many of these items also reflected a concern with masculine identities and, for some, subcultural style. For example, the following conversation about motorbikes demonstrates how subcultural affiliation links into cultural consumption:

> **Billy:** I might be floggin' my Vespa [a motor-scooter].
> **Mick:** Ah, who'd buy that . . .
> **Billy:** I wouldn't be floggin' it to you anyway.
> **Mick:** How much yuh sellin' it for?
> **Billy:** I don't know – well, I wouldn't be sellin' it to a rocker. Can you imagine a rocker on a Vespa [laughs] – looks sick!

While a concern with motorbikes clearly ties in with the lads' general predisposition towards manual labour (i.e. working on machines, see Willis, 1978), within this general culture more specific orientations towards these commodities were motivated by one's subcultural identity.

The consumer and spending patterns for upwardly mobile males followed a quite different route. These young men were more concerned to save up a proportion of their allowance in order to purchase items and they were also much more accommodative about the limits the substitute wage imposed upon their spending power. Angus mentioned that he 'got by' on the YTS allowance and even managed to put away some money each week. Nigel was even more emphatic about 'people being greedy' and wanting 'too much, too soon'. His philosophy was closely tied in with the conservative creed about young people wanting too much and being unprepared to wait for a decent wage and all that implies. However, Nigel's own upwardly mobile orientation meant that he too was concerned about spending money on things which, significantly, were quite different from those mentioned by the lads:

> **BH:** What things do you like to spend your money on?
> **Nigel:** Obviously records and um – most electrical things, I

mean I have got my stereo. And I recently did up my bedroom, that cost me a bomb and um – most things guys like really. I mean you want your own stereo and you want to go to the pictures or whatever. Obviously I'm learning to drive, I'd like my own car, things like that.

So while Nigel also expresses another side to masculine forms of consumption ('most things guys like'), it is obvious that his priorities are closely related to more middle-class youth concerns in the consumer sphere. These different orientations amongst both young men and women in the sphere of consumption will be examined in more detail in the next section which looks at the relationship between non-work activities and lifestyle.

Lifestyles and non-work activities

Non-work activities undertaken in the family home take on a new significance for young people subsisting on the substitute wage. With only £10–18 spending money per week, many trainees find that they spend not only increased amounts of time at home, but that this sphere becomes a primary site for engaging in affordable non-work pursuits. This is not to say that the home becomes an undifferentiated site of leisure for all young people. I have already referred to the differential amounts of domestic labour performed by young women and young men's escape to the public sphere. Yet, not all young women became more homebound and swamped by extra domestic tasks, nor did all young men flee to the relative freedom of the streets.

All young people engaged in some form of non-work activity in the home. The main activities mentioned were watching television, listening to music (playing the radio or record player or listening to tapes), renting videos, drinking and spending time with boyfriends/girlfriends. The existence of the 'electronic home' as an important site of non-work activity has been commented upon in other studies of the youth population (Willis, 1985). Of these, television and music are the mainstays of home-based activity.

Television was mentioned by nearly all young people as a major source of home activity.[3] It was a readily accessible and affordable form of entertainment. Interviews revealed that popular night-time soaps such as *Eastenders* and *Brookside*, both involving young people in the stories, were favourites and there were critical evaluations made of some American-made programmes which have increasingly come to dominate much of English television. The other major point worth mentioning is the increased popularity of renting video machines between groups of friends and family, an activity which proved to be sufficiently cheaper than attending the cinema.

Listening to music was also a very popular pursuit undertaken in the home. The relatively high consumption of records and tapes, considering the limitations of the substitute wage, expresses the importance music has on young people's lives and identities (Frith, 1978). Musical tastes were clearly related to lifestyle orientations as well as reflecting particular gender, racial and subcultural affiliations.

A general pattern which emerged in relation to lifestyle and musical tastes was a congruence between non-commercial preferences and upwardly mobile orientations, and the more commercial and subcultural choices made by the majority of working-class youths. This was not an all or nothing proposition, nor should there be any implication that non-commercial choices are somehow more 'refined' than popular commercial music. Some of the lads held rigidly to the music prescribed by their subcultural affiliation and this often led to arguments over the definition of a good group or to the proper categorisation of a certain type of music:

(in a discussion about 'Mod' music)

Mick: They like the Jam.
Billy: And the Selects and Specials. Mods like two-tone.
Mick: They say they like all sorts of things . . .
Chris: No, we just like the Kinks, the Who . . .
Mick: They say they like the Who, but the Who is rock music . . . They only followed the Who 'cos the Who came out at the same time they did.

Baz confined his musical preference to a single group, the Thompson Twins, and Robert who briefly became a Teddy boy in the

1982 'revival' was, for a time, heavily into traditional rock and roll.

There was a similar pattern of restricting one's taste to a single group amongst some young working-class women. This was based not upon a subcultural affiliation but rather around a particularly feminine construction of the male pop idol. Jackie, for instance, was an ardent Adam Ant fan and she bought only his records and belonged to a fan club. It is crucial that this kind of construction is not 'read' through the debilitating theory of mass culture (with a feminine twist). For in many cases this male idolisation co-existed with a concern for the meanings and social context of a particular record or song:

> **Kamni:** I like the lead singer [from U2], he's smart he is – Bono.
>
> **BH:** What do you like about their songs?
>
> **Kamni:** I think the songs have got meaning . . . Yea, they sing about love and ah – yuh know, things like war and 'cos yuh know Ireland has the most wars – 'cos there's this, I got, there's this one record out called 'Sunday, Bloody Sunday'.

The important point to note is that popular music for many young working-class people both constructs and expresses their own more specific subcultural and gendered identities.

There were examples whereby young people explicitly rejected 'pop' music culture. Interestingly enough, two of these young people happened to have upwardly mobile orientations:

> **Julie:** I'm not really that kind of person that's into all this modern music. Um, I'm not, I got me dad's past in me, yuh know, the old jazz. I mean the really old jazz like – oh, just things ah, nobody really knows about really.
>
> **BH:** What kind of music do you like?
>
> **Nigel:** I like a lot of soul and um, jazz. Jazz is very good, especially instrumental.

While it is difficult to speculate about the role of music in isolation from other social contexts, it is clear that these different orientations are part of a much broader lifestyle pattern. Other examples of how music is appropriated into a certain lifestyle and culture are not limited to social climbers. Tracy, who later became politically involved in the youth issue, attended a number of Red Wedge concerts and Dan was actually involved in the organisation of a local youth rights day, involving music and speakers from this organisation.[4] Ben, while preferring a wide range of music, also mentioned the importance of what he called 'political rock'. Garnie, meanwhile, was heavily immersed into 'soul revivals' – original recordings of various soul artists like Billy Holiday. Knowledge and possession of particular revival records were highly valued within his immediate cultural circles.

The main non-work activity engaged in outside the home was simply going out, a longstanding ritual practice engaged in by the vast majority of the youth population. The 'affluent teenager' of the post-war era was the apogee of this representation (Abrams, 1959). The precise reality of this claim and its theoretical underpinnings have been challenged by writers critical of its mass consumerist emphasis (Hall and Jefferson, 1976). Even more important, in the contemporary period, is the impact high youth unemployment and the lowering of youth wages on training schemes have on this social practice. A critical evaluation of the affluent teenager thesis is more than adequately expressed in the following comment:

Garnie: When you come down to think about it you're payin' one pound to get into a building, right? Two pound for drink, right? One pound for your girl to get into the building right? Two pound for a drink for her right? Listen to a load of rubbish music right? Come home and have a headache right? Take a taxi back home right? Two pounds to get home right? Check it down right, you got £8, yuh didn't need to spend that right? . . . That's why I don't believe in goin' to them places, man, 'cos that's when they take away your money, man.

Even if the young working class had a reasonable level of income, there is no reason to believe they would automatically become mass consumers. Many young people, unlike the image, are careful and responsible with their weekly wage.

The cost, in human terms, of being constrained by the substitute wage in going out and maintaining social relationships, is incalculable. Here one young man explains how a lack of money contributed to the termination of a relationship:

> **X:** Did you know that me and Y split up?
>
> **BH:** No, I didn't.
>
> **X:** Oh well, yes . . . It [the allowance] limits what you can do, where you can take people. 'Cos firstly, when we started off, me and Y sort of went out quite a lot and we found that we really couldn't afford it. And we used to be broke all the rest of the week, so we went out less and less – and it just went downhill. And we just sort of split up.

Despite these examples which demonstrates how the substitute wage on the YTS works to limit young people's relations and activities outside the home, the majority I interviewed were prepared to sacrifice a good proportion of their allowance in order to have a proper night out.

The general incidence of going out to a pub, nightclub or disco for most young people was limited to once a week, usually on a Friday or Saturday night. This pattern varied widely and was dependent on a number of factors, one being gender. For those young women who had a steady boyfriend there was a slightly higher number of visits to these types of venues. However, two factors – high male youth unemployment in the area and some young women's involvement in subcultures – sometimes moderated or shifted this general trend. For example, Jan and her unemployed boyfriend's combined income prevented them from going out more than once a week. Liz, who was quite involved in a subcultural/leisure lifestyle, went out every Wednesday to 'alternative night' at a local club in addition to going out nearly every night on the weekend. Most of the lads went to a pub once or twice a week in the hope someone might buy them a round, but others like Garnie and Ben mentioned that they rarely went out to or could afford these types of venues.

The social context of going out is also significant. Young women, for instance, rarely went out unaccompanied and this ties in with many of the arguments made about gender access to public space. Most went out with friends, relatives or under the 'protective' wing of boyfriends. For some, this meant that not only was their evening out structured by their male companion, their activities as well were often subject to a form of regulation:

Jackie: I go out for a drink with my boyfriend.

BH: Does he pay?

Jackie: Yea, he pays. I go to my boyfriend's home – go to discos and that, go to nightclubs.

BH: Is it expensive to get into nightclubs?

Jackie: About £3 to get in. Drinks are expensive in a night-club, so he don't let me drink too much.

The influence boyfriends had on going out appeared to cut across the careerist/domestic typology. Only Liz, who primarily went out with a group of people (both male and female), seemed to escape this gendered social context. Males, on the other hand, often went out alone, either to meet young women or friends. None of them mentioned any restrictions except the financial limits imposed by the substitute wage.

The final significant factor concerning going out is the choice of venue and how this relates to lifestyle identities. The majority of the lads chose to go to pubs which were cheaper than nightclubs and discos, in addition to not requiring expensive formal dress restrictions. Here they relied on mates, older friends or relatives to buy rounds of drinks. Some, like Chris and Mick, went to pubs which informally catered for their subcultural group. A number of young working-class women also went to pubs, usually accompanied by boyfriends or friends.

A minority of young people were critical of the pub atmosphere and chose instead to go to wine bars and nightclubs. Not surprisingly, this group saw themselves as upwardly mobile and career oriented while on the scheme. The main reason for choosing these venues was the 'atmosphere' they provided:

Nigel: Wine bars are a big establishment now, they're catching on now, wine bars. Actually, I would prefer to go to a wine bar than go to a pub. The atmosphere is different, clean atmosphere and ah, you can meet people now and again.

Julie: Um, there's nightclubs you can go to really. They're about £2–4, not a lot of money, not really. Drinking is quite expensive but the atmosphere is nice.

The hidden agenda behind the vague term 'atmosphere' clearly points towards a fusion of upwardly mobile orientations, towards work and leisure, into a caricatured middle-class lifestyle. Experiencing a slice of the 'good life' and affirming one's vertical climb into a trendy lifestyle was important, even if it was only once a week. If one of the strands of the new vocationalism seeks to convince young people that they are on the steps of the corporate ladder, then the realm of commercial leisure also plays an equally important role in the construction of a new field of identities revolving around middle-class lifestyles, for a section of working-class youth.

In summary, I have sought to demonstrate the very real limits available leisure theories have for comprehending and analysing young people's non-work experiences while on the YTS. Neither 'freedom of choice' nor youth subcultural analysis adequately deals with the impact of the substitute wage and the differentiation of working-class youth lifestyles in the non-work sphere. This is not to say that non-work identities are unimportant – youth lifestyles and subcultures can and do influence young people's overall identities and political orientations. Rather, it signals a recognition that non-work practices do not exist outside social relations, economic structures and interrelated institutional arrangements. Issues around non-work activities are clearly an important part of the life world of the young trainee and hence need to be included in the training/employment/unemployment debate.

8

Divided Youth: White Racism and Male Sexist Practice

Youth identities are not simply constructed in particular sites – such as work, the domestic sphere and non-work activity – they are also constitutive of more personalised forms of identification based around ethnicity and gender. For white working-class youth, these identities are most visibly expressed as white racism and male sexist practice. These forms are significant not only for understanding how youth itself becomes internally divided, they are also crucial elements of a wider problem of how to reconcile class cultural struggle with race and gender oppression.

The first subsection focuses on working-class youth forms of white racism. Drawing on the 'new racism' perspective and interview material, I examine the relationship between varied youth transitions and identities and the adoption of different forms of white racism. The second subsection deals with the sexist practices and identities developed through some working-class male's attachment to a culture of manual labour.

Neither of these case studies pretends to provide a complete picture or theory of working-class racism or sexist practice, nor even its youthful forms. Rather I want to raise the issue how these sources of identity link in with new and traditional working-class transitions, exploring how current explanations of these divisions create problems for developing an overall politics of youth training and employment, which goes beyond the narrow confines of a 'liberal' equal opportunity perspective.

Youth divisions and the 'new racism'

Recently, it has been forcefully argued that the focused concern of academics, political parties and social policy-makers on race

161

and race-related issues is as much a part of the problem as it is a solution (Lawrence, 1982a). Despite an exterior of positive intentions, there is a tendency in much of this commentary to remain locked into a spiralling depiction of the plight of black people, rather than dealing rigorously with the roots of racism within white society. In the current period, there has been a notable shift towards theorising race issues primarily in terms of culture (CCCS, 1982), leading to notions of 'underachievement', 'cultures of deprivation' and 'pathological family structures', all of which are reminiscent of analyses of working-class life in the inter and post-war years.[1]

This 'race-relations' perspective has, in varying degrees, informed a number of studies and reports dealing with the experiences of black youth in the education and training field. For example, the Swann Report on race and education, with its emphasis on culture, family structure and underachievement, has been criticised internally for side-stepping the whole issue of institutional and white forms of racism embedded in British society.[2] Similarly, an MSC commissioned report on ethnic minorities and the YTS (Fenton, 1984), while exposing various institutional forms of discrimination, also fails to provide a coherent theoretical explanation either for the roots or forms of racism adopted in the wider society.

Even reports emanating from a labour movement perspective (for example Pollert, 1985) say little about the need for alternative theories of the race issue and instead rely primarily on discrimination amongst employers and in the wider labour market to explain racist practices on schemes. Of course, racism on the YTS does manifest itself at the institutional level and this reflects the various racist assumptions of employers, the Careers Service and scheme personnel (Cross, 1985; YETRU, 1987). However, this type of analysis often ignores how racism amongst white workers and trainees contributes to youth divisions and hierarchies within the working-class and labour movement (Phizacklea and Miles, 1980). In order to come to terms with these issues, it is imperative to go beyond the language of equal opportunities and discrimination and begin to situate the problem within an alternative framework.

One such perspective is developed under the rubric of the 'new racism' (Barker, 1981; CCCS, 1982). Proponents of this paradigm firmly reject the race-relations perspective, with its personalised notions of bias and discrimination, and instead sees racism as a socially produced and historically developed set of ideologies and practices organised around the concept of difference. The 'new racism' as described by Barker (1981), is based around a theoretical assertion which posits that there are natural and biological reasons for 'homogeneous' communities to remain bounded and separate on the basis of a 'common way of life'. He argues that the new racist ideology arose with the development of the New Right in Britain and reflected its need to deflect attention away from the root causes of the economic recession.

The way in which the new racism is related to working-class forms in particular has been taken up by Lawrence (1982b, p. 48). He argues that the new racism is only comprehensible by exploring the symbiotic relationship between racist ideologies and 'common-sense' forms:

> In our view, the more developed racist ideologies *are popular* [his emphasis] precisely because they succeed in reorganising the common-sense racist ideologies of the white working class, around the themes of 'the British nation', 'the British people' and 'British culture' – themes which explicitly exclude black people.

In other words, Lawrence argues that such ideologies cannot become dominant without some sort of purchase on popular, common-sense forms of racism in the wider class society.[3]

While the new racism perspective is suggestive in terms of understanding white working-class forms of racism, in my view it does not go far enough in its discussion of how broader racist ideologies are linked up to common-sense forms. Neither Barker nor Lawrence deal in any great detail with how white working-class forms of racism are often the combined product of inter-class racist ideologies. Nor does the new racism perspective rigorously examine and evaluate how various members of the working class often possess quite different attachments to particular racist ideas and practices. Working-class forms appear to be unitary, popular appropriations of wider racist ideologies rather than a more fragmented and diverse response (influenced by age, gender and more specific intra-class identities).

Part of the problem then lies with the need to examine more closely the forms of white racism adopted by subsections of the working class (in this case the young) and to formulate more precise 'codes' or ideologies of white racism characteristic of different classes. Cohen (1986b), in his work on anti-racist cultural studies and schools, has distinguished three main class codes: (a) an aristocratic code of 'breeding', (b) a bourgeois/democratic variant which gave the code of breeding a scientific reading, and (c) a proletarian code, of the working class, which centres around the inheritance of labour power and territoriality. This more refined version of the new racism perspective has two main implications. First, because the working class in Cohen's (1983) overall perspective is viewed as internally divided, forms of white racism may vary substantially according to age, gender and the more specific identities thrown up in the post-war period (i.e. subcultures, new work identities, etc.). Second, it is important to understand working-class forms of racism within the context of class subordination and the unequal negotiation between rival codes. Working-class racism should be understood as highly differentiated and interactive with other dominant class forms.

Working-class youth transitions and 'common-sense' forms of white racism

The ethnographic material presented here seeks to elucidate the common-sense forms of white racism prevalant amongst young people interviewed on training schemes. As such it does not pretend to be a comprehensive examination of working-class racism or even its youthful variants. Rather, I want to examine how forms of white racism are related to various identities, transitions and divisions amongst the youth population.

It should be noted that there is evidence of widespread racism amongst young people. A *New Society* survey has shown that a significant proportion of white youngsters could be classified as racist. In the survey of 2,417 secondary schoolchildren and college students, 42 per cent of respondents 'admitted' to holding racist views.[4] More dramatically, a survey of West Midland fifth formers revealed that 14 per cent put the National Front or British Movement as their first electoral choice in a mock election, while 30 per cent picked them as their first or second choice.[5] White racism thus has a firm base of support amongst large sections of the youth population.

My interviews with white youth on the YTS support this general pattern. Survey research, however, tells us little about the different forms of white racism held by working-class youth or how these forms relate to their more specific identities. The three main forms revealed here have been labelled 'nationalist-proletarian', 'liberal' and 'left-labourist'. As the interview material demonstrates, this categorisation necessarily simplifies the complex and contradictory character of working-class youth racism. White racism as it is 'practised' by young people takes on a far more fluid and flexible make-up.

The first form identified is a nationalist-proletarian position. This form is overwhelmingly inhabited by the manual labour lads on the YTS. In this scheme, race and racism are viewed as central concepts in terms of affirming white identity and young people's desire to make sense of the present crisis (in its widest economic, social and cultural dimensions). Fundamental to the nationalist-proletarian form is the idea of the 'nation'. This includes one's insertion into and inheritance of a 'British way of life', in contrast to the 'alien' heritage of black people. Also crucial to this perspective is the specific distillation of the idea of nation down to particular class concerns over the inheritance of labour power and territoriality (Cohen, 1986b).

Due to its explicit and largely masculine gloss, the nationalist-proletarian position projects itself as the most direct and vulgar form of white racism:

(in an off-the-job training course)

Billy: I don't like Pakies. I just don't like 'em.
Berni: I don't want to hear any of that in this classroom. Is that clear?
Billy: [quietly] I'm standin' up for England, ain't I? I'm standin' up for England.

The key referent for Billy and many of the other lads is the 'nation', 'England', and 'British people' – concepts which, however vague, provide some notion of white identity and sense of belonging.

This general referent of the nation is specifically located in the two immediate contexts of male working-class life – the inheritance of labour power and territoriality. If work and neighbourhood (community) form the main planks of their experience of the 'British way of life', then these are to be 'protected' and 'defended' from outsiders in order to preserve their 'special' character:

> **Baz:**   If there weren't no coloureds or Indians there'd be more jobs for people to do – yuh wouldn't have to have youth training schemes . . . There'd be more jobs to do over here.

(in a discussion about leisure facilities)

> **Chris:**   Our park is always full of wogs and coloureds.

Here two lads explicitly discuss how, in their eyes, the inheritance of these spheres have been interrupted by black people's 'invasion' of the labour market and community. A lack of jobs, the need for training schemes and the perceived loss of territoriality for the young male working class are viewed as symptomatic of immigration rather than industrial decline and urban redevelopment.

While elements of this form clearly overlap with aspects of the 'new racism', they also contain remnants of other racist traditions. State racist ideologies, as analysed by Barker (1981), are far more careful in distinguishing between 'cultural difference' and 'racial superiority'. Common-sense forms require no such internal consistency. The construction of black people as 'alien' reaches beyond the focus on cultural difference and borrows on aristocratic images of the empire and bourgeois codes of racism as expressed through the physical body. The construction of black people as a different 'species' by the lads, for example, could be seen as a popular 'reading' of scientific and genetic theories of social difference (Rose *et al.*, 1984). The most extreme versions of this came out of some of the lads' characterisations of black people as 'animals' or even 'monsters'. Black youths were seen to behave like 'animals' during the 1985 inner city disturbances and some white youths hinted at links between the bodily disposition of Afro-Caribbeans and criminality. Mick, when describing a fight in which he was involved in the city centre, made an animal analogy when he spoke about his opponent coming 'out of the pack'. The most fantastic and lurid characterisation came from Billy's description of a black trainee on his scheme:

> **Billy:** Christ almighty, that Paki was a docile creep wasn't he? Looks like Frankenstein – the spitting image of Frankenstein.

The imagery of Frankenstein, the monster, is the ultimate attempt to define black people as virtually inhuman. The nationalist–proletarian form of racism then is not only connected to male working-class concerns about the inheritance of labour power and territoriality, it is also informed through crude appropriations of bourgeois codes of biologism, forms of popular culture, and variants of nationalism.

The second type of white racism found amongst working-class youth is far more subtle in tone and has been labelled the 'liberal' perspective. The vast majority of upwardly mobile trainees and most young working-class women fell into this category. However, some of the manual labour lads also vacillated between this and the nationalist-proletarian form, adopting one or the other depending on the situation, or holding both forms simultaneously.

In the liberal position, race is not seen as being particularly central to one's life or identity. The key referent is the individual – racism, if it exists at all, resides largely in the mind of the person. The different social conditions faced by black and white people are largely understood through the filter of personal choice, although if they appear overwhelmingly divergent they can be attributed to cultural difference rather than structural inequality. Institutional forms of racism are, for the most part, denied although individual cases of prejudice may exist.

The main locus of racism in the liberal perspective resides with the individual. Institutional forms of racism can be denied by reference to 'personal choice':

> **Robert:** Its all in your upbringing really. Like him [Baz], he's brought up like that . . . he doesn't know any better. They just put ideas into yer head. He just doesn't

like 'em . . . You can get on with a black person. It
doesn't matter what their colour is, it's personality as
well. I can get on with anybody.

Racism in the liberal perspective is defined categorically through
the actions and orientations of the individual. In a discussion of
the views held by the assistant manager of their scheme, three of
the lads holding a nationalist-proletarian position change tack and
brand him a 'real' racist:

Billy: Yea, and he's a racist cat . . .
Mick: He's an ex-copper.
BH: An ex-copper?
Mick: He's just generally a cunt.
BH: How's he racist? What does he do?
Billy: He doesn't like coloureds . . . that's it, full stop. He
         just don't like 'em.

By switching to liberal terms, some of the lads like Billy can
deflect attention away from their own racism through a comment
like, 'I used to know a lovely coloured chap.' The scheme manager, on the other hand, is a real racist because he personally
hates all black people. This individualistic view allowed some of
the lads to excuse their own nationalistic form of racism.

Underlying the rhetoric of individualism however, was an
implicit idea that choice was at least partly a matter of cultural
difference. One stance was to deny that racist-related issues had
anything to do with one's own life. Black and white people were
thought to have had 'separate' lives and black 'problems' had little
to do with white society. This perspective was clearly evident in
the following discussions concerning images of black people in the
1985 inner city riots:[6]

Julie: I don't believe in the drugs that go around there and
         I know they do. But I don't really know – I keep out
         of that.

Andy: It went from a small fight into a massive one – a big
         gang fight really isn't it? I think it was a big drug stash.
         I think it was and they tried to break it up, go and

snatch the drugs off these people and they said they beat them up or something like that. It's none of my business really.

This particular incident was viewed exclusively in terms of black people and their drug 'problem' being responsible for the riot. It had nothing to do, of course, with white racism in the police force or in the labour market. Another example of this liberal 'separateness' and 'different way of life' idea, was put forward by Jan:

(in a discussion about black youth)

Jan: I suppose that there's kids that, that hang around the street all day. They haven't got nothing, anything to do, they haven't got any money so they can't go anywhere, so it's depressing, they're depressed and – they haven't got any life sort of thing, around the street all day.

Despite the liberal tone of this statement, it is implicitly saying something about black people's 'way of life' which makes it different from that of Jan's white community. Because she does not attempt to locate the 'source' of these problems in white society, the blame ultimately falls back on to black individuals or the black community.

I have mentioned that this liberal form was adopted by many of the upwardly mobile trainees and this relates to their overall individualistic orientation. The majority of young women interviewed also adopted this position rather than a nationalist--proletarian form. This, I would argue, is at least partly explained by their own subordinate position within the class culture. Not many young women, for instance, raised the issue of jobs and unemployment in the context of immigration. Territoriality, expressed as the loss of community and neighbourhood, was not really the same issue as it was for some of the lads. Instead, white racism in the public sphere was centred almost exclusively around sexuality and criminality (i.e. the 'mugging phenomenon'). This siting is clearly expressed in the following comment by a young white woman from a neighbouring town:

BH: How have you heard about the town centre not being safe?

Pat: Well, not really – but it's not – well I don't like walkin' around the town on me own in the daytime – er, it's really the coloureds. You know, they're in groups and – I don't know really. I haven't heard about anyone gettin' attacked through them, but – I wouldn't use it, well not on me own anyway, at night I wouldn't.

The main point of this conversation is that young women's genuine fears of male harassment in the public sphere are shifted in a racist direction. Black men, rather than men in general, are seen to be dangerous and this threat lies within the realm of sexuality as opposed to territoriality.

The final form of white racism is labelled 'left–labourist'. This type was not very prevalent for two reasons. First, there were very few trainees who considered themselves to be affiliated to the labour movement. Second, of those young people who were on the left, there was generally a high degree of awareness of racism both in the wider society and within the labour movement itself. This form was mainly, although not exclusively, adopted by those trainees labelled 'politicos'. Despite this, as a general categorisation, it retains some explanatory power.

In this perspective (which could also be viewed as characteristic of the labour movement in general), racism is understood almost exclusively at the institutional level and is seen as emanating from the power blocs responsible for running the main sectors of capitalist society. The main referent is the 'institution' and the language revolves around concepts like 'discrimination' and 'equal opportunity'. Due to the fact that racism is created and practised by the dominant groups in society, there is little recognition of the new racism perspective which emphasises the importance of white ethnocentric culture as the basis of racist ideologies. This form also has difficulty in dealing with white racism within the labour movement and the working class in general.

While none of the trainees I interviewed was truly representative of this position, variations of the left-labourist position were evident in discussions concerning alleged acts of racism on schemes:

X: This, the problem with a lot of places, the schemes, the people running the schemes aren't necessarily racist. They're prepared to accept anybody, but they know it's going to be harder to try and get black people good training situations – ah work placements or positions. So I think, ah, there wasn't any clear-cut examples, but people were definitely ah, encouraged to go – like white people were saying OK, maybe you can do computer programming or something, but black people were getting told that maybe it was better for them to go work in a garage or something. And – also it is quite interesting to note that is, that throughout the scheme, it started off with say half black and half white, but as you went through the scheme the black people dropped off. So there must be something, ah, you know, they were getting unfairly treated somewhere along the line. They felt worse off than the whites.

It would be unfair to characterise this trainee's position as exemplary of the left–labourist form of white racism. Nevertheless, there are elements of this perspective displayed in the above comment. For instance, there is an underlying stress on understanding racism as institutional discrimination, situated primarily in the labour market (i.e. with work sponsors). No mention is made of the racism existing amongst the white trainees, nor is the general context of white racism, rooted as it is in British culture and social life, drawn upon. There is an implicit assumption that if only the barriers were lifted and blacks were given an equal opportunity, then somehow racism would be eradicated.

In summary, these were the main forms of white racism adopted by working-class youth on training schemes. The nationalist-proletarian position, centring around the inheritance of labour power and territoriality, although also invoking bourgeois and nationalistic variations, is taken up primarily by the manual labour lads. These young working-class males have a stronger interest in maintaining a 'white identity' in the context of the present economic crisis, because in comparison with many of the other transitions they are in a declining position, even if this has nothing to do with the presence and activities of black people. The liberal position, with its more subtle middle-class and individualistic gloss, is more characteristic of the upwardly mobile trainees and the white racism of young working-class women. With its implicit, underlying assumption of 'separateness', it is perhaps the closest approximation to the new racism perspective. In terms of young working-class women, I have argued that it is more difficult for them to feel they are losing control of the streets, parks, jobs and communities, and adopt the nationalist-proletarian position, when they themselves are either excluded from or constrained within these spheres. Instead their racism is explicitly skewed in the direction of sexuality and criminality through the mugging discourse (Hall *et al.*, 1978).

Finally, the left–labourist analysis of racism, pitched largely at the institutional level, is vaguely characteristic of that group of trainees I refer to as politicos. While it would be wrong to lump this perspective in with the other two forms, its failure to address the question of the roots of white racism often leads to an inadequate analysis of youth divisions and reflects the labour movement's own historical collusion in racist ideologies (Phizacklea and Miles, 1980). The overall analysis provided here brings to light the labour movement's failure either to construct an adequate analysis of racism in training or in the wider society (beyond an equal opportunities perspective), or to develop an effective programme for tackling white racism within the young working class.

Working-class lads' sexist practice

In this section, I focus on the specific sexist practices of a section of male working-class youth – the manual labour lads. In doing so, the analysis has implications not only for the fragmentation of the young working class but also for labour movement politics around the training issue. Like racism, sexist practice resides not only amongst employers and scheme providers, but right at the heart of traditional working-class male transitions into work. Strangely enough, studies of young male sexist practices are relatively rare and untheorised.[7] And while there is a wealth of material on women's oppression in the education/training and labour market, there are few in-depth studies linking their subordination to the precise forms, mechanisms and sites of male working-class sexism.[8]

One of the main difficulties in coming to terms with working-class sexism is that certain aspects of feminist theory have often sought to understand women's oppression by collapsing all male practices into a homogeneous category – that is, all men oppress all women in fundamentally the same ways. Evidence in support of this assertion comes from the fact that women across class, race and age barriers do face similar types of oppression and exploitation from men. However, one might conceivably argue that such points of commonality arise precisely because of the combined effect of quite different class-based sexual codes (thereby giving rise to dominant practices which may have different meanings and inflections for men of different class backgrounds). This monolithic perspective also has difficulty in dealing with the more specific forms of sexist practice experienced by working-class and black women (Carby, 1982; Griffin, 1985).

What might these class codes revolving around sexist practice and women's oppression look like? Due to the fact that sexism is also a social construction of 'difference', connected up with different class ideologies, a revised version of the racist categories utilised earlier may prove useful. Speculatively, one might distinguish them analytically as:

(a)   an aristocratic code of 'breeding' which suggests that men and women are bred into particular roles and are different physically, intellectually and emotionally. Women in this class code may be seen as 'special' yet, at the same time, inferior;

(b)   a bourgeois variant which supplements the breeding code with a scientific and biologically based justification centring around sexuality and the body as a crucial site of difference;

(c)   a proletarian code which revolves around working-class male inheritance of labour power and skills, and control over the private (home) and public spheres to subordinate women both domestically and sexually.

To suggest such an analysis is to once again argue that working-class male sexist practice, while having a degree of autonomy from aristocratic and bourgeois codes, contains 'common-sense' appropriations of these other forms and exists in a subordinate relationship to them.

It is not surprising to find that the manual labour lad's sexist practices are characteristic of the most explicit and obvious examples of male sexism. They are often blunt, bodily and expressed through a filter of bravado and physicality. They constitute, almost wholly, conventional notions of sexist practice – the wolf whistle, verbal suggestions and degradations and actual physical contact. And their overt character overshadows the much more subtle and patronising forms characterising the middle and upper classes. In this case study, these practices were located primarily around the masculine inheritance of wage labour, the sexual body and domestic sphere and male policing of compulsory heterosexuality.

The inheritance of male labour power, skills and the family wage are crucial components of the lads' sexist practice. The separate spheres young men and women inhabit in schools and their markedly different training and labour market destinations via the YTS are seen by the lads as a naturally existing phenomenon. Young women who attempt to step beyond these boundaries, by training in traditional male occupations, often find themselves ostracised and patronised by male workers (Griffin, 1985; Cockburn, 1986). High male unemployment, low scheme wages and the decline of the manufacturing sector have actually worked to heighten the defence of this traditional inheritance by a section of working-class lads. Here one lad speaks implicitly about the effect scheme wages have on his masculine identity:

> **Billy:**   Yea, 'cos say yer girlfriend's got a job right, a full-time job. Yer only gettin' £25 a week and she's gettin' about £40 to £50 a week. She takes you out, not you take her out. That ain't right.

This loss of masculinity is only recouped by reversing cause and effect and blaming women for job loss and the recession:

(in discussions about unemployment)

> **Andy:**   It's just 'cos Maggie's here. Should kick 'er out, put a bloke in.
> **Calvin:**   Never let a woman be Prime Minister.
> **Chris:**   It's these women, it's all the women's fault.

Mick: So if there's any women listenin' to this tape – [leans forward to emphasise the comment], it's all your fault.

If male working-class transitions into work are viewed as the inheritance of patrimonial skills and a masculine shop-floor culture (which by definition excludes women), then it is not surprising that increased female participation in the labour force can be seen to be responsible for the lad's blocked entry into work.

The sexual body is also a key locus of young male working-class sexist practice. This is where the lads most concretely locate notions of difference and construct male power over women. For them, the body is the most 'natural' site of sexual difference. The construction of male power in this sphere involves the simultaneous degradation of women's bodies and the celebration of 'natural' male urges in the sexual realm.

The lads engaged in this latter practice by constantly over-emphasising the strength of the male sexual urge – tracing it back to basic biological reasons. When I asked one of the lads why males and females were separated on the City and Guilds course, his answer was simply 'nature'. In other discussions, the sexual urge was always displayed as bubbling up under the surface. The lads were constantly trying to give the impression that they were always ready to 'chat up' young women for sexual reasons. The definition of being a male was shot through with the need to display sexual prowess and power.

The second mode of constructing male sexual power is through the objectification and subsequent degradation of women's bodies (Dworkin, 1981; Lees, 1986). Women, in general, can be thought of as simply objects of desire or as recipients of the sexual act. While this partly occurs through fantasy, its consequences in real life can be deadly serious. Here, one lad speaks of an imagined party game, in which a woman is viewed purely as an object to be 'won' and 'used':

Chris: It's like pass the parcel, yuh know what I mean, right? There's all boys, right, all kids, right, and there's a bird in the middle. And you pass the parcel around and there's a johnny [condom] in the parcel [others laugh]. And whoever gets the rubber gets to bang the bird.

While this scenario is pure fantasy, it is obvious that the main assumption made is that women can be treated like objects and that they exist solely for men's pleasure. The most common method of objectification used by the lads is the separation and isolation of women's body parts. In this way, women can be judged, degraded and made to feel inferior.

The sexual realm is also closely linked up with the domestic sphere and together they form an important couplet for the expression of young male sexist practice. In this short retort about the role of women, Andy sums up the basis of this dual relationship:

> **Andy:**   Only two things they're good for – the housework and
> in bed.

The foundation of this statement is derived, I would argue, from the contradictory position young women are placed in by the lads (this, of course, should not imply that young women readily accept this positioning). Women are expected to be both sexually attractive and adept domestic workers/comforters. This dual identity and the contradictions it raises are connected up with the lads' categorisation of young women as 'bad' and 'good' girls, or as Cowie and Lees (1981) put it, 'slags' or 'drags'. As Lees (1984) argues, in her interviews with young women, this positioning often places them in a 'no win' situation:

> **Girl 2:**   It's a vicious circle. If you don't like them, they'll call
> you a tight bitch. If you go with them, they call you
> a slag afterwards.

This categorisation provides the key for understanding how the sexual/domestic couplet is used to subordinate young women, while providing the lads with an ideal situation. On the one hand, the lads require females who will submit to their sexual urges (or at least young women they can speak about in these terms). At the same time, the categories of 'slags' and 'drags' allows them to evaluate their future marriage partners and domestic comforters. As the work of both Robins and Cohen (1978) and Willis (1977) demonstrate, it is usually this latter group the lads may one day think about going steady with. Spike, a lad interviewed in Willis's (ibid. p. 45) research, describes his future wife as 'clean', and 'she loves doing fucking housework'. The domestic realm then is closely tied up with the sexual sphere as a site of the lads' sexist practice.

The final area in which young male working-class sexist practice is asserted is through the policing of compulsory heterosexuality. Male sexuality is displayed readily enough through the exaggerated emphasis on male sexual urges. Yet, there is still a need for the lads to contain any tendencies which point towards a more ambiguous notion of sexuality. One method of dealing with this is to construct any 'abberation' from the male sexual 'norm' as deviant and unnatural. This occurred mainly under the guise of humour which often obscured underlying anxieties about the existence of alternative gender identities:

BH: Were there any women in the engineering course at college?

Robert: [Speaking to Baz] Besides yourself, no. Well they had a transvestite.

Baz: You were there, was yuh?

Billy: You know Boy George? It's that sort of thing now.

BH: So that's a trendy style now?

Billy: Yea.

Mick: No, he's just queer . . .

Billy: He's okay, do you like him? I like his music . . .

Mick: He's a queer, give up.

Chris: Beat 'im up, then castrate 'im.

The policing of male sexuality is expressed as a virulent homophobia and the labelling of all alternative identities as deviant (i.e. gays equal transvestites). Even the slightly ambiguous 'gender bender' image of the pop musician, Boy George, is savagely and violently attacked. The boundary lines demarcating acceptable male sexuality are so finely drawn that seemingly innocuous forms of behaviour are viewed as aberrant. This, combined with the present moral panic revolving around gayness and the killer diseases AIDS (Weeks, 1987), would appear to suggest that there is little chance of loosing the reins of compulsory heterosexuality amongst the majority of working-class males.

What explanations are there for comprehending these working-class lads' investments in sexist ideologies and practices? First, it is clear that many of them stand to gain some real material advantages from women's oppression. The forms and sites of sexist practice demonstrate how the lads consolidate their control over women economically, domestically and sexually. The male working-class expectation of inheriting labour power and its attendant skills continues to aid the social division of labour and restrict women's economic competition with men. Sexist practice organised around the body and its direct connection with the domestic sphere provides young men with the means to dominate women sexually, as well as help produce future labourers and comforters for the working-class household. Finally, the policing of male sexuality ensures that alternative identities do not take root, not only for young men but for young women as well.

Second, there is the whole issue of identity. If working-class practices do exist in a subordinate relationship to other class forms, this may partly explain why the lads engage in such overt and exaggerated displays of sexism (not only to reassure themselves, but to convince the whole of society they are 'real' men). Additionally, if working-class men are privately aware of the fact that they themselves are subordinate within a class-divided society, they may have additional reasons for attempting to maintain their domination in the more private spheres of the household and in the sexual realm.

On a more positive note, there are some factors which pose a direct challenge to male sexist practices. Young working-class women, the recipients of the lad's practices, should not be seen as passively accepting their oppression. The actual negotiated character of sexual interaction is far more complex than simple domination. Young women can and do resist sexist labelling, definitions and practices and the lads are often forced to alter their masculine posturing in actual face to face situations. There was also evidence in interviews with other working-class males, particularly those who rejected the manual labour transition and its attendant identity, of a growing awareness of male sexist practice. This was most true of those young men who had, or were developing, a political identity. And while they rejected the most obvious and visible expressions of male sexism, there were also examples of a deeper appreciation of male patriarchy and women's oppression. Male control of language, the institutional separation of men and women's work (including domestic labour) and male working-class inheritance of labour power and skill were all discussed critically by members of the male group labelled 'politicos' during the course of the research.

Sexist practice then exists not simply at the institutional level, but within the very transitions traditionally characteristic of male working class culture and organisation (i.e. trade unions and shop floor culture). For example, there are clear linkages between the lads' expected inheritance of labour power and skill and the labour movement's own historical participation in maintaining patriarchal control over the work sphere (Cockburn, 1983; Campbell, 1984). At the same time, labour movement politics directed towards young women and training must go beyond a simple equality of opportunity paradigm. It must also seek to tackle the main class cultural forms of young male sexist practice (rooted, as they are, in labour, sexuality and the domestic sphere) and unravel the contradictory linkages between male 'exclusionism' in the work sphere and the struggle over 'deskilling' taking place under the new vocationalism.

9

Youth Politics in Thatcherland

One of the most commonly held views about young people and politics is that they are predominantly apathetic about this sphere of social life. Large-scale surveys such as the Department of Education and Science publication *Young People in the 80's* (DES, 1983) gives credence to this perspective, with its finding that 75 per cent of respondents (aged 16–19) admitted to being politically apathetic, with only 2 per cent ever attending any political meetings or parties. While this apolitical model remains the dominant paradigm, an additional image of the interested minority revolves around the 'rebellious', 'idealistic' and 'extreme' nature of youth politics and organisation (Cohen, 1983).[1]

Within the strict confines of its own conventional wisdom, this dominant perspective contains a certain degree of truth. Very few of the young people I interviewed were overtly political or belonged to a political party. Despite this lack of involvement, the basis of the apolitical model requires closer scrutiny. In the first place, it must be stated that young people rarely have access to the sites of power and influence which ultimately structure British society. In fact, their right to participate, if anything, has been rolled back in the 1980s.

A further difficulty with this view concerns its limited notion of 'politics'. If such a definition is confined to party or institutional forms of politics, then this assertion is basically correct. If, however, we take politics to mean an awareness of what is happening in society, a concern over the forces and events shaping everyday life and anxieties about the future, then surely young people must be viewed as political beings. In any case, previous chapters on the YTS, work, home and public life, non-work activity and identities constructed around white ethnicity and sexist practice, seriously question the limitations of a politics based around purely party or

180

even traditional labour movement concerns. The whole issue of youth politics must be turned on its head and we need to ask how relevant existing party politics are to young people's everyday concerns.

The relationship between personal and institutional forms of politics begins with an exploration of trainee's own assessments of their current situation on schemes, before moving on to the wider issues they spring from. The most important point to stress is the linkages that exist between the various transitions and identities made available through the new vocationalism and young people's political orientations.

Why YTS? The politics of youth training

Young people's views on the politics of the YTS varied substantially and were influenced by a wide range of factors. These included previous involvement in campaigns, parties or groups, actual experiences on the scheme and, as I have mentioned, the impact different transitions into work have on political identities.

A small number of young people were politically active at an institutional level prior to their experience of the YTS. Politics was a major component of their personal identity, hence the use of the label 'politicos'. Dan's introduction to the political sphere began very early on and was primarily influenced by his parent's involvement in Labour Party and trade union politics. Finchy's political apprenticeship began in school with the student council and with his engagement in extra-curricular activities and organisations:

> **Finchy:** Yuh see I messed about at school. I didn't take exams and things and I sort of cocked everything up – kept takin' weeks off to get involved in things 'cos I was quite involved with CND and stuff then.

Prior to the YTS, both Dan and Finchy were involved in the youth section of left political organisations. In this sense they both had an overall class-based form of politics which spilled over into their involvement with a trainee action group and various youth rights campaigns. The experience of the YTS largely reinforced their existing political perspective which saw training schemes as an attack on the young working class in terms of lowering wages, expectations and working conditions. As Dan stated, 'I knew they were basically glorified slave training schemes before I started.' Dan and Finchy were also aware of how some gender and race issues manifested themselves on schemes and while critical of the labour movement, both advocated unionisation as the best form of protection for trainees.

There were other groups of young people who became politicised purely through their experience of the YTS. For simplicity, they are also referred to as politicos. However, their development and political analysis of schemes differed somewhat from this first group. Because their attitudes evolved through a disillusionment with the YTS, there was often a movement from a fairly liberal position to a more politicised version of youth training:

Tracy: When I first went on the scheme I thought, great, I'll be able to get some training in the field I want to work in. But then I couldn't get a placement in that area and I got put in a rest home instead. All I was doin' was moving people around and doin' all the shit jobs. I know now that these schemes are just slave labour.

(in an earlier written statement)

Ben: It is the people at my scheme, with their conviction, experience and belief in a future for young people which has made it one of the best schemes in the area.

(in a later discussion about the politics of the YTS)

Ben: And it's turnin' towards oppressing young people, hiding unemployment, lowering youth wages – undermining union control. 'Cos they [young people] haven't got any rights so they can't really – and if they join a union they can't get their proper rights. So it's a whole process of kicking youth in the stomach.

Due to the fact that it was the experience of the YTS, rather than a labour traditional of political activity, which shifted their

opinions, many of these young people initially viewed 'youthfulness' rather than class, gender or race as the main oppression.
As such, politics were restricted largely to issue raised on their
particular scheme (i.e. through trainee councils) and usually ended
when they finished the YTS. However, a small number of these
politicos went on to engage more rigorously with various aspects
of youth rights campaigns, as well as developing their own personalised forms of politics.

In an earlier chapter, I argued that the majority of young working-class school leavers possessed legitimate and critical knowledges of training schemes prior to their movement on to the YTS.
While many of these knowledges persist and even provide a basis
for evaluating the YTS experience, one of the intentions of the
scheme curriculum and the induction period was to begin to break
down and replace these negative discourses with far more positive
and celebrated images of training as an 'opportunity'. This was
particularly the case with those trainees who came to view their
transition on the YTS as career-oriented. 'Opportunity' and
'experience' eclipsed and masked underlying knowledges that schemes were indeed a political response to high youth unemployment:

Julie: YTS is somethin yuh can go on that gives you experience and um, you learn about um, how everything
works in a shop or in any situation 'cos you can go
into any kind of YTS. So it gives you that experience.

BH: Do you have your own ideas why they have YTS?

Angus: It's a good thing, yea, for people just leaving school
who got nothin' to do, who know nothin' about the
job or anything. It's trainin' for 'em if that's what they
want to go into.

These highly individualised explanations of the need for training
schemes tie in with an upwardly mobile orientation towards work
and training. These comments also echo the official line on YTS
as offering a 'permanent bridge between school and work' and
providing young working-class people with new opportunities to
'get on'. Implicit in them are assumptions of 'self-blame' and 'lack

of experience', rather than a shortage of jobs as the reason for training schemes.

Another subgroup of working-class youths, the manual labour lads, held quite conflicting views on the politics behind training schemes. Most of them, for example, were quite aware that the YTS was linked in some way to high unemployment and implicated in the decline of the traditional apprenticeship system. And many were highly critical of the life and social skills emphasis, the lack of craft skill training and being used as 'skivvies' on work experience placements. Yet at the same time there was a general acceptance that schemes were here to stay and that little could be done. If the YTS was the only available route into wage labour and the masculine aura of shop floor culture, then it must be endured. Being used, while unpleasant, was accepted as a fact of life. The lads' political views on the need for training schemes were also clouded by the occasional reference to young people's lack of skills and knowledge and to the impact black immigration and women's insertion into the labour force had on the lack of jobs. Overall, the lads possessed no coherent political critique of the new vocationalism and the existence of training schemes.

Other groups of young people held on to various critical aspects of training provision which were mainly reinforced through their own negative experiences on schemes. Some came to develop general critiques out of their personal disappointment with aspects of their programme. Alice, for example, became anti-YTS because of her treatment at work and the fact that she saw schemes replacing real jobs first hand:

Alice: They're takin' up all the other jobs like. Like the job I was at in the office, the other girl was supposed to be full-time but they won't take one on, they'll get a YTS scheme. And they don't have to pay yuh. So they have you workin' there for nothin' and the companies look at it and think if you get something for nothing they don't have to pay you fer it really. If they finished with YTS there'd be more jobs.

Mandy also became disillusioned when her placement didn't fulfil the criterion of proper secretarial work and she went on to develop a more political stance after getting involved in the trainee council:

BH: Why do you think YTS came about?
Mandy: Ah, mainly to keep young people off the street –
             stop mugging people [laughs].

Finally, there were some young people, like Garnie, who saw the
scheme as a political, issue right from the start:

Garnie: Two years on a YTS scheme, that is two years of
             slave labour. Two years of makin' things for other
             companies – what comes down to a lower price for
             them right? They getting all them old people out of
             manufacture place and they're puttin' young kids in.
             The way I see it, remember years ago when they
             used to have kids cleanin' the chimneys and them
             things there, that's what they're doing now.

The irony of these situations, however, was that such critiques
were rarely sustained beyond individual circumstances. Alice hap-
pily transferred to a college-based childcare scheme and Mandy's
involvement in trainee issues halted with the demise of her trainee
council. Garnie, meanwhile, stuck with his community-based
scheme because it allowed him to avoid the exploitation he spoke
about in relation to private employers.

Perhaps the largest single factor which threw up doubts about
the scheme was the persistence of high youth unemployment as a
crucial backdrop to the YTS. Even those trainees whose comments were infused with the 'official' language of deficiency and
opportunity often followed up with remarks about unemployment.
However much the government and the MSC have tried to shift
the training discourse away from unemployment, the stark reality
of the labour market for working-class youth couldn't help but
produce a consciousness of how schemes were related to a lack
of jobs. While young people developed a number of ways to
deal with their status as trainees, all of them were aware that
unemployment was a background to even the most promising
transition. The dole queue bogyman continues to haunt even the
staunchest government rhetoric which advocates training without
jobs.

Maggie's farm: understanding unemployment in Thatcherland

Unemployment then was viewed as a key component of the politics of youth training for many trainees. As a follow-up comment the question, 'Who do you think is responsible for unemployment?' was asked. Again, there was a wide variety of responses which were clearly linked to how young people understood their transition through the YTS.

One of the dominant responses linked high unemployment to the policies of the Conservative government and more specifically to the personality of the party leader, Mrs Thatcher. It was clear that there was a wide base of support for a populist 'anti-Thatcherism' amongst a large proportion of working-class youth:

>**Garnie:**   Me personally, right, would like to speak with Mrs Thatcher herself, on her own. I'll go up to her personally and I'll tell her, listen, don't give me no big talks 'cos it don't get you nowhere, just talk to me normal with little words, yuh know what I mean? And I'll bet she can't talk to me like that. She gotta use all her big words, exclusive and all this big jazz, yuh know what I mean and the only thing she's doin' using big words is makin' the world corrupted. But me personally would like to sit down here, like on this table, like me sittin' to you, 'Good afternoon Mrs Thatcher', cup a drink, put it down on the table, right. Oh yea, she don't drink does she? Sit over a cup of coffee then, right, chat to her right and chat to her vibe to vibe right? And make her chat to the rest of the million people like me, right, chat to her and see how she feel – right? She feel like a right idiot!

>**BH:**   Whose fault do you think that [unemployment] is?
>**Shanaz:**   Well, it's the government, isn't it? It's Thatcher. She's closing down all the firms and losin' jobs.
>**Daljit:**   They're bringing in all these robots.

And, in a discussion about unemployment:

Calvin: It'll never get as worse as here.

Andy: It's just 'cos Maggie's here. Should kick 'er out, put a bloke in . . .

Calvin: Look how many factories they've closed down here. It's stupid.

Andy: It ain't our fault.

BH: Whose fault do you think it is?

Chris: Maggie's.

Andy: I'll bet Maggie couldn't get a job.

Chris: Yuh know, she gets about £1000 a week.

Andy: We're only gettin' £25.

Calvin: She's gettin' all our money.

BH: She gets £1000 a week?

Calvin: She gets more than that!

Andy: Our wages right, is just her pocket money.

With the exception of Garnie's powerful statement, these somewhat sloganised explanations appear initially as almost rehearsed answers to a well-worn question. Popular discontentment with political leaders often takes the form of a 'cult of personality', which works to mask a whole series of social relationships between élites and interest groups (the relationship between political and business interests, for instance). Similarly, some of the manual labour lads' comments on the political sphere didn't exactly express a well thought out class analysis of Thatcherism.

Despite these obstacles, I would argue that there is a more complex grasp, by many working-class youths, of the political background behind the unemployment question. In the first place, populist conceptions of political leaders are comprehensible within the context of a media which projects personality over policy and individuals over social relations. Second, there is a long tradition of working-class distrust of government education and training policies which many young people continue to draw upon (CCCS Education Group, 1981). And third, these responses reflect not only perceptions of Thatcherism's public image, they also stem from a very real understanding of the connections between public figures and the effect their policies have on people's everyday lives. Many young working-class people do not require an in depth analysis of Thatcherism – they have lived through and felt the changes. A real lack of jobs and opportunities, redundancies in the household and cuts in the family benefit system are all living examples of the impact of Conservative policies.

The question remains how some of these experiences get redefined through young people's involvement in schemes and how some of the transitions created out of the new vocationalism work to shift explanations away from institutional and political factors to individual deficiencies. Two additional explanations of high unemployment were: (a) a version of a Thatcherite position, and (b) individualist-based 'blame the victim' arguments.

Initially it may seem contradictory that some young working-class people take up and expound upon government inspired economic philosophies, particularly when these implicitly seek to implicate the personal qualities of the unemployed as an explanation for their plight. However, some of the rhetoric and language surrounding Conservative views on unemployment tie in with the philosophy and upwardly mobile aspirations of a section of young trainees:

> **Nigel:**   In my mind you're talking about um, inflation, a high rate of inflation. And then you look at, the big companies go bust. Why do they go bust? I don't know. They can't get skilled workers or they're too big. And they're [the government] quite interested in, as I said, self-employed people 'cos that's where employment is gonna be in the future. And I look at it like this, look at America, they believe in their businessmen in America. And I see this Tory government is doing the same as America.

While Nigel conjures up the magic word 'inflation' to explain high unemployment, he, like the government, is not very sure about its precise meaning. Instead, he quickly elides his answer with what he sees as his future in the world of work, with the government's desire to promote self-employment. The use of Thatcherite philosophy was not just limited to the middle-management type. Elements within the lad culture were also attracted to the nationalistic flavour of Conservative explanations for high unemployment. The Thatcherite mode of casting the problem in populist terms ('everyone is to blame') enjoys some popularity amongst certain elements within the young male working class, although it clearly was not popular amongst all young lads:

(in a discussion about unemployment)

BH: Whose fault do you think it is?
Robert: It's nobody's fault – it's just a slump. It's everybody's fault if it's nobody's fault.
Baz: Well, it's gotta be the Prime Minister really . . .
Robert: Naw, she's got nothin' to do with it.
Baz: No, she's closin' down places.
Robert: She's got no choice has she? 'Cos nobody'll buy the goods they're makin' and she's not closin' 'em down.

The manual labour lads as a group were generally split over their assessment of who is to blame for high unemployment.

The other major alternative to blaming government policy as a root cause of unemployment was a philosophy of self-blame. The adoption of this option is not particularly surprising considering the stress the MSC and scheme personnel place on deficiency and individuality. Many young people's assessment of their own personal situation was literally steeped in a language of self-blame and recrimination. Other trainees, who saw their movement on to the YTS as a positive step, projected the blame towards other groups of young people:

BH: Do you think young people leaving school are lacking in skills or do you think there are no jobs?
Jan: I don't know, I mean it depends on who you are. Some people put everything into school work and get everything out of it and some people don't bother. But I think in the last few years, I mean it's sort of been a fashion to sort of not do work at school and to be a sort of a down and out lazy layabout.

Liz: I mean I know a lot of people who are on the dole. A lot of people want to be unemployed. I know a few people who are enjoying themselves.

So while there existed a basis for anti-Thatcherism around the issue of unemployment, there were also competing explanations offered by other elements of the youth population. The essential point here is that at least most young people understood, while not always agreeing with, the arguments of Thatcherism (this is crucial when we look at young people's views on Labour Party policy). Blaming oneself was self-destructive, yet there was always the fear that someone else might be taking advantage of the situation (i.e. enjoying life on the dole). These individualist philosophies only worked to create internal divisions amongst working-class youths. The connection between 'shit jobs', 'govvy schemes' and 'life on the dole' often became swept aside, only to be replaced by self-blame and social division.

'Labour's lost millions': youth views on the Labour Party

Despite the fact that there exists a broad range of opinion on the link between schemes and high unemployment, many young people do view present government policies as a feature of the economic crisis. If political parties are somehow seen as implicated in the training and unemployment debate, how are the policies and images of the opposition Labour Party perceived by the young working class? If part of the argument is that the new vocationalism has helped to construct a variety of youth transitions and identities, how are these reflected in attitudes towards Labour? What confidence do young people have in the opposition party's ability to deal with the crisis of unemployment and the youth labour market?

The response of the majority of young people was one of complete disinterest. This was particularly true of two significant groups of young people – young women and those trainees defined as career oriented. However, an overall majority never mentioned the Labour Party in connection with their experiences of the YTS. Most were unaware and unconcerned about party policy on jobs, training and education. Many had difficulty in seeing how Labour had anything to do with their everyday lives. There appeared to be little communication between the supposed party of the working class and growing up/working/class in the 1980s. It was not only that the labour movement wasn't talking their language or had failed to have a grasp of their life world – unlike Thatcherism, for many it wasn't even saying anything intelligible.

For a section of working-class males – the manual labour lads – there appeared to be somewhat of a glimmer of tradition and inheritance which still connected a small number to the labour movement. The Labour Party was at least seen as the old 'party of jobs'. However, this connection was in no way guaranteed. Elements of conservatism also ran through aspects of lad culture as the following argument shows:

Robert: The thing I'd be, if yuh put all your heart into it, yuh might make a good job of it – more and likely the, they'd expand [small businesses]. You know why this country's gone to the pits, 'cos it is a pit.
Baz: That's why we got a woman Prime Minister.
Robert: Oh Baz, that's a scapegoat, that is – it was just as bad when Labour was in.
Baz: Yea, there was more jobs then though.

For many lads, like Baz, Labour was not seen for what it positively had to offer, but rather was viewed as the only option to the 'party of mass unemployment'. Often, this choice centred around a hatred of Mrs Thatcher as a woman, rather than any explicit class-based form of politics. Other lads also criticised the present government because it was headed by a woman and people like Andy were clearly ill-informed about the Labour alternative when he remarked, 'Put Michael Foot in,' (Neil Kinnock being Labour leader at the time). Many mentioned they would vote Labour, not because of their policies, but simply to get Thatcher out.

A second view was one of extreme distrust of any political party, including Labour. Garnie, whose position was also influenced by his individualist and survivalist philosophy, adequately represents this perspective. Although contemptuous of the Tories, he was also deeply suspicious of any kind of collective structure or political organisation:

BH: What about a new government, would that change things?
Garnie: Listen – you see them government up there, chattin' their nice speech and everything. When they get in,

I'll give you this now, they'll be badder than Mrs Thatcher, I'll give you that now. We're thinking' get Neil Kinnock in. He's talking sweet talk to make everyone elect 'im. He only wants to get in there get his rise, yuh know what I mean and go home yuh know and say yes – I got the bastards now haven't I? And he'll grin his teeth man, listen.

For Garnie there was no real difference between the Conservatives and Labour. In his view, all politics are motivated by self-interest and inevitably lead to 'corruption'. His political stance was government versus 'the people' and if the people weren't ready to stand up for themselves, then individuals had to do the best they could under the circumstances. It is obvious that there is no visible connection between how Garnie saw his day-to-day life unfolding and the policies of any political party. There would appear to be an insurmountable chasm between the everyday life of a young, black working-class lad and the principles and policies of a labour tradition.

The final stance towards the labour movement was evident in the analysis of the politicos. The main view they held was summed up in a short quip by Dan who stated, 'I think the Labour Party is quite confused on the matter of YTS.' Both Dan and Finchy were highly critical of the party's failure to condemn the YTS and set up a campaign to remove labour movement support. Neither thought the party took the youth question very seriously or were aware of what was actually happening to trainees on schemes. Nor were they confident that labour had any real solutions to high unemployment except maintaining glorified schemes and 'managing capitalism' better than the Tories. They were also dismayed at the trade union movement's apparent lack of concern over trainees' rights and conditions of service. At the same time, they both advocated unionisation to protect trainees' rights and both were active in various youth campaigns (some Labour Party inspired). In other words, while critical, they both saw the labour movement as the main opposition to Conservative policy and as the only existing political forum for representing the interests of the young working class.

Other young people who became politicised while on the scheme were less sure about the labour movement's motives in dealing with the youth issue. Because their political initiation sprung out of their exploitation while on the YTS and because they did not have any real attachment to a manual culture or worker politics, they questioned the role and motivation of the labour movement for getting involved in youth affairs:

Ben: There are groups like YTURC [Youth Trade Union Rights Campaign] and LPYS [Labour Party Young Socialists], Militant youth and all that sort of stuff. I think, I can't relate to them, I don't know why. Even that Liverpool thing [a demonstration], it was a great march and everything, I just felt a bit used somehow. Because it was mainly about saving the council and I felt that somehow I'd been used to build up the numbers. I mean the youth speakers did come on and give good speeches, but after that the speakers said, you know, if you want to join any of these organisations – there's LPYS down there, there's YTURC over there – you know, come along and fight for the Labour Party. But I don't want to fight for the Labour Party 'cos they're all shit-heads, same as the Conservatives. I think there needs to be some sort of independent political body to actually fight for these rights. I don't want to be labelled anything.

If the labour movement was not an alternative and no 'independent' political body actually existed, then more personal forms of politics could be adopted. Ben went on to pursue the youth issue and his lifestyle also reflected his movement into more personalised forms of politics such as animal rights, ecology and vegetarianism. Tracy, who also fell into this category, became involved in youth issues through the cultural field (Red Wedge and media work), and developed both a class and gender-based politics in the drama field.

In summary, it is clear that the transitions thrown up by the new vocationalism have influenced the identities and politics of a whole new generation of young people. The development of varied approaches towards working life, combined with changes in the domestic and non-work spheres and the construction of identities in the ethnic and sexual realm, have resulted in a massive differentiation of working-class youth transitions. Their orientations towards training schemes and views on the causes of youth unemployment partly reflect these different transitions and identities. These changes, in turn, have had serious implications in shifting young people's political perspectives and attachments away from a labour tradition. Suffice it to say that very few of these young people see the Labour Party as a viable alternative to Thatcherism and only a tiny minority have even a 'critical' link to the labour movement. How has the movement's failure to come to terms with the working-class youth differentiation under the new vocationalism led to a crisis of confidence amongst trainees? What implications do these different transitions and identities amongst the young have for Labour Party policy and trade union action? What central issues must the Left come to terms with if it is even to begin to develop an adequate politics of relevance and regeneration amongst the new young working class? It is to these questions that I turn to in the concluding chapter.

10

Conclusion: Youth Transitions and the Labour Movement

This book began by posing some key questions about the impact training is having on the process of identity formation and growing up working class. As such, I have sought to illuminate the issue through a close examination of young people's experiences on schemes and how these relate to broader cultural processes and other social sites. The central finding of the study is that a series of diverse working-class transitions are being forged in the context of the new vocationalism and that these changes have important implications for policy-making and the future of the labour movement. In this concluding chapter, I do not pretend to provide a blueprint for any specific political strategy, or even analyse existing labour movement training policies in any detail. Instead, I want to summarise the main transitions identified, and show how they raise a series of questions and problems the Left[1] must begin to address if it is to develop any semblance of an adequate politics of regeneration amongst school leavers, trainees and young workers.[2]

The whole weight of the ethnographic presentation and analysis has sought to give credibility to a level of experience and human subjectivity which has been designated as 'cultural'. Throughout, emphasis has been placed on the creative, active and partly self-making character of everyday life – even in those moments when human beings are most subject to the constaining features of social relations and institutional structures. The new vocationalism is not simply foisted on the young working class – somewhere along the way they impart something of their culture and focal concerns on their transitions into work and adulthood.

Yet, it is equally important not to overromanticise this level or limit young people's expressions to a unitary cultural logic or singular class form. This class 'essentialism' overlooks both the

195

generational specificity of class formation and ignores social division and differentiation within the youth population. Under close scrutiny, the young and future working class has not lived up to its 'implied' heritage as a unified social grouping. I have sought to move beyond this limiting perspective by emphasising how the cultural production of a variety of youth transitions into wage and domestic labour are the result of a complex ensemble of social relations and cultural forms expressed over a range of social sites (schemes, work, the home, youth culture, non-work activities, ethnic and sexual identities, politics, etc.). It is this more complex model which must inform a renewed understanding of class relations and identities and how these relate to existing forms of political organisation.

Working-class youth transitions: old and new

This case study has categorically demonstrated the continued persistence and application of certain class cultural forms in responding to the new vocationalism. These include the desire to leave formal schooling for work, an attraction for practically based knowledge and the use of work and the wage to gain a degree of independence and identity in the world. In some instances, schemes can be perceived as a substitute for these general class concerns. On the other hand, the continued utilisation of family and community networks to gain information about schemes and the local labour market, informal modes of solidarity against the YTS curriculum and a deep-rooted suspicion of State education and training provision, continue to be important buffers against any wholesale acceptance of current training ideologies. What is clear, however, is that these old forms are being rapidly eroded and displaced and anyway are unlikely to hold back the imposition of new transitions into working life. In fact, the most worked-up form of class solidarity and organisation – trade unionism – is clearly being threatened by elements of the new vocationalism.

Youth training, in conjunction with numerous other social, political and cultural changes, has worked to alter specific aspects of traditional working-class transitions into adult life. This is not to say that these traditional forms have completely disappeared by any means – residual elements remain for almost all trainees.

However, the existence of a series of new transitions and identities amongst working-class youth demonstrate the depth of some of these changes and shows how new routes overlay some of the traditional forms.

For example, new routes for young women, presently being constructed by the new vocationalism and through other social sites such as work, politics and leisure, are beginning to mediate traditional female transitions into waged work and the domestic sphere. This does not mean they are yet fully formed or completely independent of the domestic apprenticeship pattern. For example, paraprofessional transitions for female trainees represent a compromise between having a future in a 'people-minding' career and training for one's role as a domestic labourer (Cohen, 1982). Unfortunately, critical issues such as low pay, part-time work and a lack of promotional opportunities within caring occupations are often mediated by both society's and young women's future expectations around family life.

The notion of 'glam' transitions in training appear most remote from the traditional domestic apprenticeship. The idea of a 'career' or perhaps even self-employment for young women (in admittedly, feminine businesses) provides somewhat of a buffer on family and domestic expectations. However, the extreme individualism inherent in these transitions and the substitution of selling 'feminine sexuality' on the job, in place of domesticity, blunts any real collective understanding of one's class position or gender issues. While a minutely small number of young working-class women might achieve the status of a middle-class career or business woman, the vast majority will ultimately live out their dreams at the bottom end of a feminine service industry.

Two interesting patterns thrown up by the new vocationalism are the female version of the 'politico' and the 'youth culture enterpriser.' Although both are minority patterns, these types conceivably represent alternative sources of identity to both the domestic apprenticeship pattern and the ideological notion of a 'glam' career. The politico, formed primarily through the experience of dead-end jobs on the YTS, is able to develop a political consciousness and identity to the point where traditional female transitions are rejected and new identities can be forged. While their initial motivation stems from a concern over youth issues, support and involvement of these young women in a range of activities and organisations (i.e. radical youth work, community arts and media, and other arm's length labour movement organisations) can lead to more articulate forms of class and gender politics. The feminine version of a youth culture enterpriser, although more of an unknown political quantity, at least signals a different approach to traditional orientations towards wage and domestic labour. Alternative identities based around style, lifestyle, work and leisure may be either oppositional (counter-cultural) or lean towards a kind of 'cultural Thatcherism' (selling style and subcultures). Whatever the inflection, there exists a potential for shifting work and gender roles for a small subsection of working-class women.

The gendered transition into factory culture on the YTS for young women is perhaps best representative of the continued strength of the traditional domestic apprenticeship pattern, and hence contains many of its worst oppressions (in terms of both gender and class). While this transition/orientation is perhaps the most 'class conscious' of all the female routes on the YTS, its political potential if clearly undercut by patriarchal notions of skill and the exclusivity of craft-based worker organisations (Cockburn, 1983). Also limiting here are young women's continued reliance on strong definitions of femininity and domesticity, which ultimately work to deliver them into the double burden of wage and domestic labour (Pollert, 1981).

While the possibilities and options for young working-class men have always been more open than that of their female counterparts, they too have been quite firmly anchored around traditional transitions into manual labour through a highly masculine cultural apprenticeship. Generationally, this transition has been achieved primarily through the exclusive transmission of craft skills, accompanied by the feminisation of young male workers and their integration into a masculine shop floor political culture (Cohen, 1983, 1984; Willis, 1977). With the ascendance of the new vocationalism and the destruction of craft skills and restrictive practices, this traditional route has come under strong attack and has been seriously eroded.[3]

This traditional pattern today is most symbolically represented and taken up through the semi-skilled manual labour route characterised by the 'lad culture'. While remaining one of the most exuberant and lively opponents of the 'lifeskilling' ideology, this semi-skilled transition has been clearly undermined by the new vocationalism. The attack on manual skills has eroded the lads' already weak position in relation to craft apprentices, and the construction of a new lengthened trainee status on the YTS has broken many potential linkages between the informal culture and the organs of the labour movement. Additionally, the loosening of white, male working-class control over a 'patrimony of skill' has sometimes deeped the lads long-standing attachments to ethnocentric and sexist practices, thereby further isolating them from any developing anti-racist and anti-sexist forms of politics.

A new and growing male working-class pattern is the development of a white collar, middle-management transition on the YTS. This occurs primarily in the business, retail and food sectors – areas of the economy where self-employment is often promoted. In a growing service sector, new opportunities for upwardly mobile young men to supervise and police the labours of their contemporaries are being promoted. Their adherence to forms of individualism, loyalty to the company and the adoption of so called 'progressive' people-managing techniques, reflects a growing conservative and corporate view of business. Similarly, within the realm of leisure new identities steeped around middle-class forms of consumption are also developing. While there are obvious limits to how far such working-class trainees can progress up the company ladder, move into self-employment or achieve an upwardly mobile lifestyle, this transition and accompanying identity have important implications for a future fractured class structure.

Two further (minority) identities constructed in response to the new vocationalism are male 'politicos' and what I have called 'survivalists'. The politicos are of two types. The first group were involved in largely class-based forms of politics prior to their YTS experience and they utilised this framework to further develop critiques of youth training and the erosion of young workers' rights. Some of them attempted to struggle against the worst excesses of their scheme and organised other trainees into councils or unions. Their personal identities, however, were largely defined by their engagement in politics outside the workplace (radical political movements, CND, anti-racist struggles), and they were often frustrated with the labour movement's patriarchal and patronising stance on the youth question. The second type become involved in youth issues solely through their experience of the YTS and were even further removed from a labourist political position. Instead, their truly vocational orientation (or 'calling') was initially directed towards socially useful work rather than struggles over wage labour. Additionally, they tended to be concerned with more personalised and issue-oriented forms of political activity like youth rights, ecology and questions of gender. Identity was rooted not around wage labour or workerism but around vocation, socially useful production and personal politics.

Finally, there were the survivors. Experienced in street politics and highly suspicious of any formal organisation, the survivor used the new vocationalism to develop skills without any significant attachment to wage labour. While many of the strategies adopted tended towards a certain kind of individualism, this transition is rooted around a clear distinction between 'the people' and 'them' (meaning the government, employers, bureaucrats, etc.). While work skills are valued in their own right, identity formation relies more on leisure, style and perhaps one's links with the informal economy.

The emergence of a series of contemporary youth transitions and identities developed through the new vocationalism and other social sites, has important implications for assessing the rise of what has been called the 'manpower servicedom paradigm' (CCCS Education Group, 1981) and the absence of a radical youth politics within the labour movement. In other words, they speak to some of the strengths and weaknesses of the MSC's domination of the youth question and in doing so hint at some of the reasons behind the left's inability to formulate an alternative approach to working-class employment, lifestyle and training needs.

The shifting manpower servicedom paradigm

Some of the responses young people make towards the YTS points to the important fact that neither the MSC nor the government is in complete control of the youth labour 'problem'. Trainees' exploitation of 'progressivism' to gain space for their own focal concerns, and the creative mocking of life and social skills models by some young people, provides evidence of an implicit rejection of a curriculum based on a notion of deficiency. Additionally, a lack of proper skills training and the transparency of MSC notions of training for a career are recognised by many young people, who continue to rely on family and community knowledge about schemes and the local labour market. Finally, very few trainees are taken in by the government's insistence that the allowance is a payment for training rather than a substitute wage.

The MSC's lack of overall control is also evidenced by a number of transitions inadvertently formed through the new vocationalism. For example, the fragility of their ideology is clearly expressed by the formation of politico types on the YTS. How, in effect, if schemes are so indoctrinating can this transition be explained? Yet, a sizeable proportion of young people do become disillusioned with the government's empty promises and a minority of these emerge with a critical perspective, not only of the YTS but about the entire state of youth affairs. It is this minority that often continues to be engaged in a whole range of youth and other political issues.

Similarly, other groups of young people like the survivor types utilise schemes to gain skills (sometimes for the informal economy) and shelter themselves from unscrupulous employers. Realistic appraisals of job opportunities and the poor quality of work experience placements can also produce strong 'workless cultures' amongst sections of the young population. Many of the manual labour lads and factory lasses also continue to be socialised into informal cultures of work which stresses qualities which run at cross purposes to entrepreneurship and 'corporateness' (worker/management cooperation at work). Despite its dominant position, the MSC is unable to contain these disparate knowledges and maintain a monopoly on all young people on the YTS.

These are some of the soft spots in the new vocationalism's armour. At the same time, however, the MSC and the government have always understood, albeit in often partial and distorted ways, something about working-class experiences of formal education and young people's desire to move into the world of work and adulthood. Their success in mobilising a kind of consensus around the youth training issue has been due, in part, to the way they have built upon aspects of the cultural level, while responding to changing class conditions. The MSC has in fact learned a great deal from the failure of education and from early criticisms of their own deficiency model of working-class school leavers. This original stance, whereby unemployment was disengaged from its economic and political base and reattached to working-class deficiencies (primarily in the educational sphere), while effective, hardly placed the MSC or the government in a favourable position in the eyes of young people.

In the face of continuing public and informal critiques of schemes and in order to regain credibility, I believe there has been a slow shift in the dominant manpower training paradigm (this shift also generally applies to Employment Training). The first change has been a move away from a strict 'deficiency' model to one which stresses 'opportunity' and 'choice'. This developing position is clearly consistent with the careerist ideology evident in some of the schemes examined in this case study. The shift from personal blame (a negative image) to fulfilling one's potential (a positive one) is, I would argue, a more general feature of the third term of Thatcherism. For example, the MSC's televised slogan on the YTS – 'I can't do that . . . can I?' – paints a rosy picture of progressive skill development and unlimited career prospects through training. The main element of this developing paradigm is on providing increased opportunities for already existing working-class skills and desires, through a directed and disciplined training programme.

The other key element of this new manpower servicedom paradigm is the way in which the MSC has successfully dealt with the relationship between developing careerist transitions and traditional working-class routes into work. For instance, the MSC, like the Thatcher government, has heavily promoted the idea that new career opportunities for school leavers exist in the service sector of the economy and in self-employment. These new opportunities are contrasted to the highly limited scope of traditional working-class transitions into wage and domestic labour. In this scenario, new jobs and working practices signal a move away from 'outdated' notions of class to a modernised, enterprising and socially stratified workforce. The existence of a variety of new work identities created by the YTS – such as glam and paraprofessional orientations, male white collar and middle-managers and youth enterprisers – are evidence of the pervasiveness of this growing ideology. At the same time, the new vocationalism's emphasis on 'transferable' and 'broad-based' skills and equal opportunities has begun to strip away internally the collective power of traditionally male craft occupations.

It is through this mechanism that one can see how the new vocationalism effectively contrasts the notion of 'opportunity' with the limiting nature of traditional working-class transitions, while underhandedly seeking to construct a pliable and malleable type of workforce. Such a perspective clouds real working-class issues such as decent employment rights, the desire for a skill and the unspeakable terrain of worker control and participation in industry. Socially useful production and real choices and opportunities within a truly egalitarian society are also obscured from the agenda. Nevertheless, it is here where the labour movement's own social democratic repertoire of abolishing class and creating equal access is cruelly twisted back on itself. For example, the trade unions' historical complicity in maintaining the generational, sexual and racial division of labour through the exclusiveness of the apprenticeship system is boldly exposed by the proponents of the new vocationalism. Similarly, the Labour Party's historical project of representing working-class interests are defined as 'archaic' and 'unmodern'. By appropriating elements of the social democratic project and recasting them under a more conservative agenda, the new vocationalism has effectively silenced any real alternative from the labour movement.

How has the labour movement responded to this manpower servicedom paradigm and what implications do the variety of transitions identified in this study have for the future of the movement?

Labour movement responses and dilemmas

From the perspective of the labour movement, the existing field of youth identities and transitions do not look particularly promising in terms of regenerating its base. The young working class, as a whole social group, is not interested in existing forms of party politics and, as I have argued, the very structure of schemes appears to make trade unions largely irrelevant for most trainees. Only vague links appear between the labour movement and some of the minority and declining youth transitions.

For example, one might think that the subgroup of politicos

would possess at least tacit support of trade unions and the Labour Party. Yet it is clearly the case that in addition to the politicos being produced in too small numbers to form an adequate basis of recruitment, they are, for the most part, disenchanted with the main organs of the labour movement. The male politicos are either to the left of the party, fed up with the patronising stance of trade unions, or their politics increasingly are directed towards more personalised or issue-oriented campaigns. For young women politicos there is often an uneasy relationship with the labour movement's style and mode of organisation.

A traditional base of support would also appear to lie with the male skilled and semi-skilled manual white working class and with the factory lasses. However, the construction of a trainee identity on the YTS has begun to erode existing links between informal cultures, trade union organisation and party policies. And anyway, the factory lasses, while sometimes recruited, have never been taken too seriously by manual trade unions (Pollert, 1981) or political parties. Finally, the decision to base the future of a political movement solely on a declining manufacturing workforce can only be described as a recipe for disaster.

The labour movement is perhaps more well aware of this declining base of traditional support than it is with what is being constructed in its place. The whole thrust of the new vocationalism is towards a vision of a modern, flexible and socially stratified workforce. The construction of new glamorous jobs and people-minding careers for young women and middle-management positions for young men, while largely illusory, are based around real shifts in the labour market. The infusion of these transitions with notions of social mobility and individualism are clearly barriers to any real identification with the labour movement. Similarly, the rise of entrepreneurship and the flourishing of a small business culture on some schemes does not square well with the functions and future of trade unionism. It is hard to see how the TUC's continued support for the YTS or Labour's own plan for training will halt these effects of the new vocationalism.

The labour movement then seems to be unable to respond adequately to the more varied and complex transitions and identities that characterise growing up/working/class on training schemes. This may be partly to do with the split perceptions of labour on the youth question. As Cohen (1985) convincingly argues, some sections of the labour movement remain wedded to an archaic image of the young working class, which understands the problems of youth unemployment and training through the lens of the 1930s (the labourist position). Other factions have been drawn much closer to the manpower servicedom paradigm, whereby it is asserted that equal opportunities and training for an expanding service sector economy will open up new and exciting job prospects for the young. Neither of these positions actually deals with or is based upon the wide range of practices, experiences and identities currently being constructed under the new vocationalism.

For example, the assertion that general working-class forms and cultural apprenticeships continue to have some impact on youth transitions in no way vindicates the labourist perspective. As I have argued throughout this book, even these quite general forms are worked up and applied differently by various sub-sections of working-class youth. As such, the simple existence of these forms never guaranteed any formal support for the labour movement. Even the most worked-up form (i.e. trade unionism) has produced individuals who, rather than supporting a labour tradition, become drawn towards elements of Thatcherism (i.e. supportive of tax cuts, the purchase of council houses, share ownership, etc.). Continued decline and changes within the manufacturing and craft sphere (such as new technology, the institution of flexible working practices and the demise of the closed shop) will no doubt weaken what is left of this political culture for many young people anyway.

At the same time, the service sector ideology need not imply that the new vocationalism is magically ushering in a modernised, leisured or classless youth population. New lifestyle orientations do not mean that work ceases to be an important source of identity, nor does employment in so called glam or white collar jobs signal the demise of workplace grievances or the formation of new class relations at work. The utter confusion thrown up by these blanket perspectives has virtually ensured that the debate about school leavers and the labour market has been dominated by the manpower servicedom paradigm.

I want to argue that in order for the Left and the labour movement to advance beyond these narrow perspectives, they must come face to face with two inter-related issues raised by this study of working-class youth transitions. The first issue concerns how the new vocationalism has affected and influenced the mechanisms by which the labour movement has historically regenerated itself through a manual political culture. The second issue is how the movement has sought to deal with the training needs of a differentiated young working class, almost wholly within the narrow confines of the manpower service paradigm.

Perhaps part of the reason why the labour movement has failed to respond particularly well to changing transitions and the new vocationalism has been its historical reliance on a quite archaic mode of regenerating its youth base. Cohen (1983) has argued that the movement has traditionally based itself upon a peculiarly patriarchal apprenticeship of young people, and as such has always had a hand in perpetuating the generational division of labour. This patronising attitude towards young people has often gone hand in hand with the exclusion of women and black people from certain types of labour and from positions of power within the movement. As post-war changes began to breakdown these cultural apprenticeships and as young working-class people started to construct new identities in other social sites (i.e. youth culture), the older mode of recruitment no longer appealed or functioned effectively.

For instance, the trade union movement, through the apprenticeship system, has always colluded in the generational division of labour. While this protectivism can be partly justified in relation to the forces of capital, this historical response took on a particularly patriarchal form. For instance, there is clear evidence that these cultural apprenticeships were largely beneficial to young men, with young women and black people banished to the margins of the household and the economy (Hartmann, 1979; Beechey, 1985; Campbell, 1984; Phizacklea and Miles, 1980; Lawrence, 1982b; Cohen, 1983). In their effort to maintain and protect a core section of the workforce, unions colluded in the subordination of young male workers as factory skivvies and young women as future domestic labourers. With the erosion of crafts skills (Braverman, 1974; Kelly, 1982), feminist critiques of what constitutes 'productive labour' (Fox, 1980) and with the rise of competing sites of youth identity (Cohen, 1983), the contradiction of regeneration through subordination has become even more transparent to young people.

I want to argue that despite some cosmetic changes, the trade union movement has yet to take the problem of regeneration seriously and still maintains a patronising attitude on the youth issue. Of course, the stance of different unions on the youth training debate (Eversley, 1986) and the varied perspectives of trade unionists on Area Manpower Boards (see Randell, n.d.) would require a more in-depth analysis than is possible to provide here. However, it is clear that on a general level the Trade Union Congress (TUC) has, in colluding with the YTS, been as much a part of the problem as the provider of solutions. Although critical of many of the government training initiatives, the trade union leadership has steadfastly refused to boycott the scheme, even over the issue of 'compulsion', and instead, in the words of one major union, has argued that its continued participation is 'the best way to safeguard our members in permanent jobs' and young people in training.[4] Yet, both this study and other related research (YTS Monitoring Unit, 1985) have categorically shown that the very structure of the YTS largely prevents any effective participation and interaction between trainees and trade unions. The TUC's involvement at the level of AMBs and its initial concern with existing members must be contrasted with its complete ineffectiveness at a grassroots level, and a total lack of understanding of young people's everyday experiences on schemes. This blindness to 'anti-trade union' types of transitions on the YTS and a lack of knowledge about young people's whole lifeworld has fundamental implications for the further demise of trade unionism, even though some individual unions have recently begun the task of responding to young workers.

The Labour Party, too, has been unsure of how to respond to changing patterns and identities within the working class and hence how to regenerate enthusiasm and support for its policies amongst the young. The attack on Militant as the sole reason why youth membership in the party is declining is a diversion from some of the real failures why Labour no longer connects very well with the youth issue. Like the trade unions, the party has also historically based its regeneration upon a political apprenticeship which patronisingly subordinated its youth members and sections (Cohen, 1983). The 'split perception', referred to earlier, has seriously afflicted the party's stance on the youth question. For example, the 'labourist' camp has lulled members into believing that if unemployment and training schemes are criticised enough then the young working class will automatically drift towards the party as a matter of course. Other elements, more powerful in the party, have erred in the opposite direction. They see the move away from class and a concern with promoting equal opportunities in training for new service sector jobs as the way to win young people over. In large measure, this perspective has been incorporated into what has been referred to as the manpower servicedom paradigm. Neither position is based upon a rigorous analysis of young people's transitions, identities or focal concerns either inside or outside the world of work. In other words, Labour does not quite know how to respond to a diverse youth population nor does it have a policy which situates the training/employment debate within the broader confines of an overall youth policy (which cuts across many of the social sites and cultural processes looked at here).

Instead of developing a youth politics based around people's own cultural experiences and transitions, Labour continues to rely on a past history of statist solutions to the problem, this time heavily burdened by the manpower servicedom paradigm. This reliance on statism, and the contradictions generated by it, is not, of course, limited to Labour's training policies but is linked to a set of general disjunctures between political, economic and cultural processes. Two of the most obvious limits (or contradictions) of the post-war social democratic project have been the problem of managing but not controlling the capitalist economy and the attempt to represent working-class interests through the party, while at the same time trying to eradicate class distinctions. For example, the representation of working-class educational interests through the State, whereby working-class people were deemed as objects of policy rather than as participants, clearly led to a growing distrust of state provision and laid the foundations for the Black Papers and Thatcherite visions of 'parental choice' (CCCS Education Group, 1981). Many of these contradictions are evident in Labour Party policy on training and demonstrate why they offer little alternative to the new vocationalism. A concern with access (equal opportunities) rather than with training content and control of the curriculum, reliance on 'experts' rather than popular sentiments and cultural forms and a programme directed increasingly towards economic efficiency rather than socially useful production and cultural creativity, continue to haunt the halls of party policy on employment and training.[5]

Labour is also clearly confused over how to respond to the recomposition of the young working class under the new vocationalism. The failure to grasp the intimate relationship between the new transitions and the older patterns has resulted in a virtual silencing of a radical youth policy. With a declining manual labour base and the growth of self-employment and the service industries, Labour has become caught in the middle of traditional loyalties and a lack of understanding of the new youth transitions. On the training issue, their views have largely been appropriated by the manpower servicedom paradigm – providing bigger (statist) and better (equal opportunities) youth training schemes. By plastering over some of their own historical contradictions, Labour has been forced to address the issue of youth unemployment and training at the political and even individual level (Finn, 1982), rather than pursue a whole gamut of cultural policies based around youth experiences (Willis, 1985). There is more than a grain of truth in the charge that the MSC model is, in fact, Labour's paradigm for training (CCCS Education Group, 1981).

These then are some of the weaknesses of the trade union and labour movement in relation to the youth training issue. The movement's continued reliance on patronising modes of regeneration, the inability to understand and deal with the relationship between traditional and developing youth identities and transitions (constructed across a range of social locations), a collusion in maintaining a generational division of labour and the utilisation of statist and corporate rather than cultural solutions in dealing with training and the economy, have all contributed to the crisis. These issues and contradictions must be exposed, debated and traced back to their source.

More recently, there has been a series of hopeful signs and discussions around the youth question, particularly within certain trade unions and in the party's Youth Forum.[6] As one contributor (who remains nameless) to the party debate on the youth question has put it:

Youth policy must be explicitly for, about and directed at youth. It must not be a policy by default – subsumed under or led by other policies addressed to other issues: 'training' to cover up unemployment and get the kids off the street; selection and 'realism' in education as an illusory answer to the structural problems of capitalism and contradictory demands of employers; law n' order issues finding scapegoats in youth; benefit cuts to discipline and force youth labour into low paid work. Let's *start* from the direct interests of youth and derive education, benefit and policing policies from that point – not use youth to solve or displace other people's problems.

On a grassroots level, there are individuals and organisations that are working with young people on the training and other issues (i.e. Youth Trade Union Rights Campaign; Labour Listens; Red Wedge). Some local authorities have appointed youth policy advisors and organised youth councils to rethink and reformulate their whole range of services to meet the needs of a diverse youth population (Willis, 1985), rather than opt for a simplistic 'training solution'.

Any effective and radical solution to the youth question must begin to build upon some of these wide-ranging, imaginative and fragile initiatives. Neither a traditional 'labourism' with its magical conjuring up of the 'old' working class nor a borrowed 'manpower servicedom paradigm' focusing solely around opportunities within training will suffice in providing a grassroots youth politics from below. An alternative perspective to current prescriptions is to begin the slow and democratic process of building on the existing and varied cultural transitions and identities currently being constructed in the wake of the 'long transition'.

Notes

1 Introduction: Class, Culture and Youth Training

1. The importance of schemes like the Youth Training Scheme (YTS) in displacing the 'problem' of youth unemployment is reflected in the fact that while unemployment in the 16–17-year-old age group has dropped (and is set to disappear under the new Social Security Act – i.e. this group is now ineligible to claim income support), the numbers in training have nearly doubled since 1983. By May 1988, 70 per cent of 16-year-old school leavers were joining the YTS as were 25 per cent of 17 year olds (*Unemployment Bulletin*, 28, Autumn 1988). The total in training at 30 September was 435 293 (*Employment Gazette*, vol. 96, November 1988).

   The growing importance of training in displacing unemployment and in structuring young people's movement into work should also partly offset recent suggestions that a dramatic fall in the numbers of school leavers will effectively solve the problem of youth unemployment and lead to a buoyant youth labour market. Historical research has shown that youth employment prospects have always been worse than that of the general population, even in times of economic growth (Casson, 1979). Furthermore, while the number of 16–17 year olds dropped nearly 200 000 since October 1983 (and are set to drop a further 25 per cent to 1995), numbers in training nearly doubled over this same period. Projected entrants on to the YTS alone will remain above 350 000 even up to 1990–1. Youth training (in whatever form) will remain an important structuring influence on the working lives of millions for years to come.

2. It should be mentioned that while the focus of attention has recently shifted to the government's new adult training scheme (Employment Training or ET), the YTS remains the most well-established and respected programmes in government circles. It is interesting to note that while much of the initial controversy over ET revolved around the issue of the 'voluntary' nature of the scheme, the necessary legislation making 16–17 year olds ineligible for income support has virtually made the YTS compulsory. Furthermore, it is clear that ET bears the major ideological and organisational blueprint of

211

the YTS (i.e. the combination of off-the-job training and work experience, the use of private training agencies and the twin notions of 'deficiency' and 'opportunity'), so much of what I refer to as the new vocationalism (see note 4) also generally applies to the adult scheme. An in-depth study of trainee's experiences on the YTS can in fact tell us a lot of what to expect with the new scheme. Finally, one must not forget the millions of young people who have gone through the YTS since its inception in 1983 and the Youth Opportunities Programme (YOP) before that. It should be obvious that in targeting the 18–24-year-old group, many of ET's future participants may in fact be former (disenchanted?) YOP/YTS trainees.

3. In the midst of writing this book, the 1987 Employment Bill redefined and curtailed the remit of the Manpower Services Commission (MSC) to concentrate solely upon the field of training. In doing so the name of the MSC was also changed to the Training Commission. One of the reasons for this change, I would argue, was the negative images and distrust of the MSC in the minds of many people, including the young. However, following the TUC Congress decision to boycott the government's newest scheme, ET, the short-lived Training Commission was abolished and the YTS, along with all the other training programmes temporarily became the responsibility of the Department of Employment until a new structure is put into place. It is for these reasons that I have chosen to retain the original name here. For many, training schemes will always be associated with the initials MSC.

4. Critical analyses of the MSC's views on school leavers can be found in Finn (1984, 1987), Benn and Fairley (1986) and Rees and Atkinson (1982). The 'new vocationalism' as a term of analysis has been most well developed in the work of Cohen (1982, 1984). As Cohen (1982, p. 46) explains:

> Under the old system, 'vocational courses' were a misnomer for quite specialised training in the practical skills for a particular trade or occupation, in other words a form of apprenticeship . . . In 'lifeskilling', however, the relationship is reversed – the image of apprenticeship is used to obscure the fact that the one thing most of these courses are not about is the mastery of specific techniques or skills of manual labour.

Cohen (1984, p. 105) goes on to argue:

> I want to suggest that this new approach and emphasis given to 'skilling' in both secondary school curriculum and 16–19 training provision is primarily about the inculcation of social discipline;

but this is no simple harking back to 'Victorian values'; on the contrary, it represents an attempt to construct a more mobile form of self-discipline, adapted to changing technologies of production and consumption, and to link this to a modern version of self-improvement aimed at the reserve army of youth labour.

It is interesting to note that the new vocationalism's shift from the notion of deficiency to one of opportunity (see the concluding chapter), has occurred precisely around the same time that the YTS has been effectively made compulsory.

5. While laying the blame for unemployment on so-called 'high' benefit levels and restrictive trade union practices is a feature of Thatcherism and the 'New Right', it has its origins in the doctrine of 'economic liberalism' promoted by the writings of Frederick Hayek (1980) and Milton Freedman, among others.

6. Examples of this type of analysis include Scofield *et al.* (1983), Allum and Quigley (1983) and Goldstein (1984). A more sophisticated analysis of the relationship between Thatcherism and the MSC is found in Davies (1984).

7. In prioritising the cultural experiences of young people, I have inadvertently curtailed any extended discussion of the role YTS trainers and tutors might play in developing an alternative youth politics. Instead, I have opted to show how different teaching pedagogies reflect the varied training regimes and managing strategies of training providers (primarily in Chapter 3). The absence of 'significant others' is a necessary and indeed self-imposed limitation of the study created out of a desire to reflect the least heard voices of those experiencing the new vocationalism. In defence, it should be pointed out that there has been a distinct lack of ethnographic and participant observation studies of young people's training experiences. For two studies of the Youth Opportunities Programme (the YTS's predecessor) see Williamson (1982) and Stafford (1981). Coffield *et al.* (1986) also contains a chapter on young people's views of 'govvy schemes'. For a very suggestive discussion of working-class transitions and the new vocationalism see Cohen (1984). For other relevant analyses of the cultural dimensions of working-class youth transitions and the MSC, see CCCS Education Group (1981, Chapter 11) and Finn (1983).

8. While the primary focus of this research concerns working-class youth, it is impossible to theorise class and generation in isolation to other social relations such as gender and race. Gender, for instance, forms a clear 'fault line' through class experiences, identities and destinations. Due to a history of male bias in the youth

literature, I have tried, whenever possible, to prioritise the experiences and transitions of young women in order to avoid gender from being simply tacked on to 'malestream' class theory. For a discussion of gender and the YTS see Cockburn (1987). In Part II, I try to look at the interaction between these two relations in order to explain partly how a series of diverse transitions get constructed under the new vocationalism.

The relationship between race and class is also crucial for theorising around the differential transitions and identities young people come to construct on the YTS. Institutional and personal forms of racism from Careers Officers, scheme personnel, employers, training officers and white trainees have an important impact on the responses and life chances of black trainees. The most significant empirical findings are young black people's segregation on to community-based schemes and their virtual absence on employer-led programmes (Cross, 1985; Pollert, 1985; REITS, 1985). Also important are forms of racism from white trainees and the labour movement's inadequate analysis of the roots of racism (see Chapter 8). Even white researchers have been centrally involved in helping to construct black youth as a 'problem' or 'deviant' (Lawrence, 1982a). As such, I have concentrated less on articulating specific black working-class cultural forms and instead have emphasised the issue of 'white racism'.

While I hope this analysis has gone some way in attempting to incorporate these two fundamental social relations into the development of an expanded notion of class, at the same time, it will become clear that the variety of transitions and identities within the youth population supersedes any simple combination of race, class and gender. Not all young women obediently followed the same path to the kitchen sink. Similarly, black transitions varied from manual labour orientations to white collar and careerist tendencies. That is not to say that these relations are unimportant, but rather that they can only ever form the backdrop for more specific paths, choices and actions. Additionally, like class, race and gender cannot exist as determining social relations in isolation. The point is to begin to look at multiply divided subjects in a multiply divided society. This does not negate looking at a social group through the 'lens' of one of these categories, as long as other social relations are taken into account in the analysis.

9. For example see Finn (1981), Corrigan (1979), Connell *et al.* (1982), Dwyer *et al.* (1984), Thomas (1980).

10. For two very different critiques of Willis's work see McRobbie (1980) and Walker (1986).

11. I use the qualifying term 'approximately' to make the important point that ethnographic and participant observation work is impossible to quantify in any exact way. For example, it is difficult to give every young person I interviewed the same numerical status. Some became very close friends, whom I still see, while other young people were interviewed over a shorter period of time. Coffield *et al.* (1986) also make this point.

I should also, at this point, make clear my claim of representativeness. In terms of the structure of the YTS in the area, the types of schemes trainees were chosen from constitute nearly 80 per cent of the training provision in the area (i.e. 50 per cent of places are taken up by PTAs alone, which is why they figure so highly in the study). Just under 50 per cent of the trainees interviewed were women and 29 per cent were classified as black. Both these figures are roughly representative of the overall composition of the YTS in the area. Finally, while the study does claim some representativeness in both the West Midlands and in certain comparable areas in the North of England, other regions (like the South, Scotland and Wales) would have to be looked at in terms of their own regional economies and scheme structure.

12. For a discussion of the role of ethnography in cultural studies, see Johnson (1983). For a more detailed discussion of the sociological roots of cultural ethnography see Hollands (1985c). Other writings on method that have influenced the research here are Willis (1980), Stanley and Wise (1983), Connell (1983), Finch (1984), McRobbie (1982) and Marcus and Fisher (1986). For a discussion of how the politics of method figured in this particular research see the methodological appendix to my PhD thesis 'Working Class Transitions and the Youth Training Scheme', Centre for Contemporary Cultural Studies, University of Birmingham, 1988. Unfortunately, for reasons of space, I am unable to include the chapter here.

13. Mode A has been described as being 'employer-led' with Mode B, while managed by the MSC, being farmed out to community projects, training workshops and information technology centres run by local authorities and voluntary organisation.

14. See my pamphlet 'The Great Training Robbery Continues' (TURC, 1985) for an in-depth look at private training agencies on the YTS.

2 From School to Schemes

1. Class-based experiences of schooling, although not determining, are important in understanding how young people respond to going on

to schemes and what they do when they actually get there (see, for example, the case studies in Chapter 3). Due to the self-imposed limitations of the study, I have relied on young people's major recollections of their school years. The point is not to provide a comprehensive presentation of these experiences (this has been conducted elsewhere), but rather use them to help comprehend young people's orientations towards the YTS. For discussions of schooling, see Hargreaves (1967), Sharp (1976), Willis (1977), Davies (1979), Ball (1981), Griffin (1985), Lees (1986), Stanworth (1983).

2. A large-scale survey of the young unemployed in a nearby town showed that, overall, 56 per cent of males compared to 47 per cent of females said they wanted to leave school 'very much'. White working-class males were the most overtly disaffected with school, with 61 per cent saying they wanted to leave 'very much'. See Willis (1985, p. 203).

3. For historical examinations of working-class responses to compulsory schooling see Humphries (1981) and CCCS Education Group (1981).

4. These figures are from the local Careers Service and pertain to the period in which this research was conducted.

5. While the local MSC produced a directory of the YTS in the city, it was not in a form that could be used by school leavers to choose between schemes.

3   Off-the-Job Training and Lifeskilling

1. As one of these components, off-the-job training is designed to provide young people with special opportunities to learn about basic skills, the world of work, the world outside employment, job specific and broadly related skills, personal effectiveness and the ability to transfer learned skills (labelled as learning opportunities or scheme outcomes). The eight design elements and six learning opportunities making up the one-year scheme were as follows:

Eight design elements
  (1) induction
  (2) occupationally based training
  (3) thirteen weeks off-the-job training/education
  (4) planned work experience
  (5) core areas (numbers, communication, problem solving, manual dexterity, computer literacy/information technology)

    (6)   guidance and counselling
    (7)   assessment
    (8)   reviewing and recording/achievement and certification

Six learning opportunities
    (1)   basic skills
    (2)   the world of work
    (3)   the world outside employment
    (4)   job specific and broadly related skills
    (5)   personal effectiveness
    (6)   ability to transfer skills, learning to learn, skill ownership

2. The framework of the two-year scheme is simplified into two main scheme inputs – off-the-job training and planned work experience and four outcomes – personal effectiveness, competence in a job and/or range of occupational skills, competence in a range of transferable core skills and ability to transfer skills and knowledge to new situations.

3. In fact, not long after the YTS had begun a memorandum from the Department of Employment to the MSC was leaked which contained the following quotation: 'Matters related to the organisation and functioning of society in general should be excluded unless they are relevant to trainees work experience' (*The Guardian* 12/10/83). Schemes deemed 'political' could potentially be shut down under the MSC's contract with managing agents.

4. This is not to say that all private training agencies adopted a purely 'entrepreneurial' pedagogy. However, it was clear from my various visits to different types of schemes that PTAs were generally more pro-business in their orientation. Outside the YTS, it is interesting to note that there were some 751 simulated companies organised under the Youth Enterprise Scheme (*The Guardian* 26/11/85).

5. While a larger group sense allowed for moments of solidarity amongst all the lads, these smaller grouplets were almost categorically divided along racial lines. While black youth congregated together largely to deflect institutional and personal forms of racism, the white lads' choice of mates revolved around white ethnicity and a belief in their exclusive inheritance of labour power (see Chapter 8). While some researchers have argued that there are points of contact between black and white youth cultures (Jones, 1986; Hebdige, 1979), racism remains a stable feature of white lad culture.

6. As I was physically unable to attend the residential, I have had to rely on young people's recollections of the event.

4   Work Experience and the Trainee Identity

1. While the next chapter seeks to unearth some of the more specific orientations towards work on the YTS, here I deal with the construction of a more general and abstract form of youth labour, which allows for and provides the basis for the development of more particular types of transitions into work and adulthood explored in Part II.
2. I want to re-emphasise that this 'survivalist' approach is only one response black youths develop in relation to a racist training and labour market. Despite obstacles, some in fact do conform to career-ist and middle-management ideologies. Just as there is no one single class response, neither is there a monolithic racial culture uniting all black youth.
3. For a comprehensive examination of the employment status of trainees and young workers see the Income Data Services, *Employment Law Supplement*, 51, December 1987.
4. 'Gofer' and 'dogsbody' are basically slang terms referring to the inferior way young people are often treated at the workplace ('gofer this and gofer that').
5. Some trainees gained additional satisfaction and status when work sponsors topped up their allowance. This was despite the fact that many of them only received extra money for working overtime or unsocial hours (weekends), and the level of remuneration was extremely low. In this way schemes clearly work to delegitimise employee rights and union rates of pay for overtime.
6. These cases are drawn from both personal contact with trainees and from literally hundreds of logged queries and problems concerning the scheme as relayed through a local 'YTS Helpline'.
7. Many of these same arguments apply to the debate over trade union participation on the Employment Training scheme.

5   Youth Differentiation, Training, and the World of Work

1. These elements form part of a wider ideology which has been described as the 'manpower servicedom paradigm' (CCCS Education Group, 1981), which will be examined in more detail in the concluding chapter.
2. For a comprehensive examination of how the YTS is actively involved in maintaining gendered identities and transitions into work, see Cockburn (1987). Additional material on women and training can be found in Brelsford *et al.* (1982), Wickham (1986)

and Fawcett Society (1985). Study after study has also shown that young blacks are underrepresented on employer-led schemes. See YETRU (1987), REITS (1985) and Fenton *et al.* (1984). Very few studies, however, have dealt with the more specific 'intra-class' identities and transitions constructed under the new vocationalism. For a good preliminary discussion see Cohen (1984). For a general study and discussion of working-class youth differentiation, see Jenkins (1983).

6 At Home and Out on the Street: Domestic Labour and Public Space

1. This research is reported in G. Forest, 'Abolish Kitchen Slavery', *The Next Step*, 36, September 1986. For more general discussions see Oakley (1974), Luxton (1980) and Barrett (1980).
2. In all these cases the single parent was the mother. Local statistics show that approximately 89 per cent of single parent households are headed by women.
3. For a localised and historical examination of the relationship between mothers and daughters in the area see the ethnographic studies conducted by Beasley (1985) and Duruz (1985).
4. I should state very clearly here that the primary purpose of this addendum is to use such an 'event' to combat simplistic and incomplete explanations of so-called 'hooligan' behaviour. I should also mention here that the lads' account of the fight is only one side of the story. In no way am I seeking to condone the 'negative' aspects of the situation (i.e. the expression of masculinity and the reproduction of white racism), nor am I seeking to implicate the black youths as responsible for the fight. Indeed, the exact cause of the altercation remains unknown to me to this day.

7 Non-work Activity and the Substitute Wage: The Limits of Leisure

1. There is now a wealth of material on the concept of leisure and leisure studies is a bona fide field of inquiry. Conventional definitions of leisure can be found in Parker (1972) and Roberts (1978), amongst others. Critiques of the 'conventional wisdom' of leisure studies can be found in Hollands (1988), Clarke and Critcher (1985) and Hargreaves (1986). Feminist critiques of leisure are contained

in the writings of Hargreaves (1982) and Deem (1986). For discussions of youth and leisure see Roberts (1983) and Hollands (1985b).

2. At the crux of Cohen's (1972) theory is the main thesis that working-class youth subcultures are formed out of the fragmentation of three main elements of working-class community: (a) extended kinship networks, (b) the working-class neighbourhood, and (c) changes in the structure of the local economy (particularly as they affect the young). It is important to keep in mind these economic, occupational and domestic aspects of youth subcultures stressed by Cohen when evaluating the current situation facing the young working class.

3. Clearly the whole issue of the role TV plays in the lives of young people was beyond the confines of the present study.

4. Red Wedge is a musical entourage of singers and entertainers involved in getting young people interested in the political process. While supported by the Labour Party, Red Wedge's political stance is probably best described as 'broadly' left.

8 Divided Youth: White Racism and Male Sexist Practice

1. For a survey of this latter material see Humphries (1981).

2. The Swann report rejects the view that racism is a 'white British problem' on the grounds that it exists in other countries and between ethnic groups. The full title of the report is *Education for All – The Report of the Committee of Inquiry into the Education of Children from Ethnic Minority Groups* (London: HMSO, 1985). For an internal critique of the report see Eggleston (1986).

3. In his own work, Lawrence (1982b) goes on to outline what he sees as the roots of racism in Britain's capitalist/imperialistic past, the pathology of the black family, the moral panic phenomenon revolving around black youth and notions of deprivation and underachievement in black culture.

4. This survey was reported in *The Guardian* 20/2/86.

5. This research was reported in *Multicultural Education Review*, 5, Spring 1986.

6. Many people prefer to use the term 'uprising' to explain what happened in Britain's inner-cities in 1981 and 1985. I have used the term 'riot' here to simply reflect young white people's views of the these disturbances, particularly as they perceived the role black youth played in these events.

7. Much of the material on the sexism of male working-class youth has

been part of larger pieces of work. For example see Robins and Cohen (1978) and Willis (1977). For an exception to this see Wood (1984).

8. For exceptions to this see Cockburn (1983, 1987).

9 Youth Politics In Thatcherland

1. This notion of 'extremism' is usually reserved for those organisations of the left (i.e. Militant, the Labour Party Young Socialists, etc.), rather than the youth wings of the radical right. The continuing antics of the Federation of Conservative Students and the recruitment of (largely working-class) males into the National Front are two examples of youth participation in extreme right-wing political organisations.

10 Conclusion: Youth Transitions and the Labour Movement

1. I have used the term 'Left' here to suggest that only a radicalised labour movement will be able to respond to the main issues raised here.

2. The issue of a declining youth population should also be raised once again here. One response from the labour movement might be that demographic changes in the number of young people will effectively 'solve' the youth labour/youth politics problem. I would argue that this is simply not the case. Training has, in large part, displaced, not solved, youth unemployment. Even with a dramatic decline in the number of school leavers, numbers in youth training will remain high into the 1990s. Furthermore, history shows that youth employment prospects have always been worse than that of the whole population. Most importantly, Labour must continually face an entire generation of young people who have known nothing but Thatcherism. Millions have been introduced to work through the YTS and millions more will no doubt be confronted by Employment Training. If Labour is not to lose an entire generation (for good), it must begin to develop a type of politics which first attracts and then holds on to the population as it moves through the lifecycle. Politics is not just a question of numbers, it is also a question of generations.

3. The legacy of this transition is carried on through a small minority of male youths going through what is left of the apprenticeship

system. Although observed during the fieldwork phase, they did not form a central part of this study. However, one might speculate that with the decline of the craft sector and the substitution of the YTS for apprenticeships, this select group will be even further undermined. With the exception of a minority of shop floor 'radicals' (Armstrong and Nichols, 1976), this transition could be seen to be producing a conservative workerism, or what might be described as trade union 'consumerism' (protective of its privileged position and negotiating within the boundaries set by capital and State).

4. It is interesting to note which group comes first in this introductory statement from 'YTS – How to Tackle It', A TGWU Guide for Negotiators, 1984.

5. See 'A Plan for Training' (TUC-Labour Party Liaison Committee, 1984); 'New Skills for Labour' (The Labour Party, 1987); 'New Jobs for Britain' (Labour Party, 1987) and Labour's Charter for Young People.

6. See 'Recruitment of YTS Trainees in Trade Unions' (TUC Circular No. 167, 1986–7). For the stance of particular unions see Eversley (1986). I would like to thank Phil Cohen for making available some of the written material from the Labour Party's Youth Forum.

Bibliography

Abrams, M. (1959) *The Teenage Consumer* (London Press Exchange).

Allum, C., and Quigley, J. (1983) 'Bricks in the Wall: The Youth Training Scheme', *Capital and Class*, 21.

Aries, P. (1962) *Centuries of Childhood* (London: Penguin).

Armstrong, P. and Nichols, T. (1976) *Workers Divided* (London: Fontana).

Attwood, M. and Hatton, F. (1983) 'Getting On – Gender Differences in Career Development: A Case Study of the Hairdressing Industry', in Gamarnikow, E. *et al.* (eds), *Gender, Class and Work* (London: Heinemann).

Ball, S. (1981) *Beachside Comprehensive: A Case Study of Secondary School* (Cambridge: Cambridge University Press).

Barker, M. (1981) *The New Racism* (London: Junction Books).

Barrett, M. (1980) *Women's Oppression Today* (London: Verso).

Bates, I. *et al.* (1984) *Schooling for the Dole* (London: Macmillan).

Beasley, C. (1985) 'The Ambiguities of Desire – Patriarchal Subjectivities: Memories of Motherhood, Marriage and Sex Among Birmingham Working Class Women and Their Daughters', M.A. dissertation, Centre for Contemporary Cultural Studies, University of Birmingham.

Beechey, V. (1985) 'The Shape of the Workforce to Come', *Marxism Today*, 29.

Benn, C. and Fairley, J. (eds) (1986) *Challenging the MSC on Jobs, Education and Training* (London: Pluto).

Bernstein, R. (1976) *The Restructuring of Social and Political Theory* (Pennsylvania: University of Pennsylvania Press).

Braverman, H. (1974) *Labour and Monopoly Capital* (New York: Monthly Review Press).

Brelsford, P. *et al.* (1982) *Give Us a Break: Widening Opportunities for Young Women within YOP/YTS*, Research and Development Paper No. 11, (MSC).

Campbell, B. (1984) *Wigan Pier Revisited* (London: Virago Press).

Cantelon, H., and Hollands, R. (1988) *Leisure, Sport and Working Class Cultures: Theory and History* (Toronto: Garamond Press).

Carby, H. (1982) 'White Women Listen: Black Feminism and the Boundaries of Sisterhood', in CCCS Race and Politics Group, *The Empire Strikes Back* (London: Hutchinson).

Carter, E. (1984) 'Alice in the Consumer Wonderland', in McRobbie, A. and Nava, M. (eds) *Gender and Generation* (London: Macmillan).

Cashmore, E. and Troyna, B. (eds) (1982) *Black Youth in Crisis* (London: George Allen & Unwin).

Casson, M. (1979) *Youth Unemployment* (London: Macmillan).

CCCS Education Group (1981) *Unpopular Education* (London: Hutchinson).

CCCS Race and Politics Group (1982) *The Empire Strikes Back* (London: Hutchinson).

Clarke, J. (1979) 'Capital and Culture: The Post-war Working Class Revisited', in Clarke, J. *et al.* (eds), *Working Class Culture* (London: Hutchinson).

Clarke, J. and Critcher, C. (1985) *The Devil Makes Work: Leisure in Capitalist Britain* (London: Macmillan).

Clarke, J. *et al.* (eds) (1979) *Working Class Culture* (London: Hutchinson).

Cockburn, C. (1983) *Brothers: Technology and Trade Unionism in Printing* (London: Pluto).

Cockburn, C. (1986) 'Sixteen: Sweet or Sorry?, *Marxism Today*, 12.

Cockburn, C. (1987) *Two-Track Training* (London: Macmillan).

Coffield, F. *et al.* (1986) *Growing Up at the Margins* (Milton Keynes: Open University Press).

Cohen, P. (1972) 'Subcultural Conflict and Working Class Community', *Working Papers in Cultural Studies*, 2.

Cohen, P. (1982) 'School for the Dole', *New Socialist*, 3.

Cohen, P. (1983) 'Losing the Generation Game', *New Socialist*, 14.

Cohen, P. (1984) 'Against the New Vocationalism', in Bates, I., *et al.* *Schooling for the Dole* (London: Macmillan).

Cohen, P. (1985) 'Towards Youthopia?', *Marxism Today* 10.

Cohen, P. (1986a) 'Rethinking the Youth Question', Working Paper 3, Post 16 Education Centre, University London Institute of Education, January.

Cohen, P. (1986b) 'Anti-Racist Cultural Studies', a Curriculum Development Project in Schools and Community Education, June.

Cohen, P. and Chappell, A. (1983) 'Leavers and the Three L's', *Schooling and Culture*, 13.

Connell, R. W. (1983) *Which Way Is Up?: Essays in Class, Sex and Culture* (Sydney: George Allen & Unwin).

Connell, R. W. *et al.* (1982) *Making the Difference: Schools, Families and Social Division* (Sydney: George Allen & Unwin).

Corrigan, P. (1976) 'Doing Nothing', in Hall, S. and Jefferson, T. (eds) *Resistance Through Rituals* (London: Hutchinson).

Corrigan, P. (1979) *Schooling the Smash Street Kids* (London: Macmillan).

Cowie, C. and Lees, S. (1981) 'Slags or Drags', *Feminist Review*, 9.

Cross, M. (1985) 'Who Goes Where? YTS Allocation by Race', in Cross, M. and Smith, D. (eds), *YTS and Racial Minorities* (Leicester: National Youth Bureau).

Davies, B. (1979) *In Whose Interests? From Social Education to Social and Life Skills Training* (Leicester: National Youth Bureau).

Davies, B. (1984) 'Thatcherite Visions and the Role of the MSC', *Youth and Policy* 2, 4.

Davies, L. (1984) *Pupil Power: Deviance and Gender in School* (London: Falmer Press).

Deem, R. (1986) *All Work and No Play* (Milton Keynes: Open University Press).

Department of Employment (1985) *Employment: A Challenge for the Nation* (HMSO).

Department of Education and Science (1983) *Young People in the 80's* (HMSO).

Downing, H. (1981) 'Developments in Secretarial Labour: Resistance, Office Automation and the Transformation of Patriarchal Relations of Control', unpublished Ph.D thesis, Centre for Contemporary Cultural Studies, University of Birmingham.

Duruz, J. (1985) 'The Glitter and the Gold – Motherhood, Marriage and Sexuality: Ideologies of Working Class Girls in Birmingham During the Interwar Years', M.A. dissertation, Centre for Contemporary Cultural Studies, University of Birmingham.

Dworkin, A. (1981) *Pornography: Men Possessing Women* (London: The Women's Press).

Dwyer, P. *et al.* (1984) *Confronting School and Work* (Sydney: George Allen & Unwin).

Eggleston, J. (1986) *Education for Some: The Educational and Vocational Experiences of 15–18 Year Old Members of Minority Ethnic Groups* (Trentham).

Eversley, J. (1986) 'Trade Union Response to the MSC', in Benn, C. and Fairley, J. (eds), *Challenging the MSC on Jobs, Education and Training* (London: Pluto Press).

Fawcett Society (1985) *The Class of '84: A Study of Girls on the First Year of the Youth Training Scheme*, London: Walworth Rd.

Fenton, S. *et al.* (1984) *Ethnic Minorities and the Youth Training Scheme*, Research and Development Series No. 20.

Finch, J. (1984) 'It's Great to Have Someone to Talk To: The Ethics and

Politics of Interviewing Women', in Bell, C. and Roberts, H. (eds), *Social Researching: Politics, Problems, Practice* (London: Routledge & Kegan Paul).

Finn, D. (1981) 'New Deals and Broken Promises', unpublished Ph.D thesis, Centre for Contemporary Cultural Studies, University of Birmingham.

Finn, D. (1982) 'Whose Needs? Schooling and the "Needs" of Industry', in Rees, T. and Atkinson, P. (eds), *Youth Unemployment and State Intervention* (London: Routledge & Kegan Paul).

Finn, D. (1983) 'Britain's Misspent Youth', *Marxism Today*, 2.

Finn, D. (1984) 'Leaving School and Growing Up: Work Experience in the Juvenile Labour Market', in Bates, I., *et al.*, *Schooling for the Dole* (London: Macmillan).

Finn, D. (1987) *Training Without Jobs* (London: Macmillan).

Fox, B. (1980) *Hidden in the Household* (Toronto: The Women's Press).

Frith, S. (1978) *The Sociology of Rock* (London: Constable).

Further Education Unit (1983) *Supporting YTS*.

Gershuny, J. *et al.* (1986) 'Time Budgets: Preliminary Analysis of a National Survey', *Quarterly Journal of Social Affairs*.

Giddens, A. (1973) *The Class Structure of the Advanced Societies* (London: Hutchinson).

Giddens, A. (1984) *The Constitution of Society* (Cambridge: Polity Press).

Gillis, J. (1974) *Youth and History* (New York: Academic Press).

Gilroy, P. (1981–2) 'You Can't Fool the Youths: Class and Race Formation in the 1980's', *Race and Class*, 23.

Glasgow University Media Group (1982) *Really Bad News* (London: Readers and Writers).

Goldstein, N. (1984) 'The New Training Initiative: A Great Leap Backwards', *Capital and Class*, 23.

Gorz, A. (1982) *Farewell to the Working Class* (London: Pluto).

Gramsci, A. (1978) *Selections from the Prison Notebooks* (Hoare, Q. and Smith, G. N. eds and translators, New York: International Press).

Green, A. (1983) 'Education and Training: Under New Masters', in Wolpe, A. M. and Donald, J. (eds), *Is There Anyone Here from Education?* (London: Pluto).

Griffin, C. (1982) 'The Good, the Bad and the Ugly: Images of Young Women in the Labour Market', Stencilled Paper No. 70, Centre for Contemporary Cultural Studies, University of Birmingham.

Griffin, C. (1985) *Typical Girls?* (London: Routledge & Kegan Paul).

Hall, S. (1983) 'Education in Crisis', in Wolpe, A. M. and Donald, J. (eds), *Is There Anyone Here from Education?* (London: Pluto Press).

Hall, S. (1985) 'Realignment – For What?', *Marxism Today*, 12.

Hall, S. and Jefferson, T. (1976) (eds), *Resistance Through Rituals* (London: Hutchinson).

Hall, S. *et al.* (1978) *Policing the Crisis* (London: Macmillan).

Hall, S. *et al.* (eds) (1980) *Culture, Media, Language* (London: Hutchinson).

Hargreaves, D. (1967) *Social Relations in a Secondary School* (London: Routledge & Kegan Paul).

Hargreaves, J. (ed) (1982) *Sport, Culture and Ideology* (London: Routledge & Kegan Paul).

Hargreaves, J. (1986) *Sport, Power and Culture* (Cambridge: Polity Press in association with Basil Blackwell).

Hartmann, H. (1979) 'Capitalism, Patriarchy and Job Segregation by Sex', in Eisenstein, Z. (ed.), *Capitalist Patriarchy and the Case for Socialist Feminism* (New York: Monthly Review Press).

Hayek, F. (1980) '1980s Unemployment and the Unions', Hobart Paper 87, The Institute of Economic Affairs.

Hebdige, D. (1979) *Subculture: The Meaning of Style* (London: Methuen).

Hollands, R. (1985a) 'Its Your Life! – Male Working Class Youth's Orientations Towards Educational Comics', in Points, C. (ed.), *Working Papers for 16+ Media Studies* (Clwyd: Clwyd Media Studies Unit).

Hollands, R. (1985b) 'Working Class Youth, Leisure and the Search for Work', in Parker, S. and Veal, T. (eds), *Leisure: Politics, Planning, People* (Vol. 2, Leisure Studies Conference Paper No. 23, September).

Hollands, R. (1985c) 'Working for the Best Ethnography', Stencilled Paper No. 79, Centre for Contemporary Cultural Studies, University of Birmingham.

Hollands, R. (1988) 'Leisure, Work and Working Class Cultures: The Case of Leisure on the Shop Floor', in Cantelon, H. and Hollands, R., *Leisure, Sport and Working Class Cultures: Theory and History* (Toronto: Garamond Press).

Humphries, S. (1981) *Hooligans or Rebels?* (Oxford: Basil Blackwell).

Huws, U. (1982) *Your Job in the Eighties* (London: Pluto Press).

Jenkins, R. (1983) *Lads, Citizens and Ordinary Kids* (London: Routledge & Kegan Paul).

Johnson, R. (1983) 'What Is Cultural Studies Anyway?', Stencilled Paper No. 74, Centre for Contemporary Cultural Studies, University of Birmingham.

Jones, S. (1986) 'White Youth and Jamaican Popular Culture', unpublished Ph.D thesis, Centre for Contemporary Cultural Studies, University of Birmingham.

Keat, R. and Urry, J. (1975) *Social Theory as Science* (London: Routledge & Kegan Paul).

Kelly, J. (1982) 'Useful Work and Useless Toil', *Marxism Today*, 26.

Labour Research (1983) Labour Research Department, December.

Laclau, E. (1987) 'Class War and After', *Marxism Today*, 31.

Lawrence, E. (1982a) 'In the Abundance of Water the Fool is Thirsty: Sociology and Black "Pathology" ', in CCCS Race and Politics Group, *The Empire Strikes Back* (London: Hutchinson).

Lawrence, E. (1982b) 'Just Plain Common Sense: The Roots of Racism', in CCCS Race and Politics Group, *The Empire Strikes Back* (London: Hutchinson).

Lees, S. (1984) 'Nice Girls Don't', *New Socialist*, 16.

Lees, S. (1986) *Losing Out: Sexuality and Adolescent Girls* (London: Hutchinson).

Linell, J. (1983) *YTS Curriculum Issues* (Leicester: National Youth Bureau).

Luxton, M. (1980) *More Than a Labour of Love* (Toronto: Women's Press).

MacDonald, M. (1980) 'Socio-cultural Reproduction and Women's Education', in Deem, R. (ed), *Schooling for Women's Work* (London: Routledge & Kegan Paul).

Marcus, G. and Fisher, M. (1986) *Anthropology as Cultural Critique* (Chicago: University of Chicago Press).

Massey, D. (1983) 'The Shape of Things to Come', *Marxism Today*, April.

McRobbie, A. (1980) 'Settling Accounts with Subcultures: A Feminist Critique', *Screen Education*, 34.

McRobbie, A. (1982) 'The Politics of Feminist Research: Between Talk, Text and Action', *Feminist Review*, 12.

McRobbie, A. (1984) 'Dance and Social Fantasy', in McRobbie, A. and Nava, M. (eds), *Gender and Generation* (London: Macmillan).

Meikisins-Wood, E. (1986) *The Retreat From Class* (London: Verso Press).

MSC (1977) Young People and Work (The Holland Report).

MSC (1982a) Youth Task Group Report, April.

MSC (1982b) YTS Guidelines No. 2.

MSC (1983a) Guide to Linked Schemes, August.

MSC (1983b) Guide to Managing Agents, July.

MSC (1983c) You and the Youth Training Scheme, November.

Mungham, G. (1982) 'Workless Youth as a Moral Panic', in Rees, T. and Atkinson, P. (eds), *Youth Unemployment and State Intervention* (London: Routledge & Kegan Paul).

Oakley, A. (1974) *Housewife* (Harmondsworth: Allan Lane).

Parker, S. (1972) *The Future of Work and Leisure* (London: Longman).

Pearson, G. (1983) *Hooligan: A History of Respectable Fears* (London: Macmillan).

Phizacklea, A. and Miles, R. (1980) *Labour and Racism* (London: Routledge & Kegan Paul).

Pollert, A. (1981) *Girls, Wives and Factory Lives* (London: Macmillan).

Pollert, A. (1985) *Unequal Opportunities* (Birmingham: TURC Publishing).

Randall, C. (n.d.) 'Manpower – Serving Whose Interests?', Centre for a Working World, Report, No. 1.

Rees, T. and Atkinson, P. (eds) (1982) *Youth Unemployment and State Intervention* (London: Routledge & Kegan Paul).

REITS (1985), 'YTS or White TS? – Racial Equality in Training Schemes', Coventry Workshop, April.

Roberts, K. (1978) *Contemporary Society and the Growth of Leisure* (London: Longman).

Roberts, K. (1983) *Youth and Leisure* (London: George Allen & Unwin).

Robins, D. and Cohen, P. (1978) *Knuckle Sandwich* (Harmondsworth: Penguin).

Rose, S. *et al.* (1984) *Not in Our Genes* (Harmondsworth: Penguin).

Rothaus, L. (1984) 'Punk Femininity: Style and Class Conflict', a paper presented at the Popular Culture Association Conference, Toronto, Canada, 29 March – 1 April.

Scofield, P. *et al.* (1983) *The Tories' Poisoned Apple* (Leeds: Independent Labour Publications).

Sharpe, S. (1976) *Just Like a Girl* (Harmondswoth: Penguin).

Stafford, A. (1981) 'Learning Not to Labour', *Capital and Class*, 15.

Stanley, L. and Wise, S. (1983) *Breaking Out: Feminist Consciousness and Feminist Research* (London: Routledge & Kegan Paul).

Stanworth, M. (1983) *Gender and Schooling* (London: Hutchinson).

Thomas, C. (1980) 'Girls and Counter-school Cultures', in McCallum, D. and Ozolins, V. (eds), *Melbourne Working Papers*, University of Melbourne, Australia.

Tolson, A. (1977) *The Limits of Masculinity* (London: Tavistock).

Touraine, A. (1979) 'Political Ecology: A Demand to live Differently Now', *New Society*, November.

Valli, L. (1986) *Becoming Clerical Workers* (London: Routledge & Kegan Paul).

Walker, J. C. (1986) 'Romanticising Resistance, Romanticising Culture: Problems in Willis' Theory of Cultural Production', *British Journal of Sociology of Education*, 7, 1.

Weeks, J. (1987) 'Love in a Cold Climate', *Marxism Today*, 31.

Wickham, A. (1982) 'The State and Training Programmes for Women', in Whitelegg, E. *et al.* (eds), *The Changing Experience of Women* (Oxford: Martin Robertson in association with the Open University).

Wickham, A. (1986) *Women and Training* (Milton Keynes: Open University Press).

Williams, R. (1965) *The Long Revolution* (Harmondsworth: Penguin).

Williams, R. (1977) *Marxism and Literature* (Oxford: Oxford University Press).

Williamson, H. (1982) 'Client Responses to the Youth Opportunities Programme', in Rees T. and Atkinson, P. (eds), *Youth Unemployment and State Intervention* (London: Routledge & Kegan Paul).

Willis, P. (1976) 'The Class Significance of the School Counter-culture', in Hammersley, M. and Woods, P. (eds), *The Process of Schooling* (London: Open University and Routledge & Kegan Paul).

Willis, P. (1977) *Learning to Labour* (Westmead: Saxon House).

Willis, P. (1978) *Profane Culture* (London: Routledge & Kegan Paul).

Willis, P. (1979) 'Shop-floor Culture, Masculinity and the Wage Form', in Clarke, J. *et al.* (eds), *Working Class Culture* (London: Hutchinson).

Willis, P. (1980) 'Notes on Method', in Hall, S. *et al.* (eds), *Culture, Media, Language* (London: Hutchinson).

Willis, P. (1981) *Learning to Labour* (New York: Columbia University Press, American edition).

Willis, P. (1984) 'Youth Unemployment – A New Social State', *New Society*, 67.

Willis, P. (1985) *The Social Condition of Young People in Wolverhampton in 1984* (Wolverhampton: Wolverhampton Borough Council).

Wolpe, A. M. (1978) 'Education and the Sexual Division of Labour', in Kuhn, A. and Wolpe, A. M. (eds), *Feminism and Materialism* (London: Routledge & Kegan Paul).

Wood, J. (1984) 'Groping Towards Sexism: Boy's Sex Talk', in McRobbie, A. and Nava, M. (eds), *Gender and Generation* (London: Macmillan).

YETRU (1987) *Confidential: Racism* (Birmingham: Youth Employment and Training Research Unit).

YTS Monitoring Unit (1985) *The Great Training Robbery Continues* (Birmingham: TURC Publishing).

Index

'affluent teenager' 142, 143, 157
Afro-Caribbean 25, 36
AIDS 177
allowance 80, 81, 82, 83, 113,
    126, 148, 201
apprenticeship 14, 15, 102, 118,
    206, 212n4
  cultural 14, 103, 111, 119, 198
  domestic 13, 15, 45, 57, 105,
    129, 197, 198
  political 207
  trade 34, 37, 84, 222n3
Area Manpower Boards 207
Asian 24, 36

Boy George 177
boyfriends 23, 70, 133, 154,
    158–9
Brookside 155

career 15, 40, 41, 45, 50, 66–8,
    72, 82, 83, 102, 105, 106, 109,
    113, 121, 197
  oriented 69, 70, 72, 183, 190
careerism 15, 57, 68, 73, 115
careerist 13, 73, 113, 147
Careers Service 19, 23, 38–43,
    162
cheap labout 44
City and Guilds 58, 60, 61, 63,
    64, 175
CND 181, 199
college 34, 35, 36, 44, 51, 52, 58,
    96
  scheme 65–72

Commission for Racial
    Equality 93, 94
community 15, 30, 31, 166, 169,
    172, 196, 201
Conservative
  Government 3, 17, 18, 19, 82,
    97
  Party 2, 186, 188, 192, 193
consumption 113, 142, 144,
    148–54
  mass 143, 157, 199
corporate 52, 73, 201
cultural 3, 7, 8, 195, 201
  experience 3, 8, 101, 208,
    213n7
  studies 7
culture 7–8
  counter-school 9, 10, 11, 12,
    13, 25, 60, 117
  lad 10, 11, 59, 191, 198 (*see
    also* transitions, manual
    labour lads)
  shop floor 26, 103, 152, 175,
    179, 184, 198
  work 84, 114–20

deskilling 117, 179
destinations 41, 50, 67, 66–8, 72
deviance 12, 34, 140, 141, 177
deviant *see* deviance
disabled 19, 23, 36, 66
dole 37, 43, 81, 83, 136, 137, 189
    (*see also* unemployment)
  and domestic labour 125–6
domestic labour 9, 11, 12, 67–8,

103, 121, 122, 123–31, 142, 145, 154, 198
domestic sphere 4, 7, 10, 12, 13, 14, 34, 122, 131, 132, 142, 176, 179, 197 (*see also* household)
domestic transitions *see also* transitions
doss 36, 68
'double burden' 108, 120, 130

Eastenders 155
Employment Bill 81, 212n3
Employment Training (ET) scheme 1, 2, 202, 211n1n2, 212n2n3, 218n7
enterprise culture 2
entrepreneurial 55, 56, 57, 73, 108
entrepreneurship 52, 57, 201, 204
equal opportunities 102, 161, 162, 170–2, 179, 202–3, 205, 208, 209
ethnographic/ethnography 1, 9, 10, 12, 15, 16, 101, 138, 164, 195, 213n7, 215n11n12
exams 28, 30, 35, 63, 67
exploitation 88–9, 111, 118, 173

factory transitions *see also* transitions
family 10, 31, 40, 43, 55, 57, 102, 120–3, 197, 201
    nuclear 124
    single-parent 125, 127
    wage 40
feminine 107, 108, 152, 156, 197 (*see also* femininity)
femininity 71, 103, 120, 137
feminisation 84, 118, 198
feminist 12, 173, 206
Foot, Michael 191
(Further Education Unit (FEU) 46–7

gender 4, 5, 12, 13, 15, 16, 27, 28, 33, 36, 57, 58, 66, 68, 72,

79, 84, 116, 120, 124, 125, 128, 130, 138, 148, 155, 156, 158, 161, 163, 164, 177, 182, 183, 193, 197, 198, 213n8, 214n8, 218n2
girlfriends 154
'glam' transitions *see under* transitions
'gofer' 84, 90, 218n3
grievances 74, 91, 92–4, 205

harassment 93, 94, 131, 132, 135, 170
health and safety 46, 81, 92–3, 94
heterosexuality 177
hooligan 138, 139, 141, 219n4
household 7, 10, 42, 113, 122, 123, 125, 127, 129, 145, 178
humour 26, 33, 53, 60, 70, 116, 118

impression management 25
individualism 15, 49, 50, 66, 189–90, 197, 199, 200, 204
induction period 44, 45, 46–50, 73
inheritance 14, 15, 78, 102, 103, 164, 165–6, 167, 171, 174–5, 179

'keep' 125, 145
Kinnock, Neil 191, 192

Labour Listens 210
labour movement 2, 3, 5, 14, 98, 162, 172, 179, 190, 192–3, 195–210, 221n1n2
Labour Party 181, 190–4, 203, 204, 207–10, 221n2, 222n5
Labour Party Young Socialists (LPYS) 193
labourist position 205, 207, 210
'laff' 26, 59, 60
'lasses' 53–7, 201, 204
leisure 12, 58, 108, 113, 127, 135, 153, 160, 198, 199, 200, 219–20n1

critique of 142–5
lifestyle 130
studies 143, 219–20n1
life and social skills 26, 32, 45,
    47, 49, 58–64, 65, 72, 73, 184,
    200
'lifeskilling' 44, 45, 64, 73, 198,
    212n4
lifestyle 13, 142, 144, 152, 198,
    205
    and non-work activities 154–60
Low Pay Unit 82

magazines 54, 152
managing agents 18, 44, 75, 80,
    86, 91
'manpower servicedom
    paradigm' 200–3, 205, 206,
    208, 209, 210, 218n1
Manpower Services Commission
    (MSC) 2, 3, 13, 31, 44, 46,
    51, 52, 61, 63, 65, 71, 72, 80,
    81, 84, 91, 94, 102, 148, 162,
    185, 189, 200–2, 209,
    212n3n4, 213n6, 217n3
manual labour 9, 10, 11, 14, 25,
    41, 60, 66, 68, 78, 86, 103,
    109, 111, 113, 119, 140, 153,
    161, 212n4
manual labour lads *see under*
    transitions
manufacturing 18, 19, 84, 95, 96,
    109, 110, 118, 174, 205
masculine/masculinity 10, 15, 62,
    64, 70, 78, 103, 104, 110, 113,
    118, 119, 122, 138, 140, 141,
    149, 153, 154, 165, 174, 175,
    184, 198
maths 62–3
media 7, 9, 96, 133, 187
    work 193, 198
Militant 193, 207
Mods 140, 143, 152, 155
motorbikes 153
'mucking about' 28, 33
mugging 131–3, 137, 169, 172
music 154–7

National Front 164, 221n1
New Right 163, 213n5
new technology 3, 17, 205
new vocationalism 2, 3, 8, 9, 10,
    11, 13, 14, 15, 24, 25, 27, 31,
    32, 43, 49, 50, 64, 65, 68, 82,
    84, 91, 98, 101, 102, 103, 105,
    109, 111, 114, 115, 117, 118,
    142, 145, 148, 160, 181, 184,
    188, 190, 193, 195–208, 209,
    212–13n4
nightclubs 158–60
non-work activities 142, 154–60

off-the-job training 4, 17, 18, 24,
    26, 36, 44–73, 75, 95, 106,
    107, 216–17n1

patriarchal 102, 150, 198, 199,
    206
pedagogy 45, 52, 53, 106
'personal effectiveness' 45, 58,
    63, 107
police/policing 135–8, 169
politics 3, 13, 15, 118, 180–94,
    195, 199, 201, 203
    of YTS 181–5
private training agencies
    (PTAs) 18, 51, 75, 92–4,
    108, 215n14, 217n4
'progressivism' 65, 73
    liberal 65, 68, 69, 72, 200
public space 6, 7, 131–8

race 4, 5, 16, 19, 27, 36, 79, 84,
    124, 138, 148, 155, 173, 182,
    183, 213–214n8, 219n2
Race Relations Act 81, 94
race relations perspective 162
racism 25, 61, 78, 79, 93, 133,
    137–8, 141, 199, 217n5,
    220n2n3
    the 'new' 161–4, 172
    white 161–172
'really useful knowledge' 30
Red Wedge 157, 193, 210, 220n4
reproduction codes 14–15
    theories 9, 12

residential 65, 71–2, 217n6
riots, inner-city 168–9, 220n6
Rockers 140, 143, 152

school 4, 7, 9, 10, 12, 17, 23–40,
    43, 51, 55, 59, 60, 68, 81, 125
  curriculum 28–32, 62, 64
  leavers 1, 2, 3, 17, 19, 27, 33,
    34, 36, 37, 39, 40, 43, 44, 45,
    56, 58, 66, 74, 174, 189, 201,
    202, 205, 211n1, 216–17n1
school to work transition 9, 12,
    13, 27, 31, 33, 101
self-employment 57, 65, 82, 106,
    108, 111, 115, 119, 121, 188,
    197, 199, 202, 209
service sector 17, 19, 25, 84, 85,
    199, 202, 205, 208–9
sexism 4, 10, 161, 172–9, 199,
    220–1n7
Sexual Discrimination Act 81
shop floor 10, 14, 15, 102, 117,
    118 (*see also under* culture)
siblings, and domestic
    labour 128
skill 15, 26, 41, 62–3, 85, 102,
    110, 118, 203, 212n4
  basic 45, 47, 48
  'core' 65
  'transferable' 2, 17, 202
Skinheads 136, 143
slave labour 40, 81, 84, 185
sport 71
street fighting 138–41
structuration 8
subcultures 136, 183, 140–1,
    143–5, 148, 151–3, 155, 156,
    158, 160, 164, 198, 220n2
  female 12, 133–4, 150–1, 152,
    158
subjectivity 14, 20, 50, 72, 73
'substitute wage' 123, 132, 134,
    138, 144, 145–7, 148, 150–1,
    153, 155, 158–60, 201
'survivalist' *see under* transitions

Teds 143, 155
television 154–5, 220n3

territoriality 138, 140–1, 164–7,
    170–1
Thatcher, Margaret 2, 25, 96,
    174, 186–7, 189, 191
Thatcherism 187–90, 191, 194,
    198, 202, 205, 208, 213n5,
    218n6
trade unions 3, 11, 25, 65–6, 84,
    90–2, 94–8, 118, 179, 181,
    182, 192, 196, 203, 204, 205,
    206–7, 209, 222n6
  TGWU 97, 222n4
Trades Union Congress 204,
    207, 212n3
trainee councils 92, 97–8, 183,
    199
'traineeship' 27, 80–1, 84, 86, 91,
    98, 102
Training Commission 212n3
transitions [main ones identified in
    study]
  domestic 107, 115–16, 117,
    129–30, 152, 159, 192
  factory 105, 107–8, 112–13,
    116–17, 120, 129–30, 152, 204
  'glam' 105–6, 114–15, 121,
    197, 202, 204–5 (*see also*
    upwardly mobile)
  manual labour lads 152, 167,
    171, 172, 174, 183, 188–9,
    201, 204 (*see also under*
    culture)
  paraprofessional 15, 68, 105,
    106, 114, 115, 121, 197, 202
  politicos 172, 179, 181, 182,
    197, 199–200, 201, 203–4
  survivalist 79, 138, 191,
    199–200, 201, 218n2
  'white-collar'/management 152,
    199, 202, 205 (*see also*
    upwardly mobile)
  youth culture enterprise 108,
    151, 197, 198, 202
transnational companies 18–19

unemployment 1, 3, 7, 9, 17–19,
    23–6, 34, 38, 157, 169, 174,

182–4, 185–90, 191, 192, 202,
205, 207, 210, 211n1, 216n2
upwardly mobile/upward
mobility   25, 55, 56, 57, 66,
72, 119, 135, 148, 149, 152,
153, 155, 156, 159–60, 167,
169, 171, 183, 188, 199

vocationalism   *see* new
vocationalism

wage   60, 80, 81, 126
expectations   81, 82, 111–14,
148
family   121–2, 147
wage labour   6, 7, 11, 12, 14, 78,
98, 101, 109, 114, 117, 124,
184, 198, 200
'white-collar' transition   *see
under* transitions
work experience   4, 17, 41, 42,
44, 55, 58, 74–98, 106

project-based   26, 58, 75–9, 94
work placements/sponsors   74,
84–5, 86–91, 92–4, 106–8, 109,
114–20
working-class culture   4, 8, 10,
11–12, 14, 15, 27, 30, 43, 57,
60, 64, 73, 140, 196

youth
culture   7, 142, 143, 206
differentiation   3, 101–20, 194,
196, 206
divisions   161–79, 196
policy   208–10
youth culture enterprise   *see
under* transitions
Youth Forums   209, 222n6
Youth Opportunities Programme
(YOP)   40, 44, 212n2, 213n7
Youth Task Group Report   80
Youth Trade Union Rights
Campaign (YTURC)   193,
210

ARTFORUM
INTERNATIONAL

65 BLEECKER STREET NYC 10012 212·475·4000